THESE LIVING SONGS

THESE LIVING SONGS

Reading Montana Poetry

EDITED BY LISA D. SIMON

AND BRADY HARRISON

University of Montana Press

Library of Congress Control
Number: 2014947715

Soft Bound
ISBN 978-0-9894031-9-1

Case Hard Bound
ISBN 978-0-9894031-7-7

Set and designed in
Minion by N. Putens.
Cover designed by
Jason Neal.

CONTENTS

"How do we keep
this living song alive?"

—VICTOR CHARLO

ACKNOWLEDGEMENTS

If, as someone once said, it takes a village to raise a child, it takes a good-sized state's worth of folks to realize a book on Montana poetry. A great many people have given their time, energy, good-will, resources, and more to the creation of this book, and we would like to thank those who have been most directly involved. First, and foremost, we would like to thank the contributors for their hard-work, patience, and dedication to this project: to a person, they have been generous with their time, enthusiasm, and expertise. We would also like to thank Jerry Fetz, our editor at the University of Montana Press, as well as our expert copy-editors, Mark Triana and Lynn Purl. As well, our many thanks to Montana stalwarts Sandra Alcosser, Bill Bevis, Roger Dunsmore, Rick Newby, Lynda Sexton, Annick Smith, and Lois Welch for writing letters in support of the publication of this work. More, we would like to recognize Dean Chris Comer, Provost Perry Brown, and President Royce Engstrom for their ongoing interest in and furtherance of the study of Montana literatures and cultures. Finally, and perhaps most importantly in this era of declining public and financial support for universities in general and the Humanities in particular, we are proud to acknowledge that the publication of this book was supported in part by a grant from the Baldridge Book Subvention Fund in the College of Humanities and Sciences at the University of Montana.

Lisa Simon and Brady Harrison

Photo by Brian Herbel

INTRODUCTION

Imagining Many Montanas

BRADY HARRISON *(Missoula, Montana)*

I. ORIGINS AND PURPOSES

A few years ago, at the Montana Festival of the Book, Lisa Simon organized a Poetry Salon to celebrate and promote the publication of two landmark anthologies of Montana, Western U.S., and transnational poetry: Melissa Kwasny and M. L. Smoker's *I Go to the Ruined Place: Contemporary Poems in Defense of Global Human Rights* (2009) and Lowell Jaeger's *New Poets of the American West* (2010). The salon was broken into two parts, one for each book, and a number of the contributors read their work to a diverse audience of fellow poets, scholars, and folks from Missoula and farther afield who were interested in poetry, human rights, the American West, and more. As someone tangential to the proceedings—I had contributed the introduction to the Western anthology—I was there to hear some great (and, at times, harrowing) poetry and I was struck, as I often have been since moving to Montana, by the talent in the room. Here were poets of remarkable technical, intellectual, and artistic accomplishment, masters of word and passion, brought together to share their work with anyone willing to listen. As I listened and—as unobtrusively as possible—studied the audience and their reactions and engagement, a number of thoughts occurred to me: Montanans enjoy an astonishing bounty of writers and artists; many Montanans care deeply about literature and ideas; for such a small (population-wise, that is) and remote state, Montana boasts a diversity of points of views and experiences. And, as a reader of poetry, and a scholar of Montana literature and history, I also looked about the room and considered the fact that while the state's fiction and nonfiction writers have received at least some of their critical due, the poets and their work have been somewhat neglected in studies of the Treasure State's extraordinary literary corpus.[1] In short, as I looked about the room and saw all of this talent and interest, I thought there should be a book of essays dedicated to the study and celebration of Montana poetry.

The natural person to make such a book happen was clearly the salon's organizer, and although I did not know Lisa particularly well, I mentioned the idea to her. As matters turned out, she thought that we should work on the book together, and a few hundred hours and a great deal of work by a great many people later, you now hold in hand the first-ever collection of essays devoted exclusively to the close reading and literary, cultural, and historical analysis and interpretation of Montana poets and their work. And, as even a cursory glance at the table of contents reveals, the contributors offer considerations of a rather staggering range of authors and subjects. Here, you will find studies of poets you may never have heard of, some you may know about but never had the chance to read, and some you have enjoyed for years. You will also light on an essay or two about an old friend (and Montana giant), Richard Hugo. You will find essays about writers who have received neither the critical nor the popular attention they deserve; and several others that offer fresh looks and trenchant rereadings of established figures such as Sandra Alcosser, Vic Charlo, Roger Dunsmore, Tami Haaland, Lowell Jaeger, Melissa Kwasny, Greg Pape, Henry Real Bird, James Welch, and others. You will find explorations of poems by working class and cowboy poets, detailed analyses of Native

....

1   For example, in *Ten Tough Trips: Montana Writers and the West* (1990), the ur-text of contemporary Montana criticism, only one of twelve chapters focuses on a poet. In works since, including Rick Newby and Suzanne Hunger's collection, *Writing Montana: Literature Under the Big Sky* (1996), Ken Egan's *Hope and Dread in Montana Literature* (2003), and my collection, *All Our Stories Are Here: Critical Perspectives on Montana Literature* (2009), although a number of poets receive critical attention—some for the first time—the bulk of the attention goes to writers of prose.

American poetry, stylish recountings of efforts to fashion new voices and found new—and sometimes decidedly not-male—poetic traditions, and close-yet-reader-friendly takes on such sophisticated and challenging poets as Grace Stone Coates, J. V. Cunningham, Madeline DeFrees, and Patricia Goedicke. Some of the poets considered here, such as Coates and Marjorie Frost, were at work early in the twentieth century, and some, like Heather Cahoon, Jennifer Finley, and Heather Tone, are among the emergent, tough-minded, and provocative voices of contemporary Montana writing. We hope readers of this collection will not only enjoy and learn from the essays, but—and much more importantly—read and share the poetry discussed by our scholars, dedicated readers, and poet-essayists.

If the first purpose of this collection is to introduce (or reintroduce) scholarly and general readers to the richness, variety, and superabundance of Montana poetry—and thereby to advance the study and appreciation of the state's long and distinguished poetic tradition—the second purpose arises from a clear sense of advocacy and wanting others to enjoy and admire poetry as much as we do. Our contributors not only want to enlarge and enliven the study of Montana poetry, but they also want to demonstrate *how* to read well. As part of their essays, the authors offer sustained, detailed close readings of a limited number of extraordinary works by the poets under consideration. They model, in other words, strategies for reading and exploring a wide range of poetic practices, techniques, voices, themes, forms, and more. For scholars and veteran readers, the close analyses should serve as critical steel against which to sharpen one's own interpretations. For readers relatively new to poetry—and for those who may have had bad experiences with poetry in the past—the essays have been designed from the start to be reader friendly. The contributors rely on plain, accessible writing, and even as the essays offer the depth and multidimensional cultural considerations expected of literary scholars, they remain relatively free of critical terminology and the language of high theory. All readers, we hope, are led into the poetry on the strength of narrative; each essay, told in the individual and lively voice of its author, stands on its own in smart, nonspecialized language to appeal to the readers from any background. In sum, we would like our readers to know more about the state's poets and poetry, and we offer useful (and, we hope, enjoyable and enlightening) strategies for discovering, reading, sharing, and celebrating Montana poetry. Call it a return to the sort of open-to-all, populist criticism and civic engagement practiced by William W. Bevis, Roger Dunsmore, Sue Hart, Joseph Kinsey Howard, Richard Hugo, and many others.[2]

II. IMAGINED COMMUNITIES AND MANY MONTANAS

Although the essays speak ably and engagingly for themselves, I would like—very briefly—to take a step or two back from the collection in order to assess the current state of what we might call the Montanas of the imagination. That is, at present I see a variety of centripetal and centrifugal forces at play in Montana poetry (and prose) that make this, for both the interested reader and the scholar, an intriguing time in the state's literary history. On the one hand, we see currents of the somewhat conservative, somewhat homogenizing forces and energies of what Benedict Anderson called "imagined communities"; on the other, we see an increasing diversity of voices, experiences, perspectives, values, techniques, and themes that, taken collectively, work—sometimes explicitly, sometimes implicitly— against some of the established narratives and ways of thinking and that promise new visions and representations of Montana and its histories, cultures, languages, ethnicities, and more. First, then, to the centripetal forces.

As Anderson writes, a nation "is an imagined political community—and imagined as both inherently limited and sovereign" (6). He continues: "It is *imagined* because the members of even the smallest nations will never know most of their fellow-members, meet them, or even hear of them, yet in the mind of each lives the image of their communion" (6). Although Anderson presents a too-homogenous vision of the nation, we can certainly understand his point: the diverse peoples that constitute nations—or, for our purposes, states—tell themselves stories (or have stories told to

....

2 In the Introduction to *Ten Tough Trips*, Bevis gracefully articulates his populist approach to Montana writing: "The Montana literature is so various and interesting, and the West is so intertwined with American national identity, that I thought many who do not usually read criticism or history might enjoy hearing a discussion of the books. These are personal essays, then, for a general audience" (ix). Such statements served, at least in part, as the guiding spirit for this book.

them) that bind them together, that unite disparate persons and groups into variously cooperative (or, sometimes, unruly) imaginary wholes. As nations, states, cities, towns, or communities, we tell and hear stories that work to unite us in vision, values, beliefs, and action. As Americans, we rely on tales of George Washington, Revolution, Abe Lincoln, Emancipation, Liberty, Opportunity, Justice, Free Enterprise, and so on, to make us a "nation." The equation is, of course, much more complicated, shifting, and contested than this, but we can probably agree that these sorts of homogenizing narratives pervade the culture and do a lot to stitch us more or less together. What, then, makes us Montanans?

The answer, of course, is many things—too many, in fact, to count—but the title of Bill Bevis's landmark study of Montana literature, *Ten Tough Trips: Montana Writers and the West* (1990; revised 2003), nicely captures one of the most oft-told stories: the state is a Hard Place to survive, let alone thrive in.[3] The Big Sky is an austere, daunting, sometimes hopeless, hardscrabble land, and we see this story, this vision of Montana, in writers as diverse as Nannie T. Alderson, Judy Blunt, Norman Maclean, D'Arcy McNickle, and James Welch. More, we see this vision in many of the poems explored in this collection. And, who could argue: we see hardship, fear, anger, isolation, and poverty in the work of J. V. Cunningham, Roger Dunsmore, Jennifer Finley, Ed Lahey, and Mandy Smoker. As Hugo, one of the most prolific and steadfast authors of this vision of the state, writes in perhaps his most famous poem, "Degrees of Gray in Philipsburg,"

Isn't this your life? That ancient kiss
still burning out your eyes? Isn't this defeat
so accurate, the church bell simply seems
a pure announcement: ring and no one comes? (216–17)

Ouch. According to Hugo, a Montanan has been hit so often and so hard by life that she or he seems punch-drunk, stunned, all-but-penniless, lonely, forgotten, yet one more bit of aimless detritus left over from the

....

3 For the sake of brevity, I will restrict myself to this one, primordial example, but we could name any number of others: the Ranch, Reservation, Mountain, Forests and Lumber, Mines and Cooper Kings, Cattle, Bears, and Wolves, Winter, Drought, Ghost Towns, and more.

endless cycles of boom and bust. Of course, this is only one story, and even Hugo was not without hope:

Miles from any town
your radio comes in strong, unlikely
Mozart from Belgrade, rock and roll
from Butte. Whatever the next number,
you want to hear it. Never has your Buick
found this forward a gear. Even
the tuna salad in Reedpoint is good. (204)

Against this bleak and powerful—and, in many ways, telling—portrait of our imagined Montana, our imagined, collective community, run currents that offer diverse views of Montana and its cultures, histories, peoples, writers, geographies, and ecosystems. And, although there has always been an uneven, always-in-flux, never-just-a-binary mix of centripetal and centrifugal forces at play in Montana literatures and cultures—just as they have always been at play in American literatures and cultures—the rise of feminism, civil rights, and multiculturalism across the U.S. and in the state has contributed to the increase in the diversity of voices and views especially since the 1970s: where the Montana of the imagination in the second half of the twentieth century seemed to belong particularly to Hard Place writers such as A. B. "Bud" Guthrie, Jr., Hugo, Dorothy M. Johnson, Maclean, and Welch, our contributors read the poetry of Sandra Alcosser, Minerva Allen, Heather Cahoon, Vic Charlo, Grace Stone Coates, Madeline DeFrees, Roger Dunsmore, Patricia Goedicke, Tami Haaland, Lowell Jaeger, and Lois Red Elk, among others, and find countless challenges and revisions to the dominant stories and voices and, even more, entirely new themes, ideas, techniques, and Montanas.[4]

....

4   How do new voices enter the mix? Lots of people have to make concerted efforts, from writers to publishers to readers to civic leaders to philanthropists. In terms of Montana poetry, the efforts of local and regional presses such as Farcountry Press, Lost Horse Press, Many Voices Press, and the University of Washington Press, just to mention a few, have brought forth collections and anthologies by Native American and Euro-Americans, women and men, queers and straights, Western Montanans and Eastern Montanans, and more.

What these challenges and new matters are, we will begin to see in the next section of this Introduction.

To conclude our brief overview of the current state of Montana writing, we can say that if we do not live in a golden age of opportunity and inclusiveness—far from it—we can at least say that we live at a time when, with some digging and visits to bookstores, libraries, websites, and book festivals, we can read and hear an array of voices and discover a multiplicity of imagined and re-imagined communities and Montanas. As readers of this collection must no doubt grant, there is not—nor could there ever be—a single, homogenous, unitary Montana of lived experience or of the literary imagination. On the contrary, there must be many Montanas, with no one able—at least for very long—to privilege their views, subjects, or techniques over the lives, experiences, beliefs, languages, ethnicities, cultures, histories, politics, sexualities, themes, places, geographies, environments, natures, images, metaphors, and emotions of everyone else.

III. THE ESSAYS

The first bloc of essays, "Montana Modernism," read (and laud) the work of poets whose projects and preoccupations connect them to the literary movements of the first decades of the twentieth century. Alternately witty, playful, allusive, and ironic—yet always self-aware—these poets offer sometimes biting, sometimes deeply personal and poignant responses to the new, often dizzying, complexities of a modern world. In "Finding Grace: Discovering the Poetry of Grace Stone Coates," our sparkling first essay, Danell Jones explores Coates's cultured, sharp verse and discovers a voice that not only "furtively celebrates a secret, interior life" but town politics and the sweeping landscapes of Eastern Montana as well. Jones finds Coates to be sly, sardonic, and even brilliant: why, then, did such a talent stop writing and more or less disappear from the literary landscape of Montana and the United States? From a mystery, we turn to a death and a lone, thin book of poetry. In "The Frost Family in Montana: A Story of Poetic Generations," Tami Haaland reads *Franconia* (1936), the only book of poems by Marjorie Frost Fraser, the daughter of Robert Frost, the great American poet, and the wife of Willard Fraser, later to be one of Billings's most influential civic leaders. Often ill and then dead at twenty-nine, her book published posthumously, Frost Frasier had little time to write, but

Haaland's close readings of the few poems she produced reveal a sharp and insightful mind exploring nature and life in the modern West. In the third essay, the provocatively titled "The End of Montana: Heather Tone, Gertrude Stein, and the Frontiers of Metaphor," Karl Olson argues that newcomer Tone builds upon the radical, high modernist techniques and ethos of Gertrude Stein. As Olson notes, words, in Stein and Tone's estimation, look like "dead prostitutes," and Tone seeks, in brilliant, alarming ways, to infuse them with life, "much / like vodka may be infused with roses or bacon." While Tone may not be interested in being (or being labeled) a "Montana writer," Olson finds in her work a "disavowal" of region that is also "symbiotically rooted in region."

As the essayists in the "Community" cluster suggest, poetry may be the communal art nonpareil. Exploring the work of some of the state's finest poets, the contributors examine the ways in which poetry can be used to build and sustain, or remember and sift, or challenge and reform the bonds between individuals, friends, families, and communities. The very acts of reading and writing poetry may not only call into being communities of readers and writers, but may also be some of the most important forces shaping how we think about who we are and about who and what matters. In "The Language of Dry Wind: The Poems of Tami Haaland," Sue Hart and Danell Jones argue that if, at first, her "poems appear to be quiet meditations on ordinary life in the American West," and if "her language is unpretentious, no more demanding than the daily newspaper," all this "apparent docility is merely camouflage": the poet, in her meditations on family, place, nature, and, especially, the lives and fortitude of girls and women in Montana, "draws us close to our trifling world to reveal the profound questions of human existence which reside there." For Haaland, words and poetry can transform lives and help us to know ourselves and those around us. In "From the Margins to the Center: The Populist Poetics of Roger Dunsmore," Alan Weltzien—a grandmaster of Montana and Western Studies—argues that, for Dunsmore, "some stories matter more than others." A determined populist, Dunsmore writes for and finds his subjects and stories among the lives and experiences of everyday and marginalized people. Distrusting the usual sources of cultural authority—from professors to bankers to politicians—and taking his cues from such democratically-minded poets as Walt Whitman and Gary Snyder (and such Montana writers as Mark Gibbons, Ed Lahey, and others), Dunsmore attempts to give voice to the unseen, forgotten, or neglected hovering at the rough edges of Montanan and American life.

If Dunsmore often focuses on the racial and economic divides that work to exclude or silence voices, Sandra Alcosser and Melissa Kwasny suggest that women have much more to say about bodies, desires, nature, and more than has been suggested—or perhaps authorized—by patriarchal cultures. As Caroline Patterson explains in "Of Eros and Earth: The Poetry of Sandra Alcosser and Melissa Kwasny," the work of these two nationally-acclaimed poets developed out of a community of women artists in the 1970s that defined itself, at least in part, against the masculinist culture and widely accepted (and usually male-authored) myths of the West. As Patterson writes, both artists seek to subvert "the orthodox western myths about human relationships to nature" in order to help readers to "think through the biggest questions of civilization, namely—what is our place in it? How do we respond to this world—in these bodies, in this region?" Closing this section, in "Lowell Jaeger: In First Person," Kathleen Flenniken sounds Jaeger's career-long commitment to the poetry of personal witness, to an art that affirms the individual's responsibilities to others and the world around us. We are not apart, but connected to one another and the earth. And if, as a young man, Jaeger was a poet of ferocious insight (and sometimes of accusation), Flenniken also observes in his later work an increasingly playful awareness of the technical possibilities of the first-person speaker.

In "Sovereignties," the third grouping of essays, our contributors explore, through the work of a number of poets, complex issues of Native American cultural, linguistic, political, and economic sovereignty. As Kathryn Shanley, Lowell Jaeger, and David Moore reveal, just as cultural workers have, for the last several decades, sought to preserve and reinvigorate Native American cultures, languages, histories, and more, Native American poets have sought not only to reclaim and revitalize particularly Native American ways of seeing and understanding the world, nature, and the lives of communities and individuals, but have also entered, via their art, the ongoing—and often harsh—debates and struggles over Native American control of land and natural resources. In "Renegade Worlds in the Poetry of James Welch," Shanley notes that "in a variety of intense emotional registers, Welch imagines nineteenth-century Plains Indian life from the Native point of view as well as the way that history played out in modern Native peoples' lives": "Welch's focus on the individual consciousness further grounds his aesthetics in speaking subjects rather than omniscient narrators, and to borrow Gayatri Spivak's term, they are subalterns. In other words, the powers they possess are the powers of the insignificant, the silenced or overlooked, the objectized, and the overwhelmed, yet Welch not so much speaks for them—for 'the disinherited'—as he speaks with them, or from among their company." In Welch's poetry, "the renegade who wants words wants to speak his piece in his own defense, and he rises out of erasure when his story is heard, regardless whether he can ever be truly vindicated or known."

In "Written in the Hearts of Our People: Victor A. Charlo, Lois Red Elk, and Minerva Allen," Jaeger argues that "there are limits for these three Native poets, a reticence to speak about oneself as an individual and cultural barriers surrounding what cannot be shared with persons outside the tribe." Taking up each poet in turn, he examines Native American ways of seeing life and experience, and takes up crucial questions about cultural difference and the challenges of writing for diverse audiences. If Jaeger finds a certain reserve in the poets, Moore, in "'Through the Monster's Mouth': Contemporary Indigenous Poetry and Land Rights of the Flathead Reservation" dives directly into how Heather Cahoon, Victor Charlo, and Jennifer Finley draw upon tribal values of kinship with the land in order to participate, via poetry, in ongoing (and vexed) debates surrounding management of the National Bison Range. As these poets make clear, speaking and being heard matter a great deal.

As the contributors to "Last? Best? Place?" detail in their close studies of Ed Lahey, J. V. Cunningham, Mandy Smoker, and Madeline DeFrees, Montana can be—as advertised—a very Hard Place. Surviving economically—and emotionally, spiritually, linguistically, and culturally—has not been easy for many Native Americans, both on and off the reservation. At the same time, many immigrants to the state also have not fared well and many have lost their jobs and communities and have left to try their luck elsewhere. Nevertheless, and as the work of these poets attests, Montana is also not a place without hope, and survival may just be possible. As Timothy Steele observes in "J. V. Cunningham's Montana Poetry," many readers may not know that the celebrated American poet "spent most of his formative years in Billings, Montana, and he always considered himself a native of the state." Analyzing two of Cunningham's finest poems, "Montana Pastoral" and "Montana Fifty Years Ago," Steele finds Cunningham to be both a master of the "plain style," or poetry that strives for a colloquial, accessible language and imagery, and of the "harsh and menacing landscape" of Montana that can break the lives of those who go up against it.

In "Ed Lahey: Underground Poet," novelist David Abrams sounds the depths of Lahey's uneasy relationship with the mining past of his hometown, Butte. Speaking as both a literal and figurative "underground poet," Lahey's often caustic criticism of Butte led to his divided, "heartbreak life": he came from a hard, seemingly-in-perpetual-decline town that scarcely acknowledged his poetic gifts. He was an outsider in a town of outsiders. Like Abrams, Carey Voeller, in "Montana Blue: Reimagining 'The Last Best Place' in M. L. Smoker's Poetry," finds a dark and profound current of grief in the work of an exemplary Montana poet. As Voeller contends, Smoker, in her first collection, *Another Attempt at Rescue* (2005), offers a rather different view of Montana than has been suggested in the celebratory phrase and mythos, "The Last Best Place." Writing about lives on the Fort Peck Indian Reservation, Smoker offers a much bleaker view of life in Montana, yet nonetheless recounts the "endurance and survival of American Indians." Montana may be that Hard Place, but people can survive, can endure. And if, in the first three essays in this bloc, Montana appears as a pretty grim, marginal space, in "Madeline DeFrees's Montana Renaissance," Jocelyn Siler finds that that state can also be a place of astonishing personal transformation and growth. As Siler recounts, after spending thirty-eight years as a nun, DeFrees left her order: "Amazement is still very much evident in Madeline's poetry. It's as if once she had put aside the claustrophobic certainty of life as a Roman Catholic nun she became permanently astonished by the possibilities opened by intellectual and creative exploration." In Missoula, and on the faculty of the University of Montana, DeFrees buzzed with ideas, images, boldness, and community with her peers and students.

From one celebrated teacher of poetry, we turn in our next section to another: what would a book about Montana poetry be without an essay or two on Dick Hugo? As perhaps the state's best known and most widely celebrated poet, Hugo has been the subject of biographies (both in print and in film) and scholarly studies, and has been widely anthologized and quoted. Hugo looms so large in Montana letters (and perhaps even larger in the mythology surrounding Montana letters), in fact, that any discussion of Montana poetry and writing seemingly has to include the Bard of Triggering Town. And rightly so, as the contributors to "Hugo Revisioned," our fifth cluster, suggest: not only does Hugo continue to have a profound impact on how Montanans imagine Montana, but later generations of writers have had, in the process of finding their own voice, to come to terms with his considerable legacy.

To begin our consideration of Hugo and his place in Montana writing, we return to the setting of three rather controversial poems. In "The Dixon Bards," David Gilcrest retells the story of how, after a day of fishing, Hugo, Welch, and J. D. Reed (and a rarely mentioned fourth person) stopped in Dixon and decided that all would write a poem about the bar; the poems were later published side-by-side in that apotheosis of urbane, Eastern culture, *The New Yorker*. By closely reading the poems to reveal the lurking tensions of class and race, Gilcrest's essay culminates with an analysis of a poetic rebuttal by Heather Cahoon which nicely deflates the legend of the Dixon bar poems and, in important ways, restores Dixon as "a place for plums" on the Flathead Reservation. From the boys out fishing, we turn to a woman writing about Hugo fishing. In "The Entire Poet: Patricia Goedicke's Surreal Homage to Richard Hugo," Casey Charles argues that Goedicke's homage-poem to Hugo, "The Entire Catch," written just before Hugo's death, captures "a sense of Hugo's Montana landscape in ways that are both representational and at the same time inimitable to Goedicke's image-laden and surreal poetics" and brings "an element of internationalism to [Montana], more particularly an indebtedness to the free play of thought in verse, typified by the juxtaposition of often unexpected, unrealistic, or incongruous imagery." The poem, he argues, not only pays tribute to the great poet, but at the same time works to move Montana poetics "beyond the confines of the regionalism often believed more indicative of Montana writers."

But did you know that Hugo was not the only Hugo? From Goedicke rewriting Hugo, we turn to the other Hugo, Ripley. In "Riding the Right Wind Home: Reading Ripley Schemm Hugo," Kim Anderson notes that while Schemm Hugo wrote many poems inspired by the landscape of her Montana birthplace, we are also able to locate a subtle but persistent thread in the poet's work about breaking free of the West. Looking to a handful of poems describing scenarios of escape, Anderson finds that these attempts are almost always unsuccessful, not because the poet fails but because, despite the allure of the wider world, she ultimately chooses to return home. Where Hugo seemed forever troubled about finding a home, Schemm Hugo finds a margin of peace and safety in Montana.

Our collection closes with three essays on "Poetry Activism," or the spirit of advocacy that serves as one of the guiding principles of this project. In "The In-betweenness of Home: The Advocacy of Judy Blunt and Paul Zarzyski," Nancy Cook argues that their poetry negotiates a space between two poetic practices, cowboy and literary. While their subject matter and ethical alliances suggest cowboy poetry, their techniques follow the models of literary poetry. This "in-betweenness" ultimately alters both schools; it invites the cowboy into the classroom while at the same time honors rural audiences as receptive to alternative aesthetics. Next, in "Poetry for Life's Sake: On the Road with Montana's Poet Laureates," Ken Egan, Jr. explores the work and public activism of four of Montana's Poet Laureates, Sandra Alcosser, Greg Pape, Henry Red Bird, and Sheryl Noethe. Not only offering close readings of outstanding poems by each laureate, Egan also explores the vital role of the Poet Laureate in bringing poetry (and a passion for writing and self-expression) to readers, would-be readers, *and* would-be poets across the state. As Egan writes, "Montana's poets laureate travel to reservations, schools, libraries, festivals, and more to promote poetry as a public good, a vital source of self-understanding, shared wisdom, and joy in language." He continues, "In the process they have come to realize Montanans not only read but practice poetry, often in private, and poets laureate serve as a conduit for passion and belief hardly glimpsed on the surface of our culture." Lastly, Lisa Simon argues, in "Poetry Advocacy in Montana: The Wide Frontier," that, in the words of Walt Whitman, "to have great poetry, we must have great audiences." Taking a practical approach to engaging as many readers in poetry as possible, she suggests concrete strategies to combat the ubiquitous waning of the interest in poetry. Through personal anecdotes and close reading, Simon demonstrates the power of poems to connect to readers' senses and worldly experiences without requiring specialized expertise. That is not to say, however, such higher levels do not exist, but Simon argues that the role of the advocate requires an attention to the initial stages of appreciation. Our final essay serves as a blueprint, a how-to, for sharing poetry and building communities around the written word.

IV. CONCLUSION

In the Introduction to *All Our Stories Are Here* (2009), I argued that while the contributors to that volume had gone some way in expanding the study of Montana writing, there was still much work to be done; I would say the same about the present volume. The contributors to *These Living Songs* have explored an astonishing wealth and diversity of poetry and shared treasure-chests of great ideas and insights, yet much more could be done. I have no doubt, for example, that dedicated researchers could find pages and pages of wonderful, unknown poetry in regional library, museums, and archives. In Butte alone, there may be sheaves of poems written in Armenian or Polish or Gaelic. On reservations and small towns, someone has folders of poems written by elders or ancestors. There are poems scratched on the walls of prison cells. Out there, somewhere, is a wonderful poem included among recipes for green bean casseroles in a church cookbook or alongside the latest news about the Wobblies in a union broadsheet, newsletter, or journal. And how many other books of poetry wait in libraries for someone to check them out and encounter entire worlds of thought and image? There's more to be done—we also need a book of essays on the Montana memoir—and , in good Montana fashion, the work will continue.

WORKS CITED

Anderson, Benedict. *Imagined Communities: Reflections on the Origin and Spread of Nationalism.* Revised Edition. New York: Verso, 2006. Print.

Bevis, William W. *Ten Tough Trips: Montana Writers and the West.* 1990. Norman: University of Oklahoma Press, 2003. Print.

Hugo, Richard. *Making Certain It Goes On: The Collected Poems of Richard Hugo.* NewYork: W. W. Norton & Company, 1984. Print.

THESE LIVING SONGS

PART 1 MONTANA MODERNISM

Photo by Lucy Capehart

CHAPTER 1

Discovering Grace: Coming to the Poems of Grace Stone Coates

DANELL JONES *(Billings, Montana)*

Tell me what you think of these poems, she says, handing me a brown book. I glance at the cover: *Food of Gods and Starvelings: The Selected Poems of Grace Stone Coates* (2007).

Who, I wonder, is Grace Stone Coates?

I find her name irresistible—ringing, as it does, of a gentleman's jacket, the cargo that dragged Virginia Woolf to the bottom of a Sussex river, and some unbidden, undeserved gift from God. Surely this is the name of a poet.

. . .

Who is this poet born on a Kansas wheat farm, drawn to Montana by a job in a schoolhouse, married to a Butte shopkeeper, then billeted to dusty Martinsdale until old age drove her to a Bozeman retirement home? What can one expect of a poet of Martinsdale? The clichés offer themselves too readily: a poet of mule teams and barns, antelope and campfires. Thumbing through her biography, I discover a different insight into her creative catalyst. "[A] Montana hamlet," she writes in 1925, "offers exceptional opportunities for reflecting upon the universe!" (Rostad 41). The universe? I feel a bit skeptical.

. . .

I can imagine central Montana today, but what was it like 100 years ago? This is how poet Gwendolyn Haste describes her journey to visit Coates in Martinsdale in the early 1920s:

> On we jolted, over the dusty, primitive road, around and over hills, some sage-brushy, some dressed in drought-bedraggled wheat, some left to the jack rabbit and the sere remains of old crops. . . . And, of course, the train from the east was late—hours late. . . . [T]hen boredom and heat in the station until the Pullmans and day coaches rolled in, with more hours to go while we followed the cottonwood-lined Musselshell through Lavina, Ryegate and Harlowton to the whistle stop at Martinsdale. (Rostad 37)

Martinsdale—not even substantial enough to command a place in the regular train schedule. A mere whistle stop. What universe could possibly unfold itself there?

. . .

I examine the cover of the book. It bears the browns of earth: dirt, sand, mud—the coat of a mink, an ermine, an otter. The color of bark and stones.

Before I've read a word of poetry, the portrait of Coates on the cover harmonizes with a vision I am beginning to create in my mind. She is a sepia goddess of the Gibson Girl variety: skin as pale and perfect as fresh milk; light hair billowing in waves under ribbon and bow. A decorous high collar, a modest slice of lace just past her throat followed by a rapid tide of ruffles from shoulder to shoulder. There is only one thing I don't understand: why is every inch of ruffle and lace black? Even down to the flowered ribbons in her hair. These aren't mourning clothes. I'm baffled, curious. Early twentieth-century portraits almost always depict young women in modest, demurring, sinless white. Yet here is Grace Stone Coates, dressed all in black.

A peek into Lee Rostad's biography of Coates tells me she achieved no small success in her lifetime: dozens of poems in important national publications—the *New York Times*, the *Christian Science Monitor*, the *New Republic* (Rostad 41), even Harriet Monroe's groundbreaking *Poetry: A Magazine of Verse* (Rostad 33). Stories in two volumes of the *Anthology of*

American Short Story (1929, 1930) (Rostad 43). Two books of poems and one novel. Assistant editor of the University of Montana's *The Frontier* magazine (Rostad 5); reporter for local papers. Clearly, in the 1920s and early 1930s she enjoyed some regional and even national acclaim. Then, in 1935, the poetry and fiction seemed to come to an abrupt stop. She continued editing, continued writing news stories and historical pieces, but there were no books of poetry, no more novels.

Her books went out of print. She almost slipped into literary oblivion. For decades it seemed as if she would be forgotten entirely. Then in 1988, William Kittredge and Annick Smith included her in *The Last Best Place: A Montana Anthology* (1988); a decade later, John Updike selected her story "Wild Plums" for the *Best American Short Stories of the Twentieth Century* (1999) (Rostad 43). Her novel *Black Cherries* (1931) was reprinted in 2003 by the University of Nebraska Press. Then in 2007, Rostad and the poet Rick Newby brought out the book I have before me: *Food of Gods and Starvelings: The Selected Poems of Grace Stone Oates* (2007). It gathers the poems in both books as well as dozens of uncollected pieces. The title comes from a review of *Mead and Mangel-Wurzel* (1931), Coates's first book. "[I]t isn't verse that is honey wine and hunger root," she said of that collection. "[I]t is love, which is mead when you are falling in, and mangel-wurzel when you are falling out" (Coates 20). What does she mean by wine of the gods? Food of the destitute? Time to taste.

. . .

The first poem. Lo! It is breakfast.

AT BREAKFAST

"Where were you, last night?"

"I was in bed . . . sleeping
Beside you . . . of course!"

"And I was leaping
Broomsticks, and burying Jesus,
And patting Godiva's horse." (Coates 33)

Whose voices? A husband and wife, I think, at the breakfast table. Why does she ask where he has been? The question hints at discord, but his reply comforts: he was with her in their bed. "Of course," he adds, affirming this as his rightful and customary place. Nothing irregular here. Yet, she responds with surprises. He may have been sleeping beside her, but she, she has been caught up in wild dreams—leaping, burying, patting, even flashing, as one does in dreams, through time and space, from one identity to another. At first she is a bride jumping the broom at a wedding. (Perhaps, if wives' tales hold true, she hopes to rule the household by jumping highest or hitting the ground first.) The next instant, she is at Jesus's tomb; but she doesn't say whether she is mother or Magdalene. Carried away on the wisp of a comma, the dreamer pats a noblewoman's horse. Is this the moment before or the moment just after this medieval wife rides naked through the streets?

I'm struck by the dreamer's defiant travels, their liveliness, and the worlds they unfold. And then I realize that their very abundance renders the husband's blameless sleep drearily unimaginative. These spouses are not just two bodies side-by-side, but two worlds: one, quotidian and peaceful; the other, exotic and vibrant. And each, it appears, is entirely oblivious to the other.

. . .

As I read on, I discover that Coates's poems often look at Martinsdale from the margins of respectability: she is never quite the faithful wife, never exactly the good housekeeper or the unerring neighbor. Even as a newlywed, she felt alienated from this little universe on the prairie (Rostad 10). Perhaps that's why so many of the speakers in these poems take the role of the despised woman. How wonderfully haughty, I think, to use a French expression to title a poem about a misunderstood woman: "Femme Incomprise." But the poem itself is so lighthearted, so comically illuminating of small town antipathies, I laugh out loud.

> The ladies who discuss me
> Could hardly like me worse,
> For they embroider doilies
> And I embroider verse.
>
> While they're crocheting sweaters

And knitting counterpanes,
I'm picking out new patterns
For couplets and quatrains. (199)

Even as the speaker laments the distance between her knitting sisters and herself, she also recognizes that the split is not superficial. It is an unbridgeable gap of sensibility, inclination, dedication, occupation, perhaps even morality. Yet, are their desires really so very far apart? Ironically, they share twin passions: first, a need to create, and second, a fascination with pattern.

The breach forever widens
  In spite of my regrets
That their souls dote on damask
  And mine on triolets.

As in all ridiculous conflicts, their petty competition collapses into ludicrous name-calling.

I call their laces stupid,
  They find my metres lame;
I hate their fat initials—
  But they hate my whole name! (199)

In the end, the townswomen get the decisive satisfaction: the pleasure of hating not just a short set of embroidered initials, but the whole collection of letters that make up the poet's entire, tripartite name. For reasons that are at once comic and tragic, the weavers of yarn and those of verse remain ironic enemies.

. . .

Although Coates claimed to find "Village Satiety" a hilarious poem, the only comedy I find is bitterly ironic. The speaker lashes out at the dull routines of rural Montana life. She is bored, despairs of her constricted world, and wants to triumph against it. Spending hours at her window watching "stupidity come and go," she furtively celebrates a secret, interior life. This "hidden life" is both more incandescent and more ominous than anything her neighbors know.

While I live a hidden life more sparkling

Than lights that scream on a city street,
With secret ways of thought, more darkling
Than crypt where cavern and river meet. (67)

This internal life exceeds anything in the external world whether natural
or artificial. Despite this dark, secret interior world, it is easy enough to
deceive her neighbors into believing she is nothing more than a genteel
housewife. What they don't understand—what she believes they can't
possibly understand—is that her abnormalities are themselves the source
of her transcendence.

I am deception to those who see
   Only coifed hair and tints that perish,
A flat bosom and crooked knee.
   In me is what the gods cherish. (67)

Ironically, her aberrations single her out for greatness. The alienation of
the outsider raises her above her conventional, complacent, comfortable
neighbors and makes her the golden child of the gods. The discomfort
of difference, she seems to be saying, brings her closer to the source of
creative power.

. . .

I am fascinated by Coates's ability to capture competing emotions of bit-
terness, anger, and humiliation. At once angry and vulnerable, "Turnstile"
reads like a short joke, but captures something profoundly human.

TURNSTILE

After Rabelaisian shaft
   And a kiss in mockery,
To my crazy room, as daft
   Comes my body, troubling me.

Must the turnstile of my hell
   Click its worn, accustomed way
Past the dolt who can not spell
   One bright word of Rabelais? (35)

Inspired by the wickedly funny sixteenth-century French writer, François Rabelais, the speaker's allusion celebrates the power of learning, word-play, irony, and satire. She envisions her tragedy not as one of the mind, but rather one of a body which is able to mislead the wit into the prison house of madness. Coates suffered recurring bouts of what she called "maniac-depression" throughout her life (Rostad 169). Does this poem describe the pain of that illness? The symbol of the turnstile—that prosaic counting gate—unnerves me. The turnstile separates by design, allowing only one person at a time to pass. This gateway to hell is both banal and isolating. It is also deeply humiliating. The speaker imagines a bystander who escapes its tragic click because he or she couldn't begin to understand the language of Rabelais, let alone his barbed wit. Her particular hell, it appears, is reserved for the clever, the inquisitive, the accomplished.

. . .

These are bitter, brave poems. But Coates also writes wildly dazzling, fragrant poems. The musical rhythm of "Revenants" sweeps me up from the very first stanza into a magical world.

REVENANTS

A moony spell was on the night,
    And silence in the cedar trees;
Around me came a tumbling flight
    Of swift, tumultuous, golden bees.

Its rhythm and language borrows from sixteenth-century lyrics; its Eliza-bethan sensuousness soon catches me up.

They clung upon my lips, my breast,
    I bowed my head to see them there,
And felt their jostling bodies pressed
    Against the tendrils of my hair.

A drone and odor seemed to rise
    As one, and wrapped me in its mesh.
Their vibrant wings explored my thighs
    And secret flower of my flesh

The speaker's body is erotically overwhelmed by this swarm of bees, who engulf her in a frenzy of wings and scent so intense it brings her to an expected—and unexpected—climax.

> Till, swooning to their will, I wist
>   My visitants no earthly bees,
> But dead desires keeping tryst
>   Beneath remembered cedar trees. (56)

"Dead desires," it turns out, are not dead at all. Like Proust's *madeleine*, which transports him to a place of sensuous memory with a mere bite, her encounters with ordinary things trigger involuntary memories. The experience is vivid, immediate, all encompassing, and passionate. Memory and imagination are as tangible and exhilarating as the moment itself.

. . .

I find myself impressed by Coates's dedication to the full riot of human emotions. Consider the question of love. She honors the emotional truth, however painful or paradoxical.

BEYOND ANSWER

> Do I love you? I cannot give you answer.
>   I know if a great wind sweeps over the brink
> Of a gorge, and I am borne like a madcap dancer,
>   Or if a hush falls, it is of you I think.

In moments of extremity—great noise and motion or profound stillness and silence—the beloved is present. There seems to be no state of nature that does not bring him to mind. But he is also abiding in the world of human interaction and creation.

> When the empty-minded baffle me with chatter;
>   Or a creator's golden thought shines through
> His craft, and delicate ways are all that matter
>   To life; if I am alone—my thoughts are of you.

The irritation of the nattering bore or the thrill of a brilliant work of art is always shared with the beloved. He is ever-present. He is even there as the speaker betrays him, enveloped in the arms of another lover.

When my lips are quiet under another's token,
   And my craven limbs are bared to another's embrace,
It is your name my shuddering has not spoken,
   And to your darkness I turn away my face. (49)

At the moment of sexual climax, she turns from her new lover toward the darkness. What she finds there is the deceived beloved: his unspoken name; his absent body. Her "craven limbs" may not be able to resist the allure of a new admirer, but she cannot escape the magnetism of the beloved. He is the "ever-fixéd mark" that looks on tempests, boredom, poetry, even betrayal, and is never shaken.

. . .

But there are comfortable attachments, too. Coates shared one of these with her sporting, mercantile husband, Henderson. Imagining how he would respond to her published book of poems, she writes, "[W]hen Henderson sees my book with my name full of poems that sound like chop feed to him his eyes will be so proud of me that his hand won't notice it's signing a check. I'll rub his arm with liniment! He and I are enormously good friends" (Coates 26). I expect that "To a Good Sport" is a poem to him. In it, she celebrates the differences between the poet and the sportsman. "I'm glad you do not sing erotic songs," the speaker declares,

   I'd rather see you land a fighting trout
      Upon a boulder,
   Or clamber down the shale and shelving rock
      With game on shoulder

She likes this hunting and fishing husband and moans with mock horror at the thought of being married to an artsy man.

   Than have you pick Impressionists to pieces,
      Or—rather worse—
   Patter wise nonsense when Tchaikovski ceases,
      Or write free verse! (194)

Wryly condescending, the speaker imagines having a husband who talks confidently of modern art and music, and who not only writes poetry, but the most modern poetry of all: free verse. Here she celebrates the comforting boundaries of difference. What could be worse, she seems to say, than being married to a man whose poetry was more daring than one's own?

. . .

I am drawn first to poems that are meditations of an emotional universe, but Coates also writes of the Montana landscapes. Yet, there are fewer of these than one might expect from the "dear falcon of the crazies," as a friend once called her, connecting her voice to the Crazy Mountain range that rises up from the prairie just south of Martinsdale (Rostad 316). Some of these poems describe the relationship between the land and the human psyche in surprising ways. Take "Tarnish," for example. The speaker begins by wanting to immerse herself deeply in the natural world in hopes that it will provide some kind of solace for her sense of professional failure.

TARNISH

I wish I could walk to the farthest hill,
The farthest hill under dappled sky,
Questioning life till it tell me why
I have grown tawdry, I have grown drunken,
My golden hour of promise shrunken
To a foolish word and a flaccid will.

She believes she has lost her talent and that her "golden hour of promise" is nothing but a foolish, impotent joke. Although she wanders into the hills for solace, she does not find it.

Skies that leaned, and peaks that thrust—
A wisp of vapor, a pinch of dust. (109)

It is not the great power of nature to heal that we find here, but the power of the despairing mind to defeat the natural world. By the end of the poem, the mighty sky and the giant peaks have dissolved in her mind's eye as thoroughly as her talent.

. . .

Still, let me contrast that despairing poem with these joyful lines from "The Cliff":

I shall climb the lichened boulders,
Studying red and black and orange
Mantling their aggressive shoulders;
Lean against their warmth to trace
Lovely gray-green lichen lace (172)

Is this not a writer in love with the natural world? With the prairie and the coulee? It may have been the complexities of human relationships that often fueled Coates's poetry, but one can see she also cherished Montana. She wrote of herself: "[W]hen she is away from her Martinsdale home, she remembers, never the dingy meanness of a western village but the tremendous sweep of valley from the Belt mountains to the Crazies; or the Musselshell [river], swimming in moonlight, below Gordon Butte" (Coates 17).

. . .

I don't know why a writer stops writing.

In her letters after 1935, Coates provides a number of evasive, sometimes flippant explanations for the halt in her work. "Until I am rested I can't write," she says in 1937 as she is recovering from illness in the Mayo Clinic. She acerbically adds that she cannot write "unless I fall in love, and then I'll be tired of that. Persons who have to be in love to write love lyrics are not poets" (Rostad 268). Later, she tells friend and fellow editor at *The Frontier*, H.G. Merriam, that she is not writing because she "became aware that I was trying to do this and that from outside pressure, when what I wanted to do was get outdoors and make garden. I have only one life, and if gardening is what I want, writing becomes silly" (Rostad 271). In the letter she continues to sound angry, defensive.

The only reason to write is because one has something he wants to say. And my writing is in fine shape, I'm doing what I want to do, and when I get the damned company off my hands if when as I do write, I'll be again writing what I want to write. (Rostad 271)

Corresponding with him again a few months later, she reiterates her plan to write in the future. "I haven't a new thing to offer you. One of these days I'll be writing again, and it will be when I have something I want to say, and am saying it" (Rostad 274). Is she trying to convince him or herself?

A few months later, she writes to friend and writer William Saroyan about a bad fall she has taken. "I do hurt so in all my dark corners," she explains. Then she quips, "Do you think it means I've been overeating, or that I'm going to have a poem?" (Rostad 279). Just a little over a week later, she follows with another letter returning to the same theme, this time more despondently. "I do not know why reading your letters makes me cry, except that I am not writing. Not writing is for me a way of being dead." Of course, being Grace Stone Coates, she cannot resist following this with a sardonic observation: "Being dead is all right, but not while one is alive" (Rostad 279).

. . .

But perhaps Coates did not stop writing at all. There are hints in the letters that she had been thinking of poems and stories, jotting words down. She jokes to Gwendolyn Haste in late 1938 about the people who were boarding in her house and claims she's "written poems about them" (Rostad 292). In the mid-1940s, she writes to Merriam saying, "My days would not amuse you, and of course I still write; and have nothing to submit to you just now." She talks of her war work, grading potatoes for the army, then adds, "I wrote some poems, none of which got set down on paper—"wrote" being a generic term here" (Rostad 301). At Christmas 1949, she tells a neighbor that "I no longer send cards, but to a few friends who I think will tolerate them I send rhymes in response to their cards" (Rostad 308). Even as late as the 1950s, she tells Merriam she has been working on a story and a poem. In 1960, she plans to send him a piece, but then changes her mind. She even submits something to a Denver publication, but it is rejected (Rostad 316). She may not have been publishing, she may not always be writing work down, but she is still thinking like a writer.

. . .

I don't know why a writer stops writing. I don't know why Grace Stone Coates never published another book. Perhaps she no longer had anything to say in verse. Perhaps offering her work to an editor's judgmental eye just became another kind of submission. Or, just perhaps the song of a thrush on a Meagher county thistle was enough:

YIELD

Yield—of hatreds unexplored,
  Cheated of their biting laughter—
This our empty bins afford
  After ... after ...

(Redthrust, on the thistle-fluff,
Sing clear!)
  It is enough.[1] (54)

WORKS CITED

Coates, Grace Stone. *Food of Gods and Starvelings: The Selected Poems of Grace Stone Coates*. Eds. Lee Rostad and Rick Newby. Helen, Montana: Drumlummon Institute, 2007. Print.

Rostad, Lee. *Grace Stone Coates: Her Life in Letters*. Helena: Riverbend Publishing, 2004. Print.

....

1 A "Redthrust" is not a kind of bird, although this is the word which appears in all editions of Coates's poems. It may be a local expression for a red thrush. A long-styled Thistle (*Cirsium longistylum*) is, however, native to Meagher County.

CHAPTER 2

The Frost Family in Montana:
A Story of Poetic Generations

TAMI HAALAND *(Billings, Montana)*

When Marjorie Frost married Willard Fraser in Billings, Montana, her parents, Robert and Elinor Frost, prepared to visit. The year was 1933, and Robert Frost wrote to his new son-in-law with enthusiasm about Montana in this and other letters:

> I haven't known the kind of excitement . . . your politics give us since I was a young democrat campaigning for Grover Cleveland with my father in San Francisco in 1884. We or I anyway read your Montana Year Book clean through every little while in further preparation for our visit. You will find us ready to pass examinations in the following subjects:
>
> Montana Politics National and Local (from The Progressive)
> Montana Education (from the friend [Sidney Cox] who nearly got strung up for teaching radical ethics or morals at Missoula—and I have no doubt he deserved kicking if not hanging.)
> Montana Agriculture and Stock Raising (from the Year Book)
> Montana Climate and Scenery (from the Year Book)
> Montana Homelikeness (from having you and Marj there).

To this note he added a postscript: "Has Marj written any more poetry lately? Tell her to send another as good as the last. I like my country written about that way" (Thompson 405–06).

Marjorie Frost Fraser's small volume of poetry, *Franconia*, was published in 1936, two years after her death, and the poem her father refers to is entitled "America." Compiled and edited by her parents, these poems follow the stages of her life from girlhood to marriage. They reveal not only her technical skill and knowledge of poetry, but they present her metaphorical sensibility in an eloquent and clear voice.

Born March 29, 1905, Marjorie was the youngest surviving child of Robert and Elinor Frost, whose letters indicate that she suffered from respiratory illness as a teenager and was often too weak to participate in family activities. She was hospitalized for a time in Baltimore. In 1929, she was stronger and began a course of study in nursing, but by 1931 she was living in Mesa Vista Sanatorium in Boulder, Colorado, where doctors eventually realized she had had tuberculosis for eight or more years (Thompson 376; see also Anderson 153). After a long stay, she was able to attend the University of Colorado to continue her studies, and in March 1932, Marjorie wrote to her parents to tell them that she and Willard Fraser were engaged to be married, but only after he graduated from the university and could "get on his feet" (Thompson 382). Their wedding was a quiet ceremony in Billings at the home of Willard's parents on June 3, 1933. Initially they moved to Helena because Willard Fraser was hired to work on a "weekly newspaper" (Thompson 395), but they quickly relocated to Billings, where Fraser later became involved in politics, eventually becoming one of Billings's most colorful mayors in the 1960s and 1970s.

Marjorie's story ends tragically, however, only eleven months after their marriage. Soon after she gave birth to their daughter, Robin, on March 16, 1934, Marjorie became ill and was diagnosed with puerperal, or childbed, fever as a result of unsafe conditions in the hospital. She lingered for seven weeks, sometimes with a fever as high as 110 degrees (Untermeyer 241–42). The Frosts lived in Montana with their son-in-law during the month leading up to her death, then remained after the funeral for several weeks. Doctors treated Marjorie with frequent blood transfusions, and often she seemed to rally, but the infection persisted. At last, they flew her to the Mayo Clinic in Minnesota, where she died on May 2, 1934.

In the year following her death, Elinor and Robert Frost began to consider publishing Marjorie's poetry. While Elinor wanted to see some of Marjorie's poems "in either the Atlantic or the Yale Review," she indicated that Robert was "very reluctant to broach anything to any magazine" (Grade 170). In a letter to his daughter Lesley, Robert says, "I thought we would call Marjories book If I Should Live to Be a Doll, just for the strangeness of the thing. We don't want it to savor the least bit of memorial lugubriousness. The poems are good enough for publication regularly, though I doubt if we would have the heart to submit them to public criticism" (sic; Grade 184–85). Thankfully, the Frosts compiled a small volume of 37 pages, 26 poems, divided into three sections. They named the book *Franconia* after their farm in the White Mountains of New Hampshire, Marjorie's childhood home. Joseph Blumenthal of Spiral Press designed and published the book. Only 46 copies are available in public libraries—two in Montana, with most scattered about the country, and one, oddly, at the National Library of Israel. Prior to their publication in book form, three of the poems were published in the September 1935 issue of *Poetry Magazine.*

In a letter to his son Carol, Robert Frost says:

> You know the weakness of verse: one line of it will be strong and good and the next will be almost anything for the sake of the rhyme. That's why some people cant stand the stuff. The ideal we are always striving for is an even goodness, so that neither line can be suspected of having been deflected twisted or trumpted up to rhyme with the other. That will make the verse as honest as the equivalent in prose. Sometimes I don't think there is any other test of a good poem than to see that not a single rhyme in it has hurt it. (sic; Grade 149–50)

Marjorie's poetry has the precision and "goodness" Frost describes. The early preference for ballad stanzas, tercets, and regular iambic meter in her child-oriented poems evolved into more complex patterns and variations to match a growing maturity of voice. The arrangement of the book leads readers to believe that it moves from her earliest poems to those written shortly before her death, though it would be more accurate to say that the poems simply represent the lifespan, beginning with themes of childhood and ending with themes of adult love and the separation of death. Elinor Frost indicated that "she had three brief periods of writing" which apparently parallel the arrangement of the book (Thompson 428).

Franconia opens with a poem entitled "If I Should Live to be a Doll," a two-quatrain poem that contains the playful lines "blueberry blue bluejay" and "blueberry blue blue shawl" (Fraser 7). While this poem offers an imaginary glimpse of the speaker as a "doll" that flits "from chair to chair" like a bird, the next poem, entitled "Spring," speaks about the "fear of taking wing" (8), an idea that appears elsewhere in Part I of *Franconia* as one of its unifying themes. In "Spring," the speaker clings "to tangled grass" while she listens to "Alighted robins sing / A song I dare not try." In these earliest poems there is a sense of safely inhabited space, such as a doll might have in the room of a child or the fearful child might find as she is hidden in the grass. There is also a sense of the danger that may lurk beyond the safe perimeter. It's easy to correlate this view to the safety of innocence and the fear of experience. In the earliest poems, death— perhaps the biggest threat to innocence—is transformed in various ways to become less threatening. In the opening poem, for instance, the line, "If I should live to be a doll," suggests the movement from living person to representative artifact.

Perhaps the book's title poem is the most telling, psychologically, about the themes of innocence and experience in this early work.

> Long, long ago a little child,
> Bare headed in the snow,
> Lay back against the wind—and smiled,
> Then let her footsteps blow.
>
> Lighter than leaves they blew about,
> Until she sank to rest
> Down where no wind could blow her out,
> Deep in a mountain nest.
>
> And to this day she's smiling there
> With eyes alert and wild,
> For she has lived on mountain air
> And stayed a little child. (Fraser 9)

Initially this poem may seem to be a child's death, but there is something magical in it because at the end, though this child was "bare-headed" and though she let her footsteps in the snow disappear so that she couldn't find her way back to safety, she "lived on" in the mountains "and stayed a little child." Franconia was Marjorie's home from the time she was about ten years old until the family moved away in 1920 when Marjorie was fifteen. The formative years of her youth were spent there, and this, along with other poems, indicates a desire for a permanent connection to that period. Her position as the youngest child in the family may have encouraged a prolonged innocence, but her struggle with tuberculosis during her teens and early twenties may have instilled a fear of growing up, and in particular, a fear of dying. In light of "Franconia," the first poem of the book becomes more serious than it might at first seem. The statement, "if I should live to be a doll," represents a desire for permanence and is reminiscent of Keats's admiration for the Grecian Urn or Yeats's desire to be the golden bird in "Sailing to Byzantium." The speaker in Keats's "Ode on a Grecian Urn" admires the figures on the ancient urn because they are fixed in their happy state, unlike the speaker who is subject to change and death. Similarly, the speaker of Yeats's "Sailing to Byzantium" is an aging man whose soul is "sick with desire" and who wants to cast off his body and become a golden bird, the "artifice of eternity." In both, the idea of permanence and artifice is preferable to deterioration.

In "My Place," another poem from this first section of *Franconia*, the speaker indicates the distance she feels from others:

Now always sad from outside looking on,
But never from attachment wholly torn,

As raised alone to bear an endless strife,
I watch go by a Greek-like frieze of life,

Where beady eyes make impress as they pass,
And glance at me from surfaces of glass. (Fraser 13)

The speaker is homebound and locked away. The world appears artificial, fixed like a relief sculpture, and yet she is also the object of the sculpture's gaze. It is as if the whole world has become Keats's Grecian urn, only the characters no longer appear happy or ideal but have become rather threatening. They move about in the world and the speaker, who views this "frieze," is ironically static.

In several of these earlier poems we see the writer's disillusionment with the world and a preference for nature. Her simple quintet called "Grief" illustrates this preference:

Then if by tears I only gain
A knowledge of the world's disdain,
I'll run and hurl my grief at trees
And scatter it along the breeze,
Or let it fall with rain. (Fraser 10)

She takes this theme further in "A Dying Flower." Similar to Wordsworth's "The World Is Too Much with Us," which prefers nature to the commercial, industrial world of the early nineteenth century, this poem offers criticism of American commercialism. It also presents the magical possibilities representative of the child-ego that surfaced in "Franconia."

Out in the midst of mad Times Square I'll stand
And stop converging life with lifted hand,
Till every city street is one wild mass
Of helpless mobs that can't return or pass.

Then while with traffic streams the suburbs fill
And slowly choking grow forever still,
I'll climb alone the mighty Empire tower
And be the pistil of a dying flower. (Fraser 11)

The poem depicts the imagined fall of the central commercial district in New York, which had become rough and seedy during the Great Depression. The vision at the end of "The Dying Flower" is ominous. Godlike, the speaker stops everything in Times Square and beyond "with lifted hand." The speaker will stand "alone" on the Empire tower—apparently the Empire State Building, what she imagines to be the center of Times Square—to become "the pistil of a dying flower," the sole, remaining element of fertility in the surrounding paralysis, an environment that was previously "mad" and "wild." But this is not a simple nature vs. culture dichotomy. The Empire State Building does, in fact, have a pistil-like spike at the top that was actually constructed as a mooring dock for dirigibles. Though that function didn't materialize, it allowed the building to be named the tallest building in New York City at the time. Marjorie's conversion of this spike to a pistil allows her to play with a "flowering of civilization" metaphor and point out simultaneously that the race for wealth, for the status of tallest and most impressive building in America, is hollow in her view, like a bloom that is past its prime. Meanwhile the people are moving out into the suburbs and presumably into the surrounding countryside to live the kind of life the author prefers. Yet why would she leave her speaker here in the city, the dying emblem on the highest building at the time? There is a fantastic quality to this poem. It probably predates the original *King Kong* (1933) movie featuring the well-known Empire State Building scenes, but it is likely that the anxiety of living in the Great Depression, when it must have seemed that civilization was collapsing, had an influence on her vision. More intimately, it may reveal Marjorie's own fear of death as she places the obviously female speaker, described in terms of a female sexual symbol, at the center of this paralysis and destruction.

Repeatedly, in this and other poems, Fraser juxtaposes architectural and natural images (The speaker in "My Place" is a vine climbing a "marble slab," for instance.), suggesting that this division between nature and culture, along with her own expression of separation from other people, defined her vision. The sorrow of this disconnection from place, from the past, and from an idealized world that doesn't exist appears multiple times. In a simple penultimate poem in this first section of the book, she recounts what was likely her permanent departure from the East.

COMING AWAY

I meant to walk once more
On my old, old lawn,
But it began to pour,
And I had no rubbers on.

I meant to look once more
At my old, old place,
But the taxi window wore
A veil of liquid lace. (Fraser 15)

This poem has an understated, elegant simplicity. Here, the pouring rain prevents her engagement with the "old, old lawn," and again it is the vehicle of civilization, the taxi, that takes her away. The "veil of liquid lace" on the cab window prevents a clear view, the way lace curtains might provide a barrier between self and the outside world.

In "The Sea-weed Maiden," the final selection of Part I, and in rhythmic patterns more varied and complex than those found in earlier selections, the speaker's isolation from society becomes explicit: "Above the ocean roar, borne by the fitful wind, / This was the song I heard a sea-weed maiden sing":

"All things that stir are stirred by love—
The sailor of the sea—
The homing dove,
The bee.
All, all—all things that live,
Have love to give,
But me."

The speaker concludes with another verse from the sea-weed maiden:

"All things that stay are stayed with love—
The cliffs along the lea,
The sky above,
The tree.
All things that sleep have love they keep
From me." (Fraser 16)

Isolation and disconnection characterize these youthful, imaginary, and sometimes grief-stricken poems that reflect the early period of Marjorie Frost's life. If readers were to locate these poems geographically, the East would be their most likely setting. Certainly Times Square, Franconia, and the ocean are clearly labeled.

Part II of *Franconia* turns, at least in large measure, to the West, where Marjorie spent the last three years of her life, first in the mountains of Colorado and later in Montana. The first poem of this section, "They Speak of Alpine Flowers," depends on hearsay in the first two stanzas. The speaker discusses what she has heard other people say about the flowers, and in the final of its three stanzas, the point of view shifts so the speaker addresses the flowers directly:

You are like all in vague far-distant lands,
Sweeter than if I held you in my hands,
So if I never kneel beside you there,
    I shall not care. (Fraser 19)

Once again, separation is a primary theme because she has never directly seen these high-mountain blooms, though here the separation doesn't cause as much difficulty as it did in Part I. This speaker admires the existence of the flowers even if she may never see them herself. In another poem called "Spring," she is "Content to know that it's warm enough [for others] / To stand outside and talk" even though she doesn't step out to participate (Fraser 20). The grief, fear, and feelings of isolation so prominent in Part I have receded. Instead, these poems indicate a dreamier kind of memory, an attraction to good experiences from the past and a recognition that others may have opportunities the speaker may not have. Because of chronic illness, Marjorie was often not able to do what others could, but this section of the book indicates a maturity and acceptance that was absent from Part I.

Poems like "The Long Trail Lodge" demonstrate how Marjorie is taken by the mystery of what she can't approach.

Between the mountains looming white
And the mountains looming green,
There winds a river out of sight,
Through a valley never seen,
To where a lake glows like a spark
In a forest deep and dark. (Fraser 22)

The final line of this stanza resonates with her father's line from "Stopping by the Woods on a Snowy Evening": "The woods are lovely, dark and deep" (Frost 224), which may invite readers to speculate about whether Frost had a hand in revising the poems prior to publication. My guess would be that he made no major changes. In letters to his son Carol, he offers comments that are open-ended enough so as not to intrude on the young poet's choice of language, and since he was both teacher and consultant to all of his children, I assume he offered similar respect to Marjorie's lines of poetry. Of course, she could have easily been influenced by her father's language and images.

"The Long Trail Lodge" contains much repetition. The speaker mentions the "windy tops of pine trees lean," and it concludes with these lines: "But how could I have sung my song, / Unless I'd seen it all along?" (Fraser 22). This idea represents Fraser at her Romantic best, celebrating the mysterious natural world alongside, and even with preference for, the imagination—the inner eye—that connects her to nature even if she can't immerse herself physically. Instead of mourning distance and isolation, this poem bridges the gap between the speaker and what is beyond her reach by celebrating imagined scenes.

Part II concludes with a narrative poem, "Over the Mountain," featuring two characters: a young man and a hunter. The young man has been wandering through the forest and finds himself repeatedly descending into a valley where a small stream flows. The hunter wisely explains to the young man that if he follows the stream, he will find his way out. The young man answers this way:

"But you evade my question, friend,
And tell me what I know.
Down ancient rivers you may wend,
Who have the wish to go.
I'll circle here until some day
Perchance my course will veer away." (Fraser 30)

The sensible path down to civilization is not what interests this young man, and most of this volume shows Fraser's similar preference for the natural world. "Over the Mountain" is a companion to the earlier "Franconia" with its eternal child. The young man's quest may represent Fraser's own imaginative quest to "veer away" from the limitations imposed by society, which in her case were exacerbated by illness and confinement.

The love that was so unattainable for the sea-weed maiden at the end of Part I is amply present in Part III of *Franconia*. The poet's ability to imagine the unseen river in "The Long Trail Lodge" finds an echo as this section opens with the words, "I always knew that you were there." While the first stanza of "I Always Knew" describes her lover in detail—dark eyes, fair skin, "the dew of heated hair," "curled sardonic lips"—it's clear that this lover has not arrived in her life:

> While in my heart I had to bear
> The scent of pollinated air;
> To let the utter sweetness tear
> Like phantom finger tips. (Fraser 33)

While the earlier poems refuse connection, the love poems of Part III, particularly this one, anticipate a passionate connection before the lovers meet. And now, instead of grief at loss, the speaker dwells on the sensual anxiety of how long it takes for her lover to "come to her." She says she "would never let [him] be" prior to his arrival, as though her imagination is seductively coaxing him into her life.

This section of the book is the briefest. It exhibits Fraser's most mature voice with two additional love poems, one indicating the "repose" she found in her marriage. Entitled "No Common Hand," this poem ends with a reference to death, hoping that "a hand as cool and soft" as the one that offered comfort in love will close her "dying eyes" and "lead my docile soul aloft / And lay it in repose" (Fraser 34).

Among the poems in Part III is her sonnet, "America," which appeared in *Poetry Magazine* and was chosen for the *Literary Digest* anthology of the best poems of 1935. While it only briefly makes mention of people, has nothing to say about history, and offers none of the usual clichés of patriotic poetry, it describes the country intimately, both visually and in terms of subtle sounds:

> Before my eyes, and yet so far above my praise
> I scarcely notice you for days and days on end,
> As one communes in silence with a life-long friend,
> And never once commend the million rainbow ways
> You rest my weary heart. Your self-deniers look
> For you from shore to shore; but while they rove
> I find you in some leafy sunny-speckled grove,
> or in the frozen fields the harvester forsook.
> America—they say you have no native song—
> Even among the windy pines they hear no tune—

But far from where the singing river winds along
I hear it in the stillest hour of burning noon.
And those who say no one has ever heard the words
Are leaving out of all account the voice of birds. (Fraser 36)

Addressing America as "you," she describes the country in understated and intimate terms as "a lifelong friend." How different this is from the symbols we've become accustomed to in the early twenty-first century, where statements of patriotism appear on bumper stickers and media is rife with patriotic images used as a backdrop for news or marketing. Marjorie Frost addresses those who are skeptical about patriotism, but she does so in a way that refocuses the reader's attention on the landscape, the undercurrent and physical foundation of the country, as opposed to the historical/political context that more often comes to mind. For those who argue the country has no "song," she emphasizes the "native" music of rivers and birds. Implicitly, she suggests that those who make this argument have simply not taken the time to listen and have overlooked what is most important. "America," perhaps more than any poem in the book, reflects Fraser's capacity as an observer and her imaginative vision of the breadth of her homeland.

Robert and Elinor Frost skillfully arranged their daughter's work in a chronological and thematic path from isolation to connection that encompasses a vision of the entire country. Originally Frost planned to include his poem, "Voice Ways," at the beginning of *Franconia* (1936).

Some things are never clear.
But the weather is clear tonight,
Thanks to a clearing rain.
The mountains are brought up near,
The stars are brought out bright
Your old sweet-cynical strain
Would come in like you here:
"So we won't say nothing is clear." (301)

Frost told one critic that "sweet-cynical" refers to Marjorie (Sergent 328), and the final line of the poem must then implicitly be in her voice, indicating a drive towards precision and a capacity for fair assessment.

Sometime before the book was published, Frost decided to omit this poem, perhaps because he saw how well Fraser's poetry stands on its own.

Shortly after Marjorie's death, Robert Frost wrote to his old friend, the anthologist Louis Untermeyer:

> The noblest of us all is dead and has taken our hearts out of the world with her. It was a terrible seven weeks' fight—too indelibly terrible on the imagination. No death in war could more than match it for suffering and heroic endurance. Why all this talk in favor of peace? Peace has her victories over poor mortals no less merciless than war. Marge always said she would rather die in a gutter than in a hospital. But it was in a hospital she was caught to die after more than a hundred serum injections and blood transfusions. We were torn afresh every day between the temptation of letting her go untortured or cruelly trying to save her. The only consolation we have is the memory of her greatness through all. Never out of delirium for the last four weeks her responses were of course incorrect. She got little or nothing of what we said to her. The only way I could reach her was by putting my hand backward and forward between us as in counting out and saying with over-emphasis You—and—Me. The last time I did that, the day before she died, she smiled faintly and answered "All the same," frowned slightly and made it "Always the same." (Untermeyer 241–42)

According to Untermeyer, "Marjorie was the Frosts' dearest jewel" (241).

Franconia concludes aptly with a small poem entitled "Gone." Having stepped into an empty room, the speaker can tell that someone had been there because "an ancient book, half read, lay spread upon its face." She continues, as if anticipating her own departure, "When I lay down my book, may I, too, mark my place!" (Fraser 37). Fortunately, Marjorie Frost Fraser has marked "her place" with these elegant poems, and her voice and vision persist in the small volume named *Franconia*.

WORKS CITED

Anderson, Margaret Bartlett. *Robert Frost and John Bartlett: The Record of a Friendship.* New York: Holt, Rinehart and Winston, 1963. Print.

Ferguson, Margaret, Mary Jo Salter and Jon Stallworthy, eds. *The Norton Anthology of Poetry.* 5th ed. New York: W. W. Norton and Company, 2005. Print.

Fraser, Marjorie Frost. *Franconia.* New York: The Spiral Press, 1936. Print, courtesy of Marjorie Frost Fraser's daughter and her family.

Frost, Robert. *The Poetry of Robert Frost: The Collected Poems, Complete and Unabridged.* Ed. Edward Connery Lathem. New York: Henry Holt and Company, 1979. Print.

Grade, Arnold, ed. *Family Letters of Robert and Elinor Frost.* Albany: State University of New York Press, 1972. Print.

Sergeant, Elizabeth Shepley. *Robert Frost: The Trial by Existence.* New York: Holt, Rinehart and Winston, 1960. Print.

Thompson, Lawrance, ed. *Selected Letters of Robert Frost.* New York: Holt, Rinehart and Winston, 1964. Print.

Untermeyer, Louis, ed. *The Letters of Robert Frost to Louis Untermeyer.* New York: Holt, Rinehart and Winston, 1963. Print.

CHAPTER 3

The End of Montana: Heather Tone, Gertrude Stein, and the Frontiers of Metaphor

KARL OLSON *(Missoula, Montana)*

> It is different than morphing.
> It is more like disavowing
> one of your faces.
> — from "Vertumnus" by Heather Tone (72)

> Oh dear he said, it is lovely in Montana, there are mountains in Montana and the mountains are very high and just then he looked up and he saw them and he decided, it was not very sudden, he decided he would never see Montana again and he never did.
> — from *Ida* by Gertrude Stein (638)

Contemporary poet Heather Tone was born in Glasgow, Montana, in 1979. When she was a youngster her family, like many Montanans, moved from the Hi-Line to the state's bigger cities and higher tree lines. Tone attended high school in Billings, studied biology at the University of Montana, and—after receiving her MFA at the University of Iowa in 2005—worked for several years at the Missoula Public Library and the University of Montana. She currently lives in Florida and teaches at Oxbridge Academy, a "project-based" prep school. In 2011, Tone won the prestigious *Boston*

Review poetry award for "Likenesses," a controversial choice among *BR*'s readers (if online comments are any indication), and was a finalist for the Slope Editions annual book prize. Her poems have found homes in the likes of the *Colorado Review* and *Fence*, where they surprise and captivate with the mysterious precision of exposed circuit boards. Despite a background that is deeply rooted in the Northern Rockies, I suspect Tone would not label herself a "Montana writer." Nor would she be very interested—again, I am speculating—in that rather quaint but perennial discussion on the definition of Montana literature. She moves with the natural ease of a global citizen, and her work reflects one who is at home with the uncertainties of the Millennial generation.

Which isn't to say that Montana should not claim her. The acclaimed Slovenian poet, Tomaž Šalamun, compares Tone's work to a "film projected on the night sky," full of "freedom, light, *leggerezza*, speed, and depth. Crystal abyss, 'nothing,' a touch of kabala" (66). That night sky could be a Montana sky. Our regional culture, constrained as it often is by old myths, sharp borders, and a seemingly die-cut vernacular, needs permeability, sometimes, more than definition; transition, more than "place." A little more of the esoteric wouldn't hurt. And *leggerezza*—lightness; we need that too. Like her precursor, Gertrude Stein, Tone makes "words come closer to each other than they ever had before" (Stein, "American" 229), in an effort to capture the moment things "change that is they look different" (Stein, "Pictures" 237). Heather Tone, as Šalamun assures us, offers "all of this and more" (66).

It is true that Tone's poems, with their pared down grammar and startling imagery, appear to have little in common with traditional landscape-based verse. A more obvious legacy dominates, this one associated with Europe and Modernism, and there is a particular resonance with Stein's adventurous and cryptic word play. Poetry offered Stein "a way of naming things . . . without naming them" ("Poetry and Grammar" 330). Or, as a contemporary critic, Julian Sawyer, elaborated, when "the name of anything and everything [was] dead," Stein shifted syntax to give it new life (qtd. in Van Vechten xxi). A similar idiom of mutability and reorganization runs deep in Tone. It's in the themes, where cells divide and multiply, and bodies and landscapes meld. And it's in her style, which tests the limits of categories, language, and perception. When "[w]ords look like dead prostitutes, twisted, thin," Tone seeks to infuse them with life, "much / like vodka may be infused with roses or bacon" ("Likenesses" 67). Her poetry meshes the language *of* change with narratives *about* change—metaphor and metamorphosis.

Understandably, we might resist, or sense resistance to, unraveling some regional thread from what can be perceived to be an unstable or difficult text. Surely there must be a Northern Rockies version of critic Mark Edmundson's complaint against contemporary literary standards that value "inwardness and evasion, hermeticism and self-regard: beautiful, accomplished, abstract poetry that refuses to be the poetry of *our* climate" (68). Postmodern, "post-human" (as Edmundson calls it) poetic forms challenge the vernacular of the rural-romantic American West, and are, perhaps, too furtive and too tenuous for conveying what Montana "means." This is, after all, the legendary climate of the "straight shooter," if not outright taciturnity; where a man is as good as his word, and a poet is suspect for her word choice. We take a narrow view of artistic license and the flexing nature of a language system. We do not lack metaphor: our colloquial speech is rife with *working* metaphor. But while many Montanans feel something like poetry in a phrase like "rode hard and put away wet," which equates the abuse of livestock with human hardship, they would struggle (as I do) to interpret these lines from Tone's version of the Ovid tale, "Vertumnus":

> A field full
> with pale snarls of prayer.
> One little one
> jumps from a wolf
> pale as itself. (71)

The temptation is to give up, and look the other way.

Nevertheless, it would be a mistake, I think, to assume that Montana is not to be found in the shifting lines and incongruent motifs of Tone's work. I do detect an impression of Montana in Tone—"morphing" and hovering, like encoded hypertext—and an emerging, what I will call post-Montana theory; a "disavowal" of region that is also symbiotically rooted in region. In this essay, I focus on literary precursors—especially Gertrude Stein—for context to the poet's approach to metaphor and meaning; followed by a reading of Tone's sprawling and Steinian (and spooky) playground, "Likenesses," that extrapolates a poet's approach to art, identity, and regionalism. If a pale wolf, loping across a snarled field, cannot be compared to a prayer—I don't know what can. And I would argue that Tone's regionalism is signaled everywhere by metaphoric leaps like this.

I. METAPHOR

What do you metaphor?

We tend to think of "a metaphor" as an object, a thing we make, rather than something we do. But the Greek roots of the word evoke action and movement in space. *Meta* in this case means "across" or "over"; *phor* derives from the verb, *pherein*, "to carry." Metaphor, or *metapherein*, is literally the transfer of some thing across a divide. In language, that thing is meaning, carried between two (or more) words that would otherwise have nothing in common. Take Frank O'Hara's description of a quiet moment in "In Memory of My Feelings": "My quietness has a man in it, he is transparent / and he carries me quietly, like a gondola, through the streets." There are three distinct entities: one is a state of being, another is a person, and the third an inanimate object. In the hands of the metaphoricist they are blended into one, with first the man and then the gondola performing as *vehicles* for the less tangible *tenor* (as rhetoricians call it)—"[m]y quietness." The natural boundaries between entities are broken down: a man is not a boat, but the poet blurs, if not erases, the distinctions.

O'Hara further emphasizes the shape-shifting potential of his quietness when he describes it as having "several likenesses, like stars and years, like numerals." Metaphors and similes, especially in poetry, often have a mystical quality. How, we may wonder, is quietness "like" numerals? But what the reader may perceive as a disjointed abstraction is also an opportunity to collaborate with the writer in creating meaning, to become not just a receptacle for text, but a second author. O'Hara's passage reminds me of the first time I arrived in Venice, just before daybreak. Regardless of what the poet intends, his imagery conjures the narrow *calli* in the dark, the thick quiet interrupted only by the rhythm of empty gondolas bobbing at their posts—and the old city's mysterious double street-numbering system. Another reader may form other associations. And another writer may use the same vehicle to take us down another path of imagery altogether—like this description of a lover/gondola and the beloved/city in Richard Aldington's "Images":

Like a gondola of green scented fruits
Drifting along the dark canals of Venice,
You, O exquisite one,
Have entered into my desolate city.

Humans are wired to juxtapose intangible, complex, and unfamiliar phenomena with the surface, workaday world around us. It's "what people do," says Marco Roth in *The Scientists* (2012). "[W]e can't not want there to be metaphors, even as we know there's a gap between metaphor and reality" (192). We use metaphor as a scientific method, Diane Ackerman explains in *An Alchemy of the Mind* (2004), to "dissect and organize experience" (211), and we've been doing it for as long as can be remembered. Establishing that "a thing is or is like something-it-is-not is a mental operation as old as philosophy," Susan Sontag writes in *AIDS and Its Metaphors* (1989): one simply "cannot think" without it (5). Linguist George Lakoff and philosopher Mark Johnson, authors of *Metaphors We Live By* (2003), agree: our entire conceptual system, they write, is "fundamentally metaphorical" (3). Ackerman gives metaphor added gravitas when she describes it as a survival technique. We create identity, she writes, with the use of "continually revised personal metaphors that . . . ultimately make bearable some aspects of our lives, while hiding other aspects on purpose" (214).

But as with any device, metaphor can be forced and overworked. English vernacular is so peppered with metaphoric activity that we classify much of it as "dead metaphor"—figures of speech that have all but lost the significance of their original conceptual shifts (like, perhaps, the notion of "peppering" speech with imagery), and more often, their ability to generate poignancy or surprise. Some metaphors, Sontag advises, like those equating the body with a battlefield, we should "abstain from or try to retire" (*AIDS* 5). Clichéd imagery underwhelms. William Strunk and E. B. White, mavens of *New Yorker*-style prose, object to excessive imagery. Readers, they warn, "can't be expected to compare everything with something else, and no relief in sight" (66). Metaphor "belongs," as Cynthia Ozick puts it, as much to "clarification and human conduct" (280–81) as it does to "[l]ightness of mind" and "[i]rrational immateriality" (269).

Nevertheless, this indispensable, if sometimes misappropriated, tool is also an elaborate art form. Not surprisingly, it's the character of a poet in the Bernt Capra film *Mindwalk* (1990) who most fears the possibility of an "un-metaphorical" world, insisting to his scientist companion that we "have to perceive reality in some way." Poetry, where figurative language is wielded and displayed in its utmost splendor, is metaphor's home base. Metaphor, Ozick flatly states, is the "poetry-making faculty itself" (269). Here, Lakoff and Johnson concede, there is freer range for metaphoric "extensions . . . special cases [and] innovations" (267). One way to perceive reality, Ackerman assures Capra's poet, is "lavishly"; in a twist on its utilitarian role in language, metaphor, in the hands of the artist, "transcends the ordinary" (215).

While Aristotle praised the artistic use of metaphor as a token of genius, the "poetry-making faculty" has, at least since the Romantic era, taken on the added quality of heroism. In *Where the Stress Falls* (2002), Sontag credits Modernists, the Russian Modernists in particular, with streamlining the Romantic ideal into a reaction against the oppressive dullness of "the social, the wretched vulgar present, [and] the communal drone" (5). Modernists, says Sontag, equated the prosaic with the State: bureaucratic, controlling, pedestrian. Poetry, on the other hand, was an "avatar of freedom," steering readers away from what linguists call "conventional" metaphor, and towards a more subversive purpose. This is the world Gertrude Stein stumbled upon and attempted to re-order. Literature, Stein wrote in the waning days of World War II, is "the beginning of knowing" that a democratic culture "could play and play and play with words and the words were all ours all ours" ("American" 229). She reveled in the idea that poetry fostered autonomy. Tone, in turn, inherits this Modernist legacy, and continues to test poetry's frontier with Steinian permissiveness and her own inventive spirit.

Stein, with a knack for recognizing her own genius, "discovered" poetry in 1914. For a time she decided she would rather *make* history with radical poems than to *recount* it in statist prose, and took up the cause of modernizing its components with gusto and fanfare. As soon as she felt she knew what made poetry tick, she set out to recalibrate it. She obsessed over language's capacity for change. "What is the difference," she wonders in "Patriarchal Poetry," "between right away and a pearl there is this difference" (583). And what if, Stein challenged, these "different," even oppositional, concepts were brought together, or made interchangeable in a text? Does "the relation between color and sound . . . make itself by description by a word that meant it or did it make itself by a word in itself" ("Portraits" 303). What happens, she asks in "Tender Buttons," when that which "is not recognized" is compared to that which "is used as it is held by holding"? (501). "Is there an exchange," between "stars"—which we can clearly chart at night—and "sky" which we "admit" exists but can only vaguely define? In other words, how does one transform a thing, into (as Sontag would say) "something-it-is-not"? Without "naming it," Stein was probing the very function, and limits, of metaphor.

Her breakthrough came in the composition of "Tender Buttons." "I had isolated it," she announced with triumph on the lecture circuit years later—and claimed that she had "broke[n] the rigid form of the simple noun poetry which was now broken" ("Poetry" 331). She adopted Cubist methods of dissociation and reconfiguration, and made the difficult case that art could distill the reality of a subject without reproducing it. Her description of the process—"creating it without naming it" ("Pictures" 237), or, as Sawyer qualifies it, "renaming it" (qtd. in Van Vechten xxi)—was, and is, hard for many to comprehend. Stein prized word-image relationships that she believed *recreated*, rather than *reflected*, meaning. Her epiphany, as Jonah Lehrer points out in *Proust Was a Neuroscientist* (2007), was that language is fundamentally abstract, defined "not in terms of its expressive content . . . but in terms of its hidden structure" (158).

Poetry, Stein decided, was the ideal canvas for that abstraction, a laboratory for testing connections between essence and surface, word and idea, and for "naming things that would not invent names, but mean names without naming them" ("Poetry" 330). In the flight from dead metaphor and "communal drone" writing, images would be shuffled like cards, pulled out at the poet's whim, and stand in for a subject—like the cousin in "Tender Buttons" who is compared to a carafe, or the bird in "Patriarchal Poetry" that is manifested by a bouquet of flowers:

A hyacinth resembles a rose. A rose resembles a blossom a blossom resembles a calla lily a calla lily resembles a jonquil and a jonquil resembles a marguerite a marguerite resembles a rose in bloom a rose in bloom resembles a lily of the valley a lily of the valley resembles a violet and a violet resembles a bird. ("Patriarchal" 583)

Her poems were extensions of word portraits in which she had attempted to determine "what makes" a subject by seeing "what is moving inside" them ("Portraits" 299). Traditional representation, she complained, relied on memory and created "only a thing that has become historical" ("Pictures" 237). Stein wanted essence, not history, and she cited technological advances as an analogy for what contemporary art should do. Cinema, for example, "offered a solution of this thing" in its ability to capture immediacy and nuance ("Portraits" 293).

With her typically unconventional syntax, Stein compared the "realization of existence" to "a train moving there is no realization of it moving if it does not move against something" ("Portraits" 287). When essence (what "moves inside") is imperceptible, "seeing" it requires something to gauge it against, like the immobile landscape outside a speeding train window. Meaning could be discovered by the happy accident of incongruous, even jarring juxtapositions. Granted, the shift from signified to signifier—from representing the known, to fabricating something wholly original—could be destabilizing. But eventually, Stein hoped, it would "lead to everything" ("Poetry" 336). What it frequently led to, if not everything, was dissent. Logic and experience are often limited, or limiting, when confronted with Stein's imagery.

Stein's radicalism and confident claims were often interpreted as arrogance. A case in point is her portrait of Montana, folded into the late Modernist novel *Ida* (1941). Stein never set foot in the state. But that did not keep the author of "everybody's autobiography" from giving it the Stein treatment, as demonstrated by the epigraph at the top of this essay. She had once been eager to lecture to Montana audiences, but plans to do so during her 1934–1935 U.S. tour fell through. She was left with a brief description, provided by a lone Montana-based supporter, Samuel Steward—a young English professor who had himself only recently arrived from the East, and would just as quickly make his escape. If Stein couldn't come to Montana, she would, typically, make Montana come to her. When it came to her, she wrote it down. The eponymous protagonist marries a "man from Montana" who is thoughtful, fragile, pale, and small—not really the man (or woman) our regional myth would pick to represent the Western spirit. He is the first of several husbands. "Dear Montana and how he went away," Stein writes, without explaining exactly how or why he went away, and then adds: "It does not take long to leave Montana" (*Ida* 650). For Stein, sense of place is an *idea* of a location that is gone as quickly as it appears.

Stein went to great lengths to justify her disruptions of memory, history, literature, and art—much of which is documented in her lectures—and her success is subject to ongoing debate. Her writing is "not ordinary," she acknowledges in "Tender Buttons," but Stein also insisted that it is far from "unordered in not resembling" (Tender 461). Her intent was not to hoodwink readers with meaningless exercises. Where some might see random nonsense, Stein knew there to be a method to the madness. She shrugged off accusations of incomprehensibility and obliquely hinted that the act of comparing an ostrich egg to lilies is a response to larger social pressures, with political ramifications. Better to be "not as much" understood than to be "like [the] rest," she asserts in "Patriarchal Poetry" (570).

II. METAMORPHOSIS

As misunderstood and challenged as they were, Stein's efforts to escape the prosaic and reinvent the poetic would set the stage for Tone's experiments a century later. Tone, Šalamun reminds us, brings many things to the table. But, like Stein, an easy reading is rarely one of them. The seesawing author-reader collaboration required to produce meaning from a Tone text is a rigorous performance. Consider, for example, the idiosyncratic and sinuous opening line of "Idiom: patient."

> Few of you get to see as you see me dismantle my body jar the pieces
> and stack them in crystal walls here a rare instrument a weathervane
> I think a hummingbird nudges the cells slays open the sky his throat
> should be that color should but you think his neck ripped the air
> holds no color but him and you, snags in blue film, lute shaped (9)

A reader cannot be blamed for finding the passage elusive, if not unsettling. Are we observing a medical procedure; something invasive, perhaps, that involves the transfer of cells? Is the "rare instrument" a bird, a weathervane, or something else? Is studying a patient's anatomy a metaphor for another kind of investigation? As she often does, Tone hints in "Idiom: patient" at the *issue* of meaning *in*—if not the actually meaning *of*—her lines. The poem goes on to illustrate a moment "when vision uncrams when tricked up in the sun." Pixels coalesce, revealing a "fox figure" counting "warped cells." But that vision is brief. In the last line we are informed that the "bird that was fluxing there is gone" (9).

Unlike Stein, Tone has not engaged in, or created, a public forum that takes readers behind the scenes of her process. Her poems exhibit a palpable reticence when it comes to explaining authorial choices or theorizing on one's work. "The alchemist does not have to answer," she declares in "Different,"

> as the plane begins to shift
> and toss. I'll turn
> this plane to a man.
> He'll brush his hands over
> his dusty pants and walk
> off the runway. (20)

Alchemist and poet share the same quest: to distill and transmute. They probe the ordinary for its essence, and convert essence into enchantment—planes into men, violets into birds, electricity into gold. Where life is too literal, and perhaps dull, the poet intervenes with stylistic risks. Such is the poet's prerogative: to anthropomorphize, morph, and make metaphorical—to manipulate, and shift perceptions.

The metaphoricist may not be required to break down her alchemic recipe, but this shouldn't dissuade us from guessing at the ingredients. Tone flirts with unreadability. She also scatters enough familiar cues along the way to build our own semantic nests within her skeletal designs. If the air traffic controller of "Different" sits on the secrets of her sleight of hand, the alchemist of "Likenesses" encourages us to dabble. "It's easy," she coaxes: "just close your eyes and think of a thing. Does it look / more like a little girl or a little boy?" (67). Readers are often invited to join in the work of a poem. "If you want to know / I can row," the narrator challenges us in "Vertumnus," "kayak / across the coke black / ocean" (73). By matching the poet's strokes with our own, we might come closer to penetrating the opaque surface of the text and making sense of her abstractions. Don't ask *why*, we are instructed. Just immerse in the *how*.

Does a thing look like a man dusting off his pants?

How would you describe a body that is dismantled and on display?

"Likenesses," with its encyclopedic supply of unconventional metaphor, is more than immersion. It is saturation. At nine stanzas and 140 lines, the poem features more than a hundred metaphorical transactions—a hurricane of resembling, becoming, and being.

The pint glass is a man preparing to dive off a tall building.
Paper planes look like little girls in skirts, real planes are women.
When it is dead, a fox has the eyes of a little girl.
A faun looks like a little boy, its bones like a courtyard full of
    children.
("Likenesses" 66–67)

Signified objects and their signifiers intermingle in a loose series of spaces and collections that recall the objects/food/rooms triptych of Stein's "Tender Buttons." Readers are led through suburban neighborhoods and roadside diners, along a riverbank and Fifth Avenue, into fairy tales and inside an aviary, where

A parakeet looks like a woman on her way
to a luncheon, or looks like the decorative touch
to the woman's hat. A goose looks like a little boy.
A duck looks like a little boy. ("Likenesses" 68)

Properties are exchanged. Female becomes male, man becomes machine, people dissolve into artifact, and artifacts are given life. The relentless transfiguration of little girls and little boys points to a simple, and rather obvious, tautology: the only thing that doesn't change is change. In "Likenesses," mutability is absolute.

While on the surface the poem's philosophy seems to be that anything can be subject to metaphoricism, Tone's interplay of (and I am afraid this pun cannot be avoided) tonalities raises deeper questions. On the one hand, there is an enchanting, Disneyfied quality to the poem's train of images. Tone seems to play with words until she makes them (to paraphrase Stein) "hers all hers." "Likenesses" brims with flora, fauna, objects, buildings, and characters, most of which are destined to metamorphose into a common signifier: children. Grasshoppers, paperclips, arrows, saplings, a "country church," are all transformed into "little boys"—while little girls represent snow, peach pie, foxes, candles, and sparrows. Women become the vehicles for lamps, spoons, apples, and wine glasses. Men, to a lesser extent, have their metaphoric presence as well (eagles, a computer). In this dense accumulation of metaphor a fairy tale atmosphere appears to prevail. Robin Hood, Rapunzel, and Blue Beard's bride make appearances—along with a faun, "treasonous queens" (67) and a garden that reaches out for Cinderella.

But the lightness Šalamun perceives, so active in Tone's childhood allusions and child-infused playfulness, belies darker fates: the game hunter's wild preserve in Snow White's tale, and Cinderella's inevitable return to dust. The poem is underscored by melancholy, loss, and an uneasy hint of violence. "All the birds look alive," the narrator attempts to reassure at one point, but then hedges: "for the / time being" ("Likenesses" 68). In fact, an array of metaphors involving death and decay cast a pall over the entire work. This tone is established immediately, in the first lines of the opening stanza.

> When he is dead, a man in a
> bathing suit looks most like a little boy.
> A woman in a bathing suit
> looks like a woman, unless she is quite
> thin, in which case she looks like a little boy. ("Likenesses" 66)

The dead couple in bathing suits is joined by a girl in a sundress with a mouth "as cold as a strawberry" (66). The little girl, perhaps thrown from a car, becomes a patch of snow lying on the mountainside. Then we see the car, at the moment "just before it dies," and surrounding trees emerge as boys "right before they disappear / into men with cold faces who carry hatchets" (66). Robin Hood and a robin redbreast join the casualties. It's as if we have stumbled upon a sunny, alpine vacation interrupted by tragedy.

Throughout the poem our attention is drawn to a DNA chain of graves, bones, assassins, and ghosts. The narrator is obsessed with how the dead and dying appear, and how they transform—from the musician who becomes "a little girl wasting away," to the "crashed computer" that "looks like a man killed in his prime / by a heart attack" (67). Some boys look "like stars breaking up" (66), while other children are consumed by more starlight, masquerading as moths. Even the aviary, which only appears to be full of life, holds a goose that is "more machine / than boy" (67). Characters cycle in and out of the woodwork, eternally poised between innocence and dissolution, origin and futurity, on the brink of becoming animated and being snuffed out.

Tone slows this process down in the sixth stanza to give what I think is a closer look at the poem's ambivalent tonality, as well as some evidence of her intent. To see the world in metaphorical terms, she instructs, one needs to "consider where you / would be without other people" (67). With a little imagination, a "green lawn"

> would become a man. If you are a man,
> the swimming pool will become a woman,
> cool and perfumed, with blonde highlights in her
> hair. The swimming pool, in fact, looks like a
> woman now, reflects several of them so that
> the cool, blue women are drowned. When
> drowned, such women resemble little boys. (67–68)

The youth/aging/death cycle is again brought to the foreground, as the stanza takes us from the vacant suburban landscape to a more rural scene. Here little-boy saplings go fishing, before being reincarnated as mature maple-tree women. Another sapling matures into a cottonwood tree that looks like "an old man" (68). Meanwhile,

> [t]he man who walks under the cottonwoods
> looks like an older version of himself:
> long years have sanded him down to sinewy
> essentials. That is to say that it will not
> be much of an absence in space when he
> disappears. (68)

The man/cottonwood tree is finally reduced to a white shirt in the sun. The shirt in turn is further altered into a handkerchief, waved by a woman "to pause the game" (68). The character's humanity is little more than a swimmer's damp outline left on a flat rock, at first a Rorschach test of abstract detail, and then, in sunlight—gone and without a trace.

Midway through the people/landscape transformations of the sixth stanza the narrator also pauses. "At a certain point," she remarks, as if anticipating a reader's query, "it would / be wise to ask yourself why you're doing / this" (68). Likewise, at this point, we may ask: why is *Tone* doing this? Is there more to her metaphor patterns than meets the eye?

There is the earlier claim, in stanza three, that the process of metaphoricizing is "easy": one simply needs to determine whether something resembles "a little girl or a little boy." Near the end of "Likenesses" the poet further develops this theme: What seems to make it easy is that "[m]ost fairy tales are populated by little girls / and little boys. Little girls get stuck in towers / or turned to trees and little boys must use / their knives" (68). And, as we see, the pair of scissors that is also a boy in stanza four, brandishing a knife that is also an evil queen—reappears in stanza eight to "carve" a smile upon Blue Beard's bride, who is also a little girl. Snow White turns out to be a boy here, attacked by a storm of falling apples and flying arrows—the arrows transforming into yet more boys that arc through the scene on sleds, while the apples are women, deferentially "casting off crowns" (68). "Afternoon light," the narrator adds, "lengthens / this lesson" (68).

Presumably, our extended lesson is that the tropes of fairy tale are deeply entrenched in the culture of "Likenesses," if not our own. Some metaphors are inevitable. The metaphoric form, the poem implies, anticipates our darker side and gives meaning to that which we dread. Tone's animated landscape of moths-turned-girls and boys with "parts . . . missing" (67) has Gothic roots, and points to folklore's role as a repository for societal anxieties and deviant impulses. By juggling uncomfortable incongruities, and developing an intimacy with figurative treatments of horror and loss, we acclimate to the eventual reality of existing "without others," and our own demise.

Tone's fairy tale emphasis reinforces the ubiquity and power of metaphor. Just as we are compelled to communicate concepts by replacing one image with another, we are also driven to create larger metaphoric systems— meta-metaphors, if you will, like the conventions of folklore, children's primers, or the universal jargon of computer science—to navigate the arc of human experience. What metaphor does to a word, narrative does to a collection of words. A web of meanings is crystalized, and the universe is explained, or at least made accessible. With a hat tipped to Ackerman, Lakoff and Johnson, Sontag, and Stein, "Likenesses" maintains that our entire world is metaphoric—and ours to "play and play and play with."

But the curiously phrased claim, in stanza eight, that the "delineations" of fairy tale "understand / the mind of the writer" (68) adds yet another dimension. Where an observer might state: "the writer understands the form"—Tone personifies narrative, giving *it* the ability to comprehend its human subjects. Clearly, nothing escapes the metaphoricist: even figurative language is used to describe figurative language. I also see here an allusion to a neuroscientific approach to poetry. According to the "bold claim" of the Institute of Neuroesthetics, as reported by Alissa Quart in *The Nation*, the brain is structured to produce physiological responses to art, making the artist, "in a sense, a neuroscientist exploring the potentials and capacities of the brain . . . with different tools" (qtd. in Quart 20). Metaphoric systems ("delineations") are designed around our interiority ("the mind"), fulfilling an evolutionary desire to move ideas from the abstract to the representative. We don't just understand metaphor, Tone suggests. It understands us. It is more than inevitable. It is organic.

III. ALCHEMY

When a character in the sixth stanza is finally whittled down to nothing, the poet offers little in the way of a memorial. The "essentials" of his existence are so slight that "when he disappears" he leaves behind "not . . . much of an absence in space" (68). It's an attitude that lies at the heart of Tone's work, and translates, I think, to her sense of place—or, more to the point, *dis*placement. What happens to the cottonwood man and the blue swimming pool women will happen to all of us, and to every thing. We shuttle from young self to older version, from sinew to fragment. We are elemental; eroded, lithified, and metamorphosed into raw materials for a reincarnated landscape. In its preponderance of mutating children, walking dead, decaying animals, and sprouting trees, "Likenesses" asks us to imagine what we will not consciously experience and can never fully comprehend: how the world will look after we have left it. Identity, of the self or of the place, is never constant.

This sense of reduction and alienation, the "nothing" Šalamun refers to in his praise, echoes a couple of earlier poems from Tone's MFA thesis. In

"1936 Prayer," which evokes (possibly) the High Plains of the Dust Bowl era, she pulls her listeners into the scene with an imperative mood, only to disappear them as well. "Become a space," the poet directs, "milk-thick with dust" (141). In "The End of Montana," Tone's narrator again conjures an identity, both regional and personal, that is fluid and fleeting.

> When the cowboys are reversed
> and when what they've witnessed
> glows buffalo
> over skins and the dung dressed
> lips—
>
> those real necklaces of the West—
>
> radio in the emptiness
> of their heads
>
> rattle
>
> It's a winter radio— (12)

The aging character in "Likenesses" is nullified, the "you" of "1936 Prayer" is consumed by space, and the landscape in "The End" appears to be restored of its "emptiness" when it is scrubbed of our representatives and representations. In each case, individuals cease to exist as distinct entities, and geography fills in their gaps.

But is this reincarnated geography a Montana landscape?

As I write, I am thinking of northwestern Montana, where I live, and the wilderness playgrounds that make up our (mostly metaphorical) backyards. Dangers await, unseen, behind picture-postcard slideshows of parkland beauty. It is summer, albeit a tentative summer thus far: the kind where unprepared hikers can be stranded in a Rocky Mountain snowstorm; and that same snow, metamorphosed by the sudden heat waves that come earlier each year, forms a lush, inviting—and deceptive—runoff in the valleys. Rivers have claimed several lives this season. Four hikers have plunged to their deaths in Glacier National Park thus far. For my money, this is the very vision of Montana that the tragic and melancholy lines of "Likenesses" convey.

This is essentially Gertrude Stein's Montana as well, the swerve between mountains that are lovely and mountains that will never be seen again, though she imbues them with the optimism of the armchair visitor. Stein could have referred to Big Sky Country when she exhorted readers to "[t]hink of anything, of cowboys, of movies, of detective stories, of anybody who goes anywhere . . . and you will realize that it is something strictly American to conceive . . . a space of time that is filled always filled with moving" ("Gradual" 286). She, like Tone, dwells not on physical boundaries, but on moments of change, using Montana—a place she did not and could not know—as a metaphor for an *idea*, for movement.

Tone's Montana is also found in the metaphoric transition—between cottonwoods and handkerchiefs, snowfields and girls, cowboys and emptiness. But Tone, unlike Stein, carefully encodes the geography she knows so well in the stacks of her imagery, and lets the metaphoricizing act reveal its coordinates. She avoids Stein's progressive, twentieth-century boosterism and settles on the *after* happily every after: the bust after the boom of our existence; the instant, turn-on-a-dime when the backwoods holiday is cut short by forces we cannot harness or predict. This is a region without borders and definition: an aspiritual nonlocation, an end with no beginning. Tone's sense of place is a sense of process—as perplexing as a "winter radio," as ephemeral as the here-and-gone "sky-throated" hummingbird, and, like the meta-metaphor of fairy tale, a perpetual toggling between sunlight and shadow.

WORKS CITED

Ackerman, Diane. *An Alchemy of the Mind: The Marvel and Mystery of the Brain*. New York: Scribner, 2004. Print.

Aldington, Richard. "Images." *Poemhunter.com*. June 2013. Web.

Edmundson, Mark. "Poetry Slam: Or, The decline of American verse." *Harper's Magazine* July 13: 61–68. Print.

Lakoff, George, and Mark Johnson. *Metaphors We Live By*. 1980. Chicago: The University of Chicago Press, 2003. Print.

Lehrer, Jonah. *Proust Was a Neuroscientist*. New York: Houghton Mifflin Company, 2007. Print.

Mindwalk. Dir. Bernt Amadeus Capra. Perf. Liv Ullmann. Triton Pictures, 1990. VHS.

O'Hara, Frank. "In Memory of My Feelings." *Poemhunter.com*. June 2013. Web.

Ozick, Cynthia. *Metaphor and Memory*. New York: Vintage Books, 1991. Print.

Quart, Alissa. "Adventures in Neurohumanities." *The Nation* 27 May 2013: 18–22. Print.

Roth, Marco. *The Scientists: A Family Romance.* New York: Farrar, Straus and Giroux, 2012. Print.

Šalamun, Tomaž. "Fourteenth Annual Poetry Contest: Heather Tone." *Boston Review* Nov./Dec. 2011: 66–68. Web. 1 Feb. 2013. Print.

Sontag, Susan. *AIDS and Its Metaphors.* New York: Farrar, Strauss and Giroux, 1989. Print.

———. *Where the Stress Falls.* New York: Picador, 2002. Print.

Stein, Gertrude. "American Language and Literature." *Gertrude Stein and the Making of Literature.* Ed. Shirley Neuman and Ira B. Nadel. Boston: Northeastern University Press, 1988. 226–31. Print.

———. "The Gradual Making of the Making of Americans." *Selected Writings of Gertrude Stein.* Ed. Carl Van Vechten. New York: Random House, 1990. 241–58. Print.

———. *Ida. Gertrude Stein: Writings, 1932–1946.* Ed. Catharine R. Stimpson and Harriet Chessman. Vol. 2. New York: Library of America, 1998. 611–704. Print.

———. "Patriarchal Poetry." *Gertrude Stein: Writings, 1903–1932* Ed. Catharine R. Stimpson and Harriet Chessman. Vol. 1. New York: Library of America, 1998. 567–607. Print.

———. "Poetry and Grammar." *Gertrude Stein: Writings, 1932–1946.* Ed. Catharine R. Stimpson and Harriet Chessman. Vol. 2. New York: Library of America, 1998. 313–36. Print.

———. "Portraits and Repetition." *Gertrude Stein: Writings, 1932–1946.* Ed. Catharine R. Stimpson and Harriet Chessman. Vol. 2. New York: Library of America, 1998. 287–312. Print.

———. "Tender Buttons." *Selected Writings of Gertrude Stein.* Ed. Carl Van Vechten. New York: Random House, 1990. 459–509. Print.

Strunk, Jr., William, and E. B. White. *The Elements of Style.* New York: The Macmillan Company, 1959. Print.

Tone, Heather. "1936 Prayer." *Colorado Review* 34.2 (2007): 141. Print.

———. "Likenesses." *Boston Review* Nov./Dec. 2011: 66–68. Web. 1 Feb. 2013.

———. "We Can Leave." MFA thesis. The University of Iowa, 2005. Print.

———. "Vertumnus." *Fence* V11.N1 (2008): 71–73. Print.

Van Vechten, Carl. "A Stein Song." *Selected Writings of Gertrude Stein.* Ed. Carl Van Vechten. New York: Random House, 1990. xviii–xxv. Print.

PART 2 COMMUNITIES

Photo by Brian Herbel

CHAPTER 4

The Language of Dry Wind:
The Poems of Tami Haaland

SUE HART *(Billings, Montana)*
DANELL JONES *(Billings, Montana)*

At first, Tami Haaland's poems appear to be quiet meditations on ordinary life in the American West. Dirty dishes, messy offices, and frustratingly long waits at railroad crossings all become poetic material in the hands of this Montana Poet Laureate. Even her language is unpretentious, no more demanding than the daily newspaper. But all this apparent docility is merely camouflage. In each of her two collections of poetry, *Breath in Every Room* (2001) and *When We Wake in the Night* (2012), Haaland draws us close to our trifling world to reveal the profound questions of human existence which reside there. Some of these questions have to do with the nature of our mortal coil, so mysterious, so full of possibilities, but at the same time so vulnerable. Others show the longing to understand how we make sense of our world and how we use language to describe, preserve, and transform our lives.

On the surface, for example, "Goldeye, Vole" appears to be simply a poignant description of the Montana prairie. But, as we read closer, we realize how far into the essence of our human condition Haaland is probing.

> I say sweep of prairie
> or curve of sandstone,

but it doesn't come close
to this language of dry wind

and deer prints, blue racer
and sage, its punctuation

white quartz and bone. (*Breath* 66)

Here, the prairie possesses a language more exquisite than the frail grammar of human phrases. Its beauty is not the sublime summits of granite peaks but the loveliness of things found on the ground: animal tracks, sagebrush, animal bones, and rocks. Its vocabulary is not spoken in words, but lived in the body. One learns it by moving through the land.

I learned mounds of

mayflowers, needle grass
on ankles, the occasional

sweet pea before I knew
words like perspective or

travesty or the permanence
of loss. (*Breath* 66)

The body knows the feel of "buffalo grass" and "puff ball" along the legs. It recognizes "blue lichen, gayfeather, / goldeye, vole" in their purest sense, before words like "perspective," "travesty," or "the permanence of loss" enter with their inevitable desire to fix or judge or mourn. The poet longs to reclaim this perfect language and urges the prairie muse to share her song.

—speak to me

my prairie darling, sing me
that song you know. (*Breath* 66)

The poet, poor artificer of words, aches for the magical melody she can never reproduce. Her own song, bound by the limits of human language, recognizes that it cannot match the "language of dry wind," but still it reverberates with love, wonder, and yearning for the beauty beyond its grasp.

For Haaland, a primal yearning for the best lost place defines our human condition. In "Brambly Place," she imagines her speaker arguing with a fallen Adam and Eve about their longing to return to Eden. It is hard to know who this slightly exasperated speaker might be. A human observer? An angel? God himself? What frustrates the speaker is our first parents' conviction that the Eden which lives in their memory still exists.

> You say Eden,
> I say silted waterways, overgrown blackberries,
> bindweed, never mind the snakes. Go there
> and eat the withered fruit, fine. It's not the same. (*Wake* 22)

Determined to make them understand the effects of time, she explains that untended gardens become overgrown, unpicked fruit withers, and snakes multiply. Even if they could return, she implies, Eden is not as they remember. When this argument fails, she turns to reason.

> There are reasons you ate
> and ran, reasons for someone to guard
> the gate. Didn't the path lead away
> for good reason? Thorns, yes, but take those away
> and where are the roses, their mealy fruit?
> No one said it would be easy. (*Wake* 22)

Gently nudging them toward self-awareness, the speaker reminds them that not everything was perfect in their garden. Nostalgia, she implies, blurs their vision.

If "Genesis" is an allegory of growing up, the surrender of the innocent paradise of childhood for the complicated world of adulthood, then the speaker is the mature adult trying to comfort our first parents as they put away childish things. Much like the stoical mothers in other Haaland poems, this speaker points them toward a pragmatic course: it is best to try to understand what has happened and then make the best of it. Fallen roses may have thorns, but they also have fruit. Perhaps sensing that her dispassionate advice fails to convince the covetous pair, the speaker ends her short monologue with a sorry platitude meant to cut short the conversation: "[N]o one," she tells them, "said it would be easy." This final line exposes the fatal flaw of her philosophy. As practical as her advice may be, she appears incapable of grappling with Adam and Eve's profound sorrow at their loss.

The vulnerability of human existence makes this stoical attitude difficult to achieve. In "Your Emergency Awaits," the speaker assures readers that it is just a matter of time until they will endure their own crisis:

If you haven't met it, you will.
It sits somewhere on a sofa watching reruns
until the time is right.

[. . .] No matter how you think it will look,

how you may have planned,
it will find ways to surprise you. (*Wake* 69)

Haaland creates the feeling of imminent disaster by imagining the emergency taking up unseen residence in the intimacy of our own homes. Although it may seem no more threatening than a television-watching couch potato, its apparent inaction only ensures it will catch the victim off guard. This guise of idler only makes the lurking misfortune more terrible.

But, if time is catastrophe's tool, it is also its corrective.

Your emergency has offered you
this gift. It will lean into you. It will become
a familiar weight against your shoulder. (*Wake* 69)

Over time, the emergency will lose its sense of urgency. It will become something to which one grows accustomed, like the weight of a dog or child leaning against one's body. In time, the poem assures us, today's emergency will be

[. . .] as subtle

as the scar where a pine splinter
from the playground drove into your shin.
At the time it seemed like terrible damage. (*Wake* 70)

In the face of pain, the poem suggests, we are eternal children, unable to measure the true scope of our suffering. Only through experience do we learn that seemingly great wounds eventually heal, sometimes leaving only a fading scar. The poem embraces the resilience of the human constitution—spiritual, physical, and emotional—to recover from life's bewildering assaults.

Such resilience animates the central figure of "Spring Burning in the Pasture," one of the many resilient, independent women of Haaland's poetry.

> Afterward she sees the brittle
> ash tree, broken and ablaze.
>
> She drags the hose, comes back
> for a cane to make herself steady.
>
> Inside and out. A little rest and
> back to the task. No one to help. (*Wake* 26).

Relying on a cane to steady her and brandishing nothing but a garden hose as her weapon, the old woman battles the burning ash tree all day by herself. She does not shirk from her solitary battle despite age and infirmity. Determination and fortitude, the poem demonstrates, are not the prerogatives of young men. She refuses to surrender even when the fire continues to burn the next day. Ultimately, she tames the blaze, but she never defeats it. "For days, / she can see it smolder" (*Wake* 26). The poem ends in an uneasy truce, but that, it appears, is enough. It is not the outcome of the battle that is important as much as the supreme dignity the woman achieves by engaging it.

Haaland finds further evidence of this feminine fortitude in the austere landscape of the Montana prairie farm. "August" opens with harvest time, and the women's obligation to care for the men working the land.

> My cousin was five.
> We walked with her to the granaries
> to ask the men if they needed food,
> to ask if they needed water to drink. (*Breath* 10).

The grass was a little "dry and crackly," but "[t]he crop / was pretty good" (*Breath* 10). As the speaker, her cousin, and her mother walk toward the field, they hear the sizzling rattle of the snake coming from the grease house. In the world of Haaland's poems, little girls and the women they become do not call men for help; they do what needs to be done. "I pulled my cousin's arm," the speaker says, "flipped her belly-down / behind me. She didn't cry" (*Breath* 10). The mother then dispatches the rattler by cutting off its head. "She cut three times / to separate the head from / its coiled body" (*Breath* 10). With the fangs of the severed head biting into the air, the unflappable mother calmly

> dug a hole
> beside the cottonwood trees
> and buried the open mouth there.
>
> She told us to leave that place
> alone, told us to watch
> so the dogs wouldn't dig. (*Breath* 10)

The mother cares for her men and protects her children without drama. And like the elderly woman fighting the fire, she feels little complacency in today's triumph. Although the snake's head may be buried, the danger always persists. In this world, venom is always ready to be unleashed by forces as banal as curious dogs.

Although the archetype of the resilient, long-suffering woman commands a powerful role in many of Haaland's poems, other poems question and resist it. In "To Cinderella on the Stair," Haaland wittily puts the reader in the place of Cinderella as the clock strikes midnight, and she flees the ball.

> You lift your skirt
> for speed, the fabric a sail in your wake.
> The clock strikes. Your heart hesitates.
>
> But look at the pearls, the white satin.
> Must every woman wear this dress? (*Wake* 27)

Haaland invites us to imagine ourselves as Cinderellas contemplating our various choices. In the fairy tale, the glittering ball with its handsome prince appears to be the most seductive opportunity. Haaland asks us to question this idea. If we look beyond the dazzle, she suggests, we might see a disconcerting orthodoxy requiring a high degree of conformity. "Must every woman wear this dress?" It is possible that pearls and satin may be their own kind of trap. Next, Cinderella considers the pumpkin-turned-carriage:

And in the shadows you see
the carriage, still a carriage,
ready to take you to the open road. (*Wake* 27)

What if Cinderella had imagined taking the carriage not back to her demeaning stepfamily but to the "open road," Haaland asks. What if she could see beyond the castle walls to all manner of roads and their respective possibilities? What if she had enough imagination to rewrite her own story?

The last stanza poses two essential points.

Consider whether to return to the hearth.
Think how long you might wait. (*Wake* 27)

In the fairy tale, Cinderella always returns to the sooty hearth to wait for Prince Charming. But Haaland's poem expresses urgency for Cinderella to act now and act for herself, to reject her usual self-denying role even if that is always how the story has been told.

Downtown Billings, Montana, serves as a modern-day hearth for contemporary Cinderellas in "Kathy Catches a Train." While driving to meet a friend at a local coffee shop, the speaker gets stuck in traffic at a railroad crossing where she finds herself, like an obedient Cinderella, "[w]aiting and waiting" (*Wake* 90). From her car window, she watches Kathy, a seemingly ordinary woman in a "brown plaid jacket" as she "strides past the fallen arms and climbs the engine's stairs" (*Wake* 90). The speaker realizes that Kathy "plans to step down / the stairs to this side of the tracks," but the train unexpectedly begins moving. Afraid of falling, Kathy hangs on as the train carries her out of town and out of sight.

The incident fires the speaker's imagination. She wonders what will happen to Kathy on the train. Will she "go inside" the car or will she "hang on until they find her and pry her loose" (*Wake* 90)? She wonders when her absence will be noticed at work and what her husband will do. But these prosaic questions soon evolve into fantastic possibilities. She tells herself that the train makes stops and Kathy "could / get off wherever she likes" (*Wake* 90), yet in the vivid world of the speaker's imagination Kathy doesn't get off; she doesn't try to come home. Instead, the speaker imagines that

[. . .] I'll hear from her. She'll call
and tell me about the island she inhabits or her winter vacation

in Brazil. I'll tell her how she looked that day, boldly impatient
when her road was blocked, the machine taking her from her settled life.
　(*Wake* 90–91)

Of course, almost everything that happens to Kathy takes place in the
speaker's imagination. Kathy's defiant refusal to be patient ignites her
observant friend's mind with a vivid story of escape. Ironically, it is too
great a leap even for the bold Kathy to take of her own volition. The sedi-
ment of one's life is so strong, apparently it can only be escaped through
a happy accident. Yet, the very act of being able to imagine what Kathy
might do changes the world. By allowing herself to imagine a different,
more exciting life for Kathy, the speaker also begins opening up such
possibilities for her own "settled life."

Driving around town with the windows down, observing the world and
letting the wind whip their hair, the two young women of "Liar" contem-
plate this profound power of storytelling. When they drive past a couple
fighting, they tease out different versions of what will happen next. At
first, they adhere to familiar narratives of passion. One says the man will
"speed around the block, feel guilty, / return, and insist she get in" (*Wake*
15). The other believes the woman will have to "get there another way, /
hitch hiking maybe or a long walk" (*Wake* 15). Intuitively, they recognize
that the stories they know have something to do with themselves.

> The ending is the same and we both know it,
> the way we know there are only so many stories,
> perfectly formed, and they enter us
> each time in shadowy variation. (*Wake* 15)

Even though they are young, they know that a narrow range of stories
shape women's lives and that their future will be limited to one of them:
a woman becomes a nurse, schoolteacher, waitress; she gets married, she
has children. In this scenario, girls are merely the "shadowy" variations
of their mothers. Because they are both blond, they understand their
particular stories are even more limited: "[w]e are the kind of women
they joke about, / another kind of story" (*Wake* 15). But as smart young
women, they question the received wisdom. "[M]aybe," the speaker sup-
poses, "there are as many stories / as stars" (*Wake* 15), as many ways of

living as one can imagine. Realizing this imaginative possibility, they reject the trajectory of the arguing couple.

> But we are smart enough to guess how this story
> will end for the girl, smart enough to know
> that if we keep on driving maybe
> there's a better version up ahead just waiting
> to pull its comb through our tangled hair. (*Wake* 15–16)

Eager to discover stories beyond those they know, the young women sail optimistically ahead, confident that they will find the story which, like a comb running through hair, will make beautiful sense out of their lives.

Haaland devotes an entire section of *When We Wake in the Night* (2012) to the idea that there are as "many stories / as stars." The eleven poems of "Inquest" explore the aftermath of a man's suicide from several points of view. The parents' stories achieve heartbreaking intensity as they remember their son and try to make sense of what happened. "Penmanship" poignantly evokes the dead man as a gangly boy lackadaisically doing his homework.

> He chewed the end of his pencil,
> sometimes bit the eraser almost off.
> We'd tell him to stop and get to work.
> He'd sit at the kitchen table, feet dangling,
> copy in his penmanship book. (*Wake* 45)

The gnawed pencil, the dangling feet bring to life the gawky boy through his parents' tender eyes. He has killed himself, but he still lives in their words. They ache with powerful memories tainted by self-doubt.

> He made us feel like he was

> the best boy. Lucky then, but what could
> we have done, and when? To have it back. (*Wake* 45)

Anguished by the death they were unable to prevent, they torment themselves with self-reproaching questions. For them, answers remain ever out of reach.

The philosophical narrator of "Now This" brings the readers into the story in order to demonstrate that no one is immune to such tragedies.

Except for those with foresight,
no one knows. You and I, for example,
are forever at the kitchen table

reading the paper, sipping coffee,
until the next thing happens,
and we look up in surprise. (*Wake* 46)

Crises catch us off guard, interrupting our mundane routines. Those who
suffer are no different from ourselves, this poem explains, and their grief
provides the opportunity for reflection on our shared vulnerability.

The speaker of "The Nurse's Story" refuses to believe the man's death
could be anything other than suicide. She provides an itemized list which
explains why no other conclusion is possible. "No one could have / gone
into the cell," she argues, "[n]o one could have / opened the door." It is
absolutely clear to her that "No one could have / done this" (*Wake* 47).

No one
opened the door.

No one had a key.
No one tied the sheet. (*Wake* 47)

In her methodical world, there is no one to blame but the man himself.
"Who," she asks, "could hang a man / if he didn't want / to be hanged?"
(*Wake* 47). Her conclusion admits no impediments. There is no mystery
here, no confusion, no questioning. From her perspective, the reason for
his death can be simply answered: he wanted to kill himself and he did.

For the offhanded clerk in "Paperwork" the suicide is "all about getting
you / into the filing cabinet" (*Wake* 48).

Sure, we're sorry,

but kill yourself
and everything after that
is mop up: make sure

no one killed you, make sure
you did it yourself, make sure
you died as the coroner said. (*Wake* 48)

For the clerk, the man's death is a matter of bureaucracy. It is about organizing the reports and getting them in the right drawer. For him, the death is not about the story of a life, but about another round of boring paperwork.

The witnesses and medical reports presented during the inquest lead to the conclusion that the cause of death was suicide, but "The Verdict" shows that for the loved ones this result cannot answer their most profound questions.

> You've seen the pictures, the autopsy
> report. You know how capillaries
> explode in the head when air and blood
> can't circulate. A soft ligature, they said.
>
> That's one truth. And the paperwork, another. (*Wake* 51)

For the parents, the story that is missing is their son's, the person they loved. The explanations given by nurses and clerks don't add up because they can never penetrate the mystery which they are unable to solve satisfactorily: what happened to our boy? The problem is that they resist any story which says their son took his own life. Suicide is a story that makes no sense in their world. The speaker in "Fury" grasps for other, better versions of the man's death.

> Better to be bitten
> by a snake than this.
> To fall from a mountain,
> or have a cougar grab him
> by the throat. More reason
> in that. More sense.
> Better a bear in spring,
> a river over boulders,
> better disease than this. (*Wake* 52)

The speaker could have understood, she believes, if nature had taken him. She could understand what it would mean to have him killed by a wild animal or even devastated by disease. Those may be unlikely scenarios, but they are familiar and acceptable. They can accept death, they tell themselves, just not this kind of death. That he should end his own life feels fundamentally wrong. Suicide violates their way of making sense of the world.

The short final poem of the sequence, "In Secret I Make My Plea," powerfully captures a parent's raw grief.

> I look at his picture.
> *Don't die*, I say. The face
> looks back. *Don't.* (*Wake* 55)

In private, the speaker looks at the photograph and speaks to the dead. She begs him to live. As powerful as a stoical mother might be, here she collapses in grief. She cannot accept how things are; she cannot get on with it. Her words press hard against death. If she can keep on talking to her son, begging him to return, she is then able to continue a conversation which she cannot bear to see end.

This intersection of time, memory, and story ignites not only sorrow but moments of supreme joy. In "No Hands," a girl, "[p]ack on her back, hair in ponytail" (*Wake* 92) passes the speaker during a morning walk.

> . . . only I am a morning
> walker, and she, a no-hands rider
> steering her bike down a curving street.
> Sun out, it could be any summer. (*Wake* 92)

The sight transports the speaker out of time and into her own childhood.

> And now I am ten, a no-hands girl with hair
> caught in wind. This is a dirt road, a prairie,
> a world of blue above. The girl becomes
> me, then it's she and I, then she. Time loves
> this trick, knows I will trip in a moment, skip
> into memory, body sailing, hands free. (*Wake* 92)

Haaland is interested here in not just remembering, but in the process of memory. The mind flits among identities—"the girl becomes / me, then it's she and I, then she"—as the imagination flares into action. Importantly, the process is as physical as it is mental. Although the woman is now grown, the memory of this childhood sensation threads through her body even as it lights up her mind. She knows that once time does its "trick," she will again feel the joy of her "body sailing," her "hands free." This memory draws her once again to that perfect language which the prairie speaks to the body. Through memory, she will once again feel the dirt roads with a "world of blue above." She may be older and far away from the buffalo grass, goldeye, and vole, but even in memory, she is still able to surrender to the "language of dry wind" (*Breath* 66).

WORKS CITED

Haaland, Tami. *Breath in Every Room*. Ashland: Story Line Press, 2001. Print.

———. *When We Wake in the Night*. Cincinnati: WordTech Editions, 2012. Print.

CHAPTER 5

From The Unvoiced Margins to the Center: The Populist Poetics of Roger Dunsmore

O. ALAN WELTZIEN *(Dillon, Montana)*

Roger Dunsmore's *Greatest Hits 1969–2006* (2007) opens with a prose statement, "From the Great Lakes to the Backbone of the World," which could be called, after William Wordsworth's example, the growth of a poet's mind. His use of the Blackfeet phrase for the Northern Rockies ("Backbone of the World") attests to his career-long advocacy of Native American literatures and belief systems. After his Michigan and Pittsburgh youth, Dunsmore migrated west to Big Sky Country, enacting in his own way Thoreau's celebrated advice in "Walking." In this autobiographical sketch, Dunsmore defines his calling, "[t]he act of poetry," as "the practice of try-ing to enter into the life of perishable things" (*Greatest Hits* 8). To create poems out of the "perishable" is to freeze frame the transient, to recover and redeem it. Nothing remarkable here. But some kinds of stories matter much more than others. Later in the sketch, Dunsmore, looking back on his early years in Missoula, declares, "I felt lost in much of the language and ideas of conceptual academic talk" (8). Elsewhere he repeats that he disliked "the tones of certainty / in the voices of my colleagues" (*Tiger Hill: China Poems* 79–80). For Dunsmore, academic jargon represents a false authority and knowledge, and rings hollow. The best kind of stories hail from less privileged voices and places. Inside those places, Dunsmore found his identity as a poet.

In the mid-nineteenth century, Walt Whitman famously widened the subject and style of poetry, claiming for it a fundamental value for men and women of all colors in all walks of life. For Whitman, poetry meant giving voice to all people, not just refined folks. Every generation revisits and extends the democratic purpose and audience of poetry. In modern Montana poetry, Richard Hugo used small towns and blue-collar lives to "trigger" his long-line verse, and through the 1970s he gained a national reputation. His books and presence helped create literary Missoula. Dunsmore arrived in Missoula in 1963, the year before Hugo. Like Hugo he devoted himself to the "democratic vistas" announced by Whitman, though he did it more quietly, and his particular territory and his line were markedly different. Dunsmore took his cue from Gary Snyder, not Theodore Roethke, Hugo's mentor. Like Snyder, Dunsmore writes a tight, imagistic lyric, one infused with indigenous voices and inspired by classical Chinese poetry as well as Zen Buddhist thought. In his career, Dunsmore has defined his own distinct, populist poetics, one that hasn't varied since the 1970s.

Back in *Blood House* (1987) Dunsmore first published "Deerlodge (Montana State Prison)," a poem he selected for his *Greatest Hits 1969–2006* twenty years later. In his *Greatest Hits* sketch, he narrates the poem's genesis: inmates he'd been working with watched a documentary, *The Hunters (1957)*, chronicling "a thirteen-day giraffe hunt in southern Africa's Kalahari Desert by K'ung Bushman [sic]." The poem captures their post-film discussion: "It does one of the things I try for in my poetry: getting down the voices of ordinary people saying extraordinary things; this time, a conversation between Indian and white convicts in our state prison" (*Greatest Hits* 11). Obviously, prison inmates aren't exactly "ordinary," but "Deerlodge (Montana State Prison)" contrasts their own expressions of "wildness" with the wildness of giraffes or zebras—or K'ung, for that matter—in presenting an interracial exchange. The book and film triggered this remarkable conversation by brown- and white-skinned men who had acted inappropriately "wild." Dunsmore bears witness to the down-and-out, and this poem quietly, ironically plots the variable boundary between wildness and the rest of our morality:

He [half zebra, half horse] was just plain wild—that's all.

Bad Horse laughs—
"Hell, that's what got me in here in the first place,
that wildness" (*Blood House* 22–23).

That kind of ordinary voice transcending its ordinariness epitomizes Dunsmore's populist sensibility from the beginning. Since his *On the Road to Sleeping Child Hotsprings* (1972; rpt. 1977) he has highlighted marginalized voices, since he believes those contain a culture's most essential stories. Dunsmore privileges the words of those usually unvoiced, ignored, and forgotten. Perhaps that has expressed itself most powerfully in his career-long fascination with American Indian literature (as it used to be called). This conviction is evident in his recent essay on four Montana poets—Mark Gibbons, Vic Charlo, Ed Lahey and David Thomas—titled "All My Stories Are Here" published in a collection of Montana literary criticism edited by Brady Harrison (2009). That phrase not only captures Dunsmore's credo but underlines his priorities: the hitherto marginal (and marginalized) becomes the center. Dunsmore created this self-referential phrase when discussing Mark Gibbons's poem "In the Blood," concluding, "These stories are the generations of connective tissue to this place" ("Stories" 23). That "connective tissue" transcends the inherent truth of "perishable things," the chronic pressure of mortality.

In his essay's conclusion, defining Gibbons, Charlo, Lahey, and Thomas, he also describes himself: "They may be mad, impoverished, Indian, alcoholic, laborers, or they may be saints, teachers, chiefs, creators, sane, or all of these things together. Mostly they have been found by language…" To hear these stories requires rolling up your sleeves: "[Y]ou will have to get your hands, even your pretty souls, dirty, bloody, or perhaps broken . . . if you are to experience the best of the culture here" ("Stories" 35). For Dunsmore, to discover or record or read the best stories requires guts and a willingness to explore unconventional paths. He pulls us out of our comfort zones as we attend to what we too often ignore—or don't even see.

This poet has trod those paths since his beginning. He lived along them in the 1970s and 1980s in Missoula, a bad boy who taught in the Missoula campus's Humanities program and helped energize grassroots environmental education. In his early poem "Aberfan" he honors "dead children / [dug] out of the black, flowing sludge, / out of the waste" (*On the Road* [1972] 8): he unflinchingly gazes into human ugliness, whether manifested in war or relationships gone sour. That steady gaze exposes, at times, graphic, horrifying images that also belong to the sweep of human experience (like Whitman) and should be recognized, not avoided. Like Whitman, he doesn't ignore prostitutes or venereal sores. His commitment to the dispossessed strongly manifests itself in "Taking Leave of a Tramp by a Cook-fire Under the Madison Street Bridge." Most of the poem unfolds in the tramp's own voice:

> [he] shows me which boxcars are going east,
>   which west, which are empties.
> "Some bulls won't let ya build a fire.
> Say, you ain't thinkin of hoppin a freight are ya?" (*On the Road* [1977] 50).

Dunsmore favors this pattern, lending most of a poem to a neglected subject. We glance over entire lives, like cuttings of dramatic monologue, and imaginatively taste the world according to their lights.

Dunsmore's commitment to American indigenous voices manifests itself in "Carver, Outside the Market," which appears in his second chapbook, *The Sharp-shinned Hawk* (1987). In this tribute, the poet transfers the animal imagery of the carver's totem pole to the carver himself, and includes a brief conversation. In his deep respect for the carver's craft, he asks if the carver is

> the man that carries
> the strength-stone from Spearfish
> to Celilo Falls, seven miles
> and more without rest,
> two hundred pound stone
> glowing in your arms, light,
> as it lifts you upriver like wings? (*Sharp-shinned Hawk* 7)

The poem concludes, "you are that man": the carver possesses the energy and beauty of the "killer whale" that "swims into your face." In "Humus" most of the poem is spoken by Willie, a Crow friend (and the poem's dedicatee), who elaborates the etymological connections between "human—humus—humble." The poem sustains Dunsmore's primary chthonic theme, expressed by the gifting of deer "parts that can't be eaten, / [fed] to the river" and the consolation of connection after "[t]he morning Elaine dies." Dunsmore is so fond of that Crow "saying," "you're just dirt," that he titled his newest collection with it (*You're Just Dirt* [2010]). As the poet instructs us through Willie, "dirt" means, in Crow tradition, humility, not white-trash or scum:

> When somebody is bragging themselves up
> we have a saying,
> *you're just dirt,*
> only it doesn't mean the same
> as when white people say it—dirty.
> It's like to be humble,
> like that human, humus on the board." (*You're Just Dirt* 21–22;
>   emphasis mine)

That definition embraces both the Book of Genesis (from dust were ye made, etc.) and modern ecology, and expresses that "connective tissue" Dunsmore exposes and celebrates in this essay. In his view, we've lost track of the Crow meaning of dirt, and need to recover and embody it, instead of the prevailing white meaning, more than ever before.

Dunsmore doesn't consider his poems complete after publication; he habitually revises, sometimes publishing a newer version or edition. In the newer version of "You're Just Dirt," he concludes, through Willie's voice,

> The earth is my body.
> You're in sorry shape
> if you can't feel it. (*You're Just Dirt* 22)

Plenty of us are "in sorry shape" in the wired twenty-first century, and contemporary urban/suburban densities suggest he's right. Early in *Blood House* (1987), "Earth's Mind" asserts that "We have lost our mind" because intellectualized First World peoples, whether white or not, have fundamentally lost their kinship with the natural world, and cannot discern the stories arising from plants and animals (e.g., orca whales). The poem seeks to restore that kinship by way of touch and smell:

Rub sweet juniper into your face and hair.
Take your time.
Earth's fragrant Mind. (*Blood House* 15)

Dunsmore teaches "the primal value of relatedness" (*Earth's Mind* 13). That totem pole carver outside Seattle's Pike Place Market, or Willie, or the Crow teacher, demonstrate the kind of knowledge most Americans no longer possess but desperately need.

Blood House (1987), Dunsmore's second book, shows the poet again tracking the margins in search of those voices carrying the most neglected but essential stories. "What Dale Said," almost entirely in Dale's voice, begins and ends by affirming Dunsmore's poetics: "We live in the day of our language." Dale's own language more authentically expresses those stories most necessary for our physical and spiritual health. Dale, another Indian, teases about the supposed white authority who claims "we eat the placenta / after our babies are born," and he extols the value of eating tripe and undergoing sweats in a sweat lodge, since both symbolize rebirth:

You see yourself inside your mother's womb again
only you're not a baby anymore.
And you've got to pray right.
The steam is her breath. (*Blood House* 70–71)

That last phrase hammers home the analogy. Renewal comes from closer contact with the earth, whether rubbing "sweet juniper" or taking a sweat.

In "Eclipse," dedicated "to my [unborn] son [Jack]," we listen, along with the baby "six months in the belly," to four diverse voices in the poem's three sections. In the first, old Anna, who "steered clear" of "Indians," tells the story of her mother taking kids to the cemetery's shade trees, only to be frightened by "a band of braves / who made over [the children] / the way they always do." In the second, old Ernie, also "no Indian lover," "tells of the abandonment, / [of] a whole generation of horses," and the poet's mixed-blood wife advises him to "'Imagine the animals.... / Think simply. / Forget everything you know." Only by such "forgetting" can whites overcome old Anna's fear. The third section depicts National Guard pilots in an "F-106" flying "1200 mph," photographing a full solar eclipse, which causes a "school child," in the final section, to imagine he is "going to get blinded." The braves' affection for the children picnicking is eclipsed by the tractors replacing horses and advanced warfare (F-106s and "missile silos hidden underground") potentially annihilating the "people driven here— / Indians, sheepherders, poor-whites" (*Blood House* 64–67). It's a satiric progression. No wonder the poem instructs us to "forget everything you know," because what we know climaxes in potentially fatal destruction: the Cold War. If we forget, we might be able to learn anew the right stories, ones leading away from "weapons of mass destruction," the infamous Iraqi War rationale, and institutionalized paranoia.

"Navajo High School," which closes *Earth's Mind: Essays in Native Literature* (1997), distills the poet's experience as "Humanities Scholar in Residence at the largest Indian high school in the U.S., at Tuba City, Arizona" (*Earth's Mind* 205-13), in 1988–1989. (Dunsmore subsequently published a far shorter version, "Fort Sumner History Lesson—Navajo High School" (*Greatest Hits* 23–24).) Again, poems aren't "over" after initial publication. During that school year, Dunsmore taught the teachers—and discovered, from varying sources, resistance to Navajo knowledge. After he has taught "Story from Bear Country," by Leslie Marmon Silko, "the head of physical education blurts, 'You expect us to believe that?'" Such products of teacher education programs just don't get it, missing one of those ancient, vital stories we call myths, as the poet answers the jock:

> "[K]now that this child's
> transformation
> into a bear
> is one of the oldest,
> widest spread stories in the world" (*Earth's Mind* 207)

Dunsmore challenges all of us: "[B]elieve what you want'" (*Earth's Mind* 209). This story contrasts with the painful absence of story in the poem's third section, when an old Navajo woman in the classroom recommends, through a translator, learning "the white man's language / [to] get a good job." When asked for one of her stories, the translator painfully fails, and we recognize the tight bond between *Dine* language and traditional story:

> "I don't know the word for story,' he says,
> deeply embarrassed.:

Do any of you know the word for story,
how to ask her to tell us a story?"
More silence." (*Earth's Mind* 207)

This silence and loss, a fundamental failure in intergenerational commu-
nication, is precisely the sort of disappearance that Dunsmore's poetics
fights against. In "the English" we've been following the wrong stories
and must search and find the right ones, often indigenous, to regain our
way and health.

Tiger Hill: China Poems (2004), his third book, distills Dunsmore's
experiences in Shanghai (and elsewhere) as an exchange professor (1991,
1997). Unsurprisingly, he foregrounds the life stories of Chinese acquain-
tances, which refract the horrors of Japanese occupation during World
War II and the brutal austerities, incarcerations, forced relocations, and
Cultural Revolution of the Mao dictatorship. The book's third poem, "For
a Chinese Friend," chronicles the friend's uncle's life arching from mul-
tilingual employment to a decade in jail, terminal illness, and muteness.
The short, final stanza generalizes a theme of the book:

These bright
pools of pain
just beneath
the surface
of family after family
in China. (*Tiger Hill* 14)

Dunsmore echoes this theme in his "After-Word," citing "the pools of
unexpressed pain one can feel beneath the surface of nearly every Chinese
I met" (*Tiger Hill* 107). The poet's job is not only to bear witness but to
express the unexpressed, as Dunsmore states in the book's final sentence
(*Tiger Hill* 111). He has consistently stalked the unexpressed, however
shocking or painful, in his career.

"Nuclear Peach" describes an exchange between the poet and "*Blue
Stone*," the dedicatee who "taught me Chinese silence" as well as the "old
song / about every grain of rice / spilled from anyone's bowl," which the
poet includes: "Who knows that the rice in every bowl, / every grain of
it, is precious?" His lesson in hunger and thrift is more than matched by

the poet's story of the "Seri Indians," whose "second harvest"—extracting and washing the "undigested seeds" from their "saved" "feces"—would strike Western readers as "filthy" (*Tiger Hill* 81–82). As is often the case in Dunsmore, the poem enacts an exchange of understandings between the poet and a subject who functions as teacher. "Looking for Marx's Chair" (included in *Greatest Hits* with a different dedicatee) represents the kinds of biography-tribute Dunsmore prizes. The dedicatee, who calls the poet "as tough as a daffodil in the snow, / but [with] the heart of a child," embodies both a nation and most of a century of oppression:

> "I want to tell what happened
> to my family, to close friends,
> so the world will know China
> this last one hundred years." (*Tiger Hill* 84–87)

To witness and commemorate such a voice allows it to rise above those "bright / pools of pain" (*Tiger Hill* 14). The poet publicizes her uncommon, common story of survival, including the survival of her own impulses to love, which otherwise might be lost. In Dunsmore's poetics, the witnessing and inclusion of the otherwise silenced voice amounts to a sacred duty.

You're Just Dirt (2010), Dunsmore's fourth book, contains several tribute poems ranging outward from the familial. "Taking All the Iron Out " tells Otto's story as a junkyard man whose job and way of life are ending because of "those goddamned environmentalists, / all their expensive solutions." Part of the poet's achievement consists in his honoring opinions sometimes divergent from his own. The poet humanizes Otto, a generous recycler who sees a corporate takeover ruining his local, self-sufficient system of salvage. Though Otto claims "You've got to have dirt in the air" and derides "this clean air bullshit," he also knows iron "is no good for the ground" (*Dirt* 49), so he extracts and resells scrap iron to poor people. Otto, though, goes the way of his operation, forgotten except for this poem.

In "Quita-Le Los Huevos," an angry political poem documenting killings and torture in El Salvador and Guatemala, he raises a fundamental question also treated in *Tiger Hill: China Poems* (2004):

> What are poets for?
> The pain of the people, of the land.
> Their generosity

after generations
of torture.
Their beauty." (*You're Just Dirt* 78–81)

As he has since his early years, Dunsmore sustains a hard focus upon sundry acts of inhumanity, including torture and death. In his view, poetry always matters because it bears witness to human pain and celebrates the endurance of morality despite it. It celebrates the survival of compassion (e.g., "Their generosity") despite sustained degradation.

You're Just Dirt (2010) includes "The Sharp-shinned Hawk," the title poem of Dunsmore's second chapbook (1987) and, in many ways, an epitome of his career. It measures, once again, the vital losses accruing from our neglect of the Navajo "grandfathers" everywhere among indigenes on the planet. This central poem summarizes several strands of Dunsmore's poetics, as it dramatically contrasts the knowledges embodied by the (mostly white) "university" and the "medicine man" who comes to teach. Dunsmore likens the latter to the mimetic motions of the title, totemic bird and, in the second section, expresses his homily:

There are coherences of the mind,
the body,
coherences of the breath or lips,
way out beyond this English.

Paraphrasing Hamlet's rejoinder to his friend, Horatio, there are more things in heaven and earth than are dreamt of in [our] philosophy, our First World intellects. In the closing, he echoes this statement of earth's mind:

There are coherences of the wrist,
the lips,
coherences of the breath
(hawk feathers and dried grasses),
far out beyond this English,
this five thousands of years,
with which we jam our minds." (*You're Just Dirt* 93–96)

Dunsmore's career and example have consistently promoted our collective "unjamming" such that we might discover, and abide by, some of those "coherences" that exist before and beneath the modern world. These voices constitute the extraordinary to be discerned through the lens of the ordinary (e.g., "this English"). In this populist, intermittently neoprimitivist view, the oldest stories, often shuffled aside, remain the most vital. This senior poet has always recommended we attune ourselves to earth's mind. Just as Walt Whitman's poetics enfolds and embraces all humanity, so Dunsmore's poetry embraces the marginalized and indigenous in teaching us to listen to their stories, which belong in our cultural center.

WORKS CITED

Dunsmore, Roger. "All My Stories Are Here: Four Montana Poets." *All Our Stories Are Here: Critical Perspectives on Montana Literature.* Ed. Brady Harrison. Lincoln: University of Nebraska Press, 2009. 21–36. Print.

———. *Blood House.* Vancouver: Pulp Press Book Publishers, 1987. Print.

———. *Earth's Mind: Essays in Native Literature.* Albuquerque: University of New Mexico Press, 1997. Print.

———. *Greatest Hits: 1969–2006.* Columbus: Pudding House Publications, 2007. Print.

———. *On the Road to Sleeping Child Hotsprings.* Vancouver: Pulp Press, 1972. Print.

———. *On the Road to Sleeping Child Hotsprings.* 1972. Vancouver: Pulp Press, Revised 1977. Print.

———. *The Sharp-shinned Hawk.* Nobleboro: Blackberry Books, 1987. Print.

———. *Tiger Hill: China Poems.* Seattle: Camphorweed Press, 2005. Print.

———. *You're Just Dirt.* Kanona: FootHills Publishing, 2010. Print.

Thoreau, Henry David. "Walking." *Walden, and Other Writings.* Ed. Brooks Atkinson. New York: Random House, 1950. 625–63. Print.

CHAPTER 6

Of Earth and Eros: The Poetry of Sandra Alcosser and Melissa Kwasny

CAROLINE PATTERSON *(Missoula, Montana)*

Two of Montana's foremost contemporary poets, Sandra Alcosser and Melissa Kwasny, share many surprising similarities beyond the fact they are female Montanans who have written award-winning collections of poetry. They both live in cabins up dirt roads on either side of the Continental Divide—Alcosser outside Florence, Kwasny outside Jefferson City. They both grew up in Indiana no more than thirty miles apart—Alcosser in South Bend and Kwasny in LaPorte—in working-class towns built by early immigrants. Alcosser's family ran an auto body shop which, as she describes in her second collection, was a space of *"paint fumes, grease pans, sparks flying"* (*Except* 32). Kwasny's grandparents were tenant farmers who also worked in the woolen mills. Her parents and paternal grandparents owned The 3-Star Lounge, a Polish bar in LaPorte. Both women came to Montana in the 1970s—Sandra to teach poetry in the schools and to study with Richard Hugo, (whom she had met at a YMCA in New York); Melissa to go to school at the university with "the cheapest undergraduate education in America" (Kwasny, personal interview). Both have served in poets-in-schools programs and as university professors. Both have amazing intellectual energy. Kwasny's is deep, quiet, intense; Alcosser's is at once precise, blooming, and far-ranging. They both are, in Kwasny's words, "unlikely girl poets from the backwoods of America" who have been "influenced by and, in a way adopted by [Richard] Hugo" ("An Appreciation" 94).

They also share an engagement with the natural world. This is a traditional subject of writers who identify with the American West, as well as of women writers, who have often been associated with descriptive pastorals rather than more frenetic urban or revolutionary political poetry. On the surface, their similarities line up with the lineage of Western writers. Yet careful readers will find these engagements deliciously subversive to the orthodox Western myths about human relationships to nature, especially nature's conventional associations with women. They proceed in these resistances in very distinct ways. Alcosser follows a path of the sensual, embracing Eros as a quest while condemning the culture that punishes her for doing so. Kwasny's tack is to examine nature through a variety of intellectual perspectives that challenge the dominant European models. Alcosser's poems sing the body electric—they dance, buzz, perfume the air. Kwasny's resist by holding up marginalized or cast-off world views as equal, if not superior, to the western European worldview that has dominated normative cultural values for the last centuries.

My friendships with these women were launched more than thirty years ago in Richard Hugo's creative writing classes and renewed over and over again throughout the years. While the bonds of friendship influence my reading, my dedication to their work derives from more than admiration. I continue to read each book they create because they rigorously engage in a type of cultural problem solving that directly speaks to my life as a woman, writer, Westerner, and human being struggling to crack the unwritten codes inherited from a European-based culture.

Over the three decades of their careers, they take seriously the calling of poets to listen, observe, and question. Most important to me, their poetry renders into language a resistance to cultural values held up as "normal." These poets are helping us think through the biggest questions of civilization, namely—what is our place in it? How do we respond to this world—in these bodies, in the West? I read their poetry to learn, to see them advance the inquiry further, to absorb their intellectual, artistic findings. To paraphrase a description used for Gertrude Stein, Alcosser and Kwasny each act as a Marie "Curie of the laboratory of vocabulary"

(Loy 94), behaving as much as scientists, or cultural anthropologists, as poets. By examining the distinct ways that these poets resist that inherited normalcy of human interactions with "nature" (and even that word is contested), they have altered the conversation and expanded the way we talk about the physical world in poetry. The condition for writers in Montana, especially women, is far from the one they entered, and their work—distinct, yet equal in rigor—will offer young women writers more authority from which to start writing. But first, let me begin by telling you a bit about who they were almost forty years ago.

1976: CREATING COMMUNITY

I first met poet Melissa Kwasny in 1976, when we were undergraduates in Richard Hugo's graduate poetry workshop. She rushed in, late, having just bicycled in from her apartment in East Missoula. She was bohemian, shy, immensely talented. Twenty years later, I met her again, this time on the lime-green sofa in Patricia Goedicke's living room—she was studying with Patricia to complete her MFA at the University of Montana. She had the same shy smile, but a new, fierce confidence and two books under her belt, *Modern Daughters of the Outlaw West* (1990) and *Trees Call for What They Need* (1993).

Kwasny had spent some of the years in between in Basin, 45 miles south of Helena—a dying silver mining town on the east side of the Rockies—where a group of women were buying old buildings and businesses and creating a community of their own. For Kwasny, it was a formative time, "being young and coming out" in this "small funky town," along with the numerous other lesbian musicians, painters, and writers who had gravitated there from across the country. It was there, she said, "I met all these women. I didn't have to answer to anything. It was where I learned to live a creative life" (Kwasny, Personal interview).

I also met Sandra Alcosser in Hugo's graduate poetry workshop, in 1980, around a blonde veneer conference table in the bland world of the University of Montana's Liberal Arts building. Alcosser epitomized glamour and adventure, having just arrived from New York, where she'd worked at *Mademoiselle* and directed Central Park's Poets in the Park program. Now she lived in a cabin with her husband in Rock Creek and taught poetry workshops for the National Endowment for the Arts.

Alcosser and I got to know one another well in the 1980s, when we were part of the Rattlesnake Ladies' Salon, held at the home of Connie Poten. This group of women included writers Deirdre McNamer, Kate Gadbow, Patricia Goedicke, Marnie Prange, Megan McNamer, and Annick Smith. Winters we gathered around a fire in the living room and summers in a gazebo in a lily-filled backyard, a lively, raucous group that read and critiqued one another's work. We commented on poems of Sandra's that became part of *A Fish to Feed All Hunger* (1986) and *Except by Nature* (1998). Early drafts of "Salvation Army" and "Dancing the Tarantella at the County Fair" filled me with awe, admiration and envy—like some kind of heady champagne.

Why is it important to locate Kwasny and Alcosser in their communities? Because these communities were vital to women artists in Montana. In the 1970s and 1980s, women were trying to articulate new versions of themselves, new visions of what it meant to be female writers writing about the West, and we needed one another to nurture our visions. We were trying to articulate those visions in an unabashedly male-dominated writing scene. It wasn't that women were not welcomed or represented—Richard Hugo and Madeline DeFrees nurtured many female students, but women's voices weren't particularly heard when it came down to the publishing end of things. This was the glass ceiling in the world of Western literature: take all the workshops you want, write all poems you want: then just see who gets published. Take a look at a table of contents at any anthology from the 1970s and 1980s and count the women authors. There will be, say, 18 males, maybe 2 females. That was known, at the time, as diversity.

So women clustered to support one another, to keep their writing alive. Kwasny went to Basin where, with the support of a community of women, she learned to live a creative life. Alcosser was party to the lively Rattlesnake Ladies' Salon and she was out in the world, teaching at Louisiana State University (1982 to 1985), and then San Diego State University (1985 to present) where she started the MFA Graduate Program.

What the two of them were doing was re-seeing women's relationships to nature. Instead of seeing the landscape as a woman's body, Alcosser experienced a landscape as her body. Instead of seeing the landscape as an image or a setting—something separate from the speaker—Kwasny went back to the lost ways of looking at the world—the Romantics, the Native Americans—in order to restart a conversation with the natural world.

Anthropologist Sherry Ortner observed in her 1974 essay "Is Female to Male as Nature Is to Culture?" that almost universally across cultures woman is associated with nature and is thus viewed as uncultured and inferior, while man is synonymous with culture and civilization. Alcosser plays with the hierarchy: man is to woman as culture is to nature. As Alcosser writes in "Skiing by Moonlight,"

> ... Eros is the wound.
> White will go to shadblow. White will go to orchid bloom.
> Except by nature—as a woman, I will be ungovernable. (*Except* 60)

She rejects the culture as being the governing force, and instead turns to nature, the shifting nature of Eros, of touch, of sensuality as her governor, inverting as she does even her own language so that the object, nature, is what comes first, then the subject: the narrator as woman.

EXPLORING THE DIVIDE BETWEEN HUMAN AND NONHUMAN: MELISSA KWASNY

On May 28, 2012, Kwasny and I meet for coffee in a wooden booth at Helena's General Mercantile. As we sip lattes, she tells me about her new book, *Earth Recitals: Essays on Image and Vision* (2013), which focuses on the life of the image and its role in visionary experience. An image, she says, "is where the "spiritual and the sensual meet." (Kwasny, Personal interview). She explores "the potential of the image—particularly the natural image, the image from the nonhuman world—to bridge the increasing rift between human consciousness and nature's consciousness, to investigate how 'the shaping spirit of Imagination,' as Samuel Taylor Coleridge called it, might help unite 'the living self to the living outer world'" (*Earth* 2).

This exploration of how vision bridges the natural world and human consciousness is a refinement of conversations between human and non-human worlds that Kwasny has been conducting over the years. Kwasny's conversations with the natural world have grown larger and more wide ranging over the years, from her narratives about talking with trees (*The Archival Birds*, 2000), to poems about talking with plants (*Thistle*, 2006) to poems juxtaposing the nineteenth-century Romantics' views of nature with those of Native Americans (*Reading Novalis in Montana*, 2009). These are part of a communication Kwasny is interested in; she writes in the literary journal *Willow Springs*, of "a speaking and a listening, between the human and nonhuman" (5).

Although, as Kwasny's poems regularly engage "various thinkers and 'philosophies of the land,'" in *Reading Novalis in Montana* (2009), she chooses to view the world through the lens of nineteenth-century German Romantic poet Novalis, who, she states in a *Coldfront* interview, believed in the "correspondence between the natural and spiritual worlds and its emphasis on the dialectic between inner and outer realms of thought" ("Possibility"). She then set Novalis's insights alongside Native American views of the natural world. We see one expression of that separation between ourselves and the world in "Reading Novalis in Montana," when Kwasny quotes Novalis as saying, "*All that we experience is a message*" (*Novalis* 3). Kwasny turns that separation on its head in section 5 of "The Waterfall." As the narrator watches the whirl of birds drunk on chokecherries and the clouds of insects, she mourns not just the separation of humans from the language of nature, but the lost conversation—a conversation that we hear only in fragments, that we are simply unable to translate, a conversation in tongues no longer accessible to us, in voices we can no longer hear:

> Before us, the birds
> dive-bomb the chokecherry, crass and clumsy on its wine.
> We live as if in a foreign land, the soil consecrated
> to spirits we don't know, who do not know us. We are blind,
>
> yet a brilliance flies through us, angled, belated,
> last of the butterfly days. The yellow glue from their bindings
> dries and breaks. Wings fall from each other, unweighted.
>
> Which world do insects fall through, ours or theirs, confiding
> a life too precious, too astute? (*Novalis* 33)

The natural world, Kwasny observes, could serve as a "mirror or lens...for the divine presences," or as a "correspondence between inner and outer worlds" ("Possibility"). In this image of a blighted paradise—the birds drunk on chokecherries, the butterflies flying, then breaking apart, like glue from old books, broken—she asks a more undermining question: is this our world after all? Or theirs? On this ground consecrated by spirits we do not know, did not ever care to find out about, what world is it these animals are living in? Or that we are living in? Tromping through? Digging up and plundering?

Kwasny is interested "in a process where the voice becomes indeterminate," she says in *Willow Springs*. "We can't tell—is that you speaking or is that the plant speaking? Is that you listening or is that the plant listening? In a communion, one doesn't know exactly where the "I" is" (5).

These correspondences between the inner and outer worlds parallel some American Indian beliefs and practices where the features of the earth— sun, moon, Chief Mountain, Sweetgrass Hills, to name just a few—are themselves divine. Through that lens, Kwasny examines paradoxes of life in contemporary Montana, a mountainous paradise where the landscape is regularly pitted by mines, a place where "pictographs and petroglyphs from visionary ceremonies a thousand years ago...are now often the site of beer parties and racist graffiti" ("Possibility"). And this isn't a new tradition. Consider the numerous peaks, creeks, and mountain ranges given the derogatory name "squaw," or the Tetons in Wyoming, the French name for breasts. If Western society weren't a patriarchy, if landscape wasn't considered akin to a woman's body—and therefore the domain of the male—would Euro-Americans have felt as free to ravage the landscape as they did? Is it coincidence that the intensive drilling in the Bakken oil fields in Eastern Montana and North Dakota coincides with what appears to be an increase of violence against women in the West?

In *Reading Novalis in Montana* (2009), Kwasny enlarges the conversation to portray the contradiction between our spiritual conception of the natural world and our actual engagement with it. In juxtaposing the world view of the German mystic poet Novalis and eighteenth-century Romantic poets and that of life in contemporary Montana, Kwasny examines this notion of "correspondence between the natural and spiritual worlds and its emphasis on the dialectic between the inner and outer realms of thought" ("Possibility"). Is our perception of the human and the natural world as separate as the original sin—our original break from the natural world? In the ninth section of "The Underworld" she portrays this heart-wrenching separation of the human from the earth:

When I broke with the earth, in grief, the animals still gathered. The iris skimmed the pond, turning it to azure. I felt the coolness on my arms.

Re-pressed. Implying the property of buoyancy. Re-petition....Though the soil still clings to me. Though I drag my bootleg pain....Deep need, I am bending into you....Help me to remember who I am. (*Novalis* 77)

What if, she asks, there is no divide between the human and the nonhuman? This is the question she explores in more depth and at an ever more personal level in her next book, *The Nine Senses* (2013). In an attempt to live more in resonance with the natural world, she asks of those she encounters, including the nonhuman, "Who are you?"

"Attention is the prayer of the soul" (7), Kwasny quotes Paul Celan in an interview in *Willow Springs*, and indeed, her poems, in their seeking of this lost unity of human with nonhuman, are a spiritual meditation moving us from brokenness to wholeness. Her poetry reminds us "to be alive to our worlds and our relationships." Inherent in this, is the hope that "we, as creative beings, could see *into* the mystery that is the wholeness of the world" ("Possibility").

MAPPING THE WORLD THROUGH THE SENSES: ALCOSSER

Alcosser describes herself as "a natural savorer," (Interview) as the two of us sit at a table, eating almonds, in a pool of light from her cabin window. Alcosser's first book, *A Fish to Feed All Hunger* (1986), implies, as Alicia Ostriker writes in *Poetry*, "a kind of connection between woman and nature which is both old and new" (237). In *Except by Nature* (1998), Alcosser's careful observation of this connection deepens into immersion. In some poems, we enter an entire, self-contained world, like a doll spinning inside a jewelry box. Tactile, rich, sexy, earthy, as Judith Moore points out in her interview in *Poetry Daily*, "the poems serve as tiny museums to store domestic details that otherwise might be lost to us" ("Conversation"). Whether she is portraying a nine-year-old girl trying to dance away the shame of being forced to perform for the old people in the county home, moving faster and faster to "*blow the stink off*" in "Dancing the Tarentella at the County Farm" (*Except* 33) or grizzly bears that ". . . swirl / as they bat snags of color / against their ragged mouths" (*Except* 47); this world is tactile, swarming with color, movement, sensuality.

The poems are not just about sensuality on the page; they are about how the words feel in the reader's mouth, the Eros on and off page. It's the slow draw of a finger along a crystal glass—and the implied ringing—in her poem "Azaleas," where Alcosser writes: "Tell me about a lover, she'd say, causing a lip of wine to sing under her index finger. Or: "[O]ur dresses lifted and fell those hours between the wicker and dying rafters like opulent clouds of steam" (*Except* 9). It is feeling words crunch in the mouth in "What Makes the Grizzlies Dance," ". . . Shaping / the lazy operatic vowels, / cracking the hard-shelled / consonants like speckled / insects between your teeth" (*Except* 47). Alcosser orchestrates sound and image into a dizzying, hypnotic dance to make steamy New Orleans heat or the shaggy head of an *Ursus horribilis* rise from the page.

In *Except by Nature* (1998), it feels as if the world must pass through the poet, a world returned in its most sensual level, a world experienced on its most basic level: taste, touch, sight, sound, and smell. In the three sections of *Except by Nature* (1998)—Sugary Heat, Sweat, and By the Nape—we are taken respectively on a kind of hellish sense journey through a Louisiana bayou, then through the body shops and mills of Alcosser's home ground in South Bend, Indiana; and finally we land in a benign, but wilder place, her acquired home in the Bitterroot Mountains. "I have touched everything," she writes in "Throughout the Duration of a Pulse a Heart Changes Form," as the narrator prepares a homecoming for her husband. "I put out a bowl of pecans. I sweep / the white tile floor one, two, three times" (*Except* 57).

Each item is taken on and examined through the senses, moved through the body, a process similar to "Worms," who "can eat anything— // two by four, dog, human" (*Except* 11). As the farmer tells Alcosser:

> . . . I know where
> we come from, and despite all our slick
> designs, I know where we return.
> This town's passed more than once
> through the slippery tunnels of worms. (*Except* 11)

Though the poem itself takes on the racism of the Louisiana bayou town where once a black man passed a white woman and was burned alive—it takes us down to worm level where all creatures, white and black, are the same. A worm can eat anything, as the poem points out, "two by four, dog, human," so at this level, man and nature are one as well. As the worm farmer points out, even the ". . . whorls of your fingertips / will vanish" (*Except* 11).

Through the sensual world, Alcosser delves further into wildness. She explores the erotic, humid heat in New Orleans in "Azaleas," where "[s]isters climb the bedroom window, lay themselves on the night table like pink fish, like negligees and soap slivers, diaphanous, pale veined" (*Except* 9) to a more staid, two-dimensional Eros portrayed at the opening of the "Sweat" section, that of "*calendars of women with bombshell breasts and skirts*" (*Except* 32; italics in original).

In the third section, she turns to a different form of wildness: wildlife. In poems such as "Wildcat Path," Eros is felt not only in the speaker's syntax ("foul breath and baby cry"), but in the mysterious, sensual presence of the cougar that stalks a woman and attacks her.

> *Hadn't I always wanted to hike the maple canyon*
> *with my teacher dress in shreds?*
> *Oh sure I was frightened. Thrilled too.*
> *Falling into a cougar's eyes, yellow stripes*
> *under cool green, like gooseberries.*
> *Have you heard a wildcat scream?*
> *Foul breath and baby cry.* (*Except* 48; italics in original)

Here the epitome of a civilized woman, the teacher, is attacked by the mountain lion, but is excited by being "chosen," excited by the charge, the "shredding" of her dress, her identity, and her "falling into" the pure strangeness of the sight and sounds of this large cat at such a close hand. Instead of greeting the attack with fear, the woman is thrilled at the encounter, at the shedding of her "civilized" self—at the merging of woman and wildcat.

In the lovely prose poem at the beginning of the book's third section, titled By the Nape, Alcosser presents a child and her grandmother. The child, who has not yet learned the division between culture and nature, "*curl*[s] *in the crotch of a sugar pear and dream*[s]" as her grandmother, who is distant enough from the hierarchy of things to do as she pleases, naps, surrounded by "*birds . . . draped in cobwebs*" and butterflies with "*pollinia like slippers on their feet*" (*Except* 46; italics in original). "*We were given to ecstasy, my grandmother and I,*" Alcosser writes, "*We were just the right distance from civilization to be invisible*" (*Except* 46; italics in original). The two of them drowse, immersed in the heat, the afternoon, the birds, the world around them, then Alcosser pulls back and swings one into the stands with this remarkable statement: "*A body grows from its erotic entanglement, and then is reprimanded, as if nature and culture were opposed*" (*Except* 46; italics in original).

Alcosser explores the erotic as a "method, as politics, as battlefield between nature and culture." As she moves through the Eros of the body, from sexual awakening to another kind of eroticism associated with her past—that of the body in motion, working or hiding (the girl in the pear tree, the grandmother dozing in the "*warmwater sleep of afternoon*") her exploration widens outward from the human species into other species, other types of wildness, as in wildlife—a world more mysterious, more unknowable. As she states in the poem that opens By the Nape,

> Sometimes I don't know who I am—
> my age, my sex, my species—
> only that I am an animal who will love
> and die, and the soft plumage of another body
> gives me pleasure, as I listen for the bubbling
> and drumming, the exaggerated drinking
> of a lover rising vertically from the sedges
> to expose the violet streaks inside his body,
> the vulnerable question of a nape. (*Except* 64)

In that admission of vulnerability lie the seeds of Alcosser's activism. It begins, she says, by "the vulnerable question of the nape." The nape —for all of us—is a vulnerable part of the body. Is this to acknowledge our vulnerability? To acknowledge that we are all needy, precariously perched on this earth? Does this acknowledgement eliminate the hierarchy between humans and animals?

"Human and earth share the same root in more than one language." Alcosser talks of this relationship in an interview with Amy Ratto in *Poetry Digest*. She quotes two lines from her poem, "The Blue Vein," in which she describes this relationship : "To be human is of the earth, crumbling / . . . / Is humus. Is humility" (Ratto 1). Again, Alcosser puts us in the dirt. This is the basis of our humility: to be one with the dirt. To acknowledge that leveling is to acknowledge the meaninglessness of our existence. And that, she says, is the first step to learning to be a human again on this land. Not just "human"—note—but human "again" on this land. Obviously, it is a lesson that we didn't learn so well the first time.

Kwasny writes of Alcosser's *Except by Nature* (1998), "Eros inhabits the space between ungoverning and ungovernable" ("An Appreciation" 95). Where Kwasny wants to erase the Western world's hierarchy between man and nature by reframing the conversation between the human and nonhuman, between speaker and object, Alcosser interrupts the hierarchy between woman and nature. "Eros disrupts," Kwasny writes. "[T]hough eros is pleasant, it is also dangerous, a threat to what has been established, a threat to peace" ("An Appreciation" 95). In Alcosser's work, the fusing with our animal selves is dangerous, sexy, amusing, and, well, fun. It can be the dangerous attraction between the woman and the mountain lion in "Wildcat Path," where a woman's identity becomes fused with the cat that tries to attack her. Now she becomes not just "*mother, wife, teacher*," but the "*woman who walked with a lion*," who was attracted to her "*. . . for just the warm scent of my flesh / and the crackle of a nylon dress*" (*Except* 49). Or, it can be the thrill of pure intensity, as in "Woodpecker":

> After all, have you never wanted
> to drive at top speed,
> to slam into a tree or dive
> from a ledge or catch fire
> or slit your wrists
> and let the fluids geyser?
>
> Not suicide, but its burning . . . (*Except* 70)

Who hasn't wanted, Alcosser asks us, to feel life to its fullest and then go over the edge—ending it all at "top speed"—when the passions are running at their highest? Isn't this what those teenage songs about car wrecks and love are all about? Riding out the passions to their fullest? Not the "crumbling" decline into middle age, taxes, and arthritis.

Or, it could be the mere animal pleasure of doing ". . . the dance / of the smart, hardheaded, // flashy creatures of the world" (*Except* 69).

> . . . on the long day
> of the summer solstice

when the world spins
silly with light, we do
the dance of the woodpecker,
twirling our skirts. (*Except* 70)

MENDING THE RIFT

Spirit guides or seductresses, the works of Kwasny and Alcosser guide us
to reevaluate our relationship to the natural world, to mend this rift from
the natural world, by recalling the wisdom of Native American elders or
the Romantics or Coleridge, or by forging paradigms for this conversa-
tion. Here, at the level of the earth, the worms, the plants, the spittlebug,
the common blue, the poets are telling us we must start over. It is at this
micro level that we must begin a new conversation in order not to repeat
the tragic lessons of our past—the ravaged lands, the massacres, the graffiti
on sacred sites, the lessons learned, then cast away.

In section 11 of "The Waterfall," Kwasny writes:

There is a certain emptiness between the ancient years of roaming
and the end of roaming, the old song and dance gone, the gods
waiting for their complements. How huge this country is and
how we've filled it. The woman in the desert subdivision leads
workshops in correct listening, although it would be a different
place here, blue dragonfly, dry species, without the Roman
columns, without irrigation.

Whether or not we are part of this, should we still feed their
angels, we who love our quick summers of breath? Fog by the
wayside, freckled and blue. If we forget the new series, the
undercoat of lupine, and have to piece it anew day by day? If profit
isn't involved, should we be interested? (*Novalis* 41)

Come close, they are telling us. Listen to the bear. The owls and the mice.
The fat flicker. The common blue. Feel the wings flutter the air, the vibra-
tion of its being.

Then listen again.

WORKS CITED

Alcosser, Sandra. *Except by Nature*. Saint Paul: Graywolf Press, 1998. Print.

———. Personal interview. 6 May 2012.

Kwasny, Melissa. Interview by Brett Ortler and Maya Zeller. "A Conversation with Melissa Kwasny." *Willow Springs*, 2006. 1–10. Web.

———. Interview by Melinda Wilson. "The Possibility of Wholeness." *Coldfront*, 2011. Web.

———. "Sandra Alcosser: An Appreciation." *Drumlummon Views* 1.1–2 (Spring/Summer 2006): 94–98. http://www.drumlummon.org/images/PDF-Spr-Sum06/DV_1-2_Kwasny2.pdf. Last accessed May 2, 2013.

———. *Earth Recitals: Essays on Image and Vision*. Spokane: Lynx House Press, 2013. Print.

———. Personal interview. 28 May 2012.

———. *Reading Novalis in Montana*. Minneapolis: Milkweed Editions, 2009. Print.

Loy, Mina. *The Lost Lunar Baedeker: Poems*. New York: Farrar, Straus and Giroux, 1996. Print.

Moore, Judith. "Sandra Alcosser in Conversation with Judith Moore." *Poetry Daily*. Lannan Foundation, 1998. http://www.cstone.net/~poems/alcinter.htm. Last accessed August 17, 2013.

Ostriker, Alicia. "The Tune of Crisis." *Poetry* Magazine 149.4 (Jan. 1987): 231–37. Print.

Ratto, Amy. "Interview with Sandra Alcosser." *2006 Poet's Market*. New York: Writer's Digest, 2006.

CHAPTER 7

Lowell Jaeger: In First Person

KATHLEEN FLENNIKEN *(Seattle, Washington)*

Lowell Jaeger is a gifted practitioner of the first person lyric poem. His first two collections, *War on War* (1988) and *Hope Against Hope* (1990), are intensely personal and emotional examples of the first-person form—furious, tender, and despondent at turns. These are a young man's poems, full of fierceness, but reflective enough that their speakers are self-aware, self-deprecating, as implicated as any other actor. Published twenty years later, Jaeger's two recent collections, *Suddenly, Out of a Long Sleep* (2009) and *We* (2010), still favor first person but adopt a more universal speaker and veer toward first-person plural. A close look at a few of Jaeger's first-person poems reveals his evolving poetic sensibility and maturity.

I first discovered Lowell Jaeger at a time when my life was changing. It was the mid-1990s and I was just barely beginning to enter the world of poems. I was in my thirties, married, home with two small children and on leave from my career. I was reading poems and writing poems, some-times as I stood at the counter with a child on one hip, stirring a pot of spaghetti. My friend brought me Jaeger's second collection, *Hope Against Hope* (1990), from Montana to add to my collection of poetry books, which probably numbered fewer than ten at the time. "Hope Against Hope" is the opening poem; I remember reading it for the first time, overwhelmed by the pell-mell rush and panic that made my heart race uncomfortably.

And you between. With shattered birds
faltering at your feet in the mire
of backyard play where I suppose,
too many years after, maybe your mother
was right: nothing should make you cry.

What else could I do?
You'd storm open my back door,
your trembling hands cupping a nest for twisted beaks,
battered wings; your muddy heels
anchored on linoleum waxed
against despair.

It can't last, your mother
behind closed doors insisted
I should encourage you not to try.
She doubted me better than I knew how;
I couldn't face your pain, your reluctance
to toss those bloody feathers back in the bush
where half-dead birds belong.

That's just life, I guess, both sides.
I've been foolish enough to find myself
panicked in the rummage of upstairs closets,
kitchen drawers, assembling another armload of shoe box,
rags, eye-dropper,
whole afternoons of anxious knots and bad news.

Afterwards you wouldn't come near me
for days. *I hope someday you learn,* your mother
scolded me.
    And you,
Girl-child, I couldn't wake you
that night. I knelt. Whispered
deep in the ear of your dreams:

Someday I hope you don't. (*Hope* 1–2; italics in original)

Poetry connects us to the human experience. We strap ourselves into another existence. We are handed borrowed senses—the screen door slams, we rush and fumble, our eyes search the jumble in the closet, we enter a dark room humid with the breath of a sleeping child. We're plunked down in the midst of it all, asked to make sense of it, asked to take sides. "Hope Against Hope // And you between." The mother can't bear to see the unrealistic, unmanageable, emotionally fragile parts of her daughter that are most like the father; she knows no good can come of lost causes and the inevitable suffering. For the father, it's not a choice. Against his better judgment and the mother's warnings, he permits and abets his daughter's doomed acts of charity; he's essentially luring his daughter to be more *his*. "That's just life, I guess, both sides," and we hear in that line not just the dark and light of life, our capacity for empathy and pain, but also the battle of mother against father, father against mother. The very details that make this poem singular—the daughter's trembling hands trying to save these broken birds, the harsh rebuke of the mother, the "linoleum waxed / against despair," the palpable anxiety—invite us, and this is the magic of poetry—to see ourselves in that anxious scene, to face our own circumstances.

That discomfort I felt as I read "Hope Against Hope" was partly the result of the sometimes head-over-heels syntax—"*It can't last*, your mother / behind closed doors insisted / I should encourage you not to try," and partly due to the dizzying zero-to-sixty intimacy and magnitude of the subject. The poem seemed to tumble forward like the father, tearing open the cupboards, rummaging through drawers. The speed and rhythmic shifts of the topsy-turvy language tightened the knots in my stomach made by the poem's circumstances. And part of the poem's power came of its address to "you"—daughter, "*Girl-child*," the only innocent person in this poem, the object of love. I immediately felt myself squarely in the shoes of the speaker, never "you." If I were looking only at pronouns, "you" would be a reasonable role assignment, but Jaeger immediately defines "you" with "shattered birds / faltering at your feet," so I buckled myself in and became "I," a flawed actor caught in this upheaval, and to this day, the next line sometimes comes to me out of nowhere: "She doubted me better than I knew how."

Here's a poem that asks us to choose a side, from its adroit title (Hope [*pitted*] *Against* Hope) to its showdown in the last line, in which the speaker/ father lays down all his cards—*I want you to be my daughter more than hers*. If we imagine this scene relayed by some omniscient god-speaker instead of a first-person actor, how would the poem be different? From the height of our new (and neutral) remove, we could see clearly the cruel ways we, as parents, manipulate our children to feel better about ourselves, that protecting our children from pain is sometimes more truthfully self-protection. Some couples compete to be the "good" parent; that god-voice poem might comment wisely (and more pointedly) on the way children often become pawns in bad marriages. It might well be a more philosophical and political poem, but would it be as close? as true? as necessary?

I'd argue that the speed and rhythms of "Hope Against Hope" are the result of that first-person voice. If I, the reader, imagine myself as a camera, what is my perspective? I am at linoleum-level, my hands reach into the medicine chest, I lean down to cup those child hands cupping a bird. It is impossible not to get caught up in the distress—there is no scrim between me and that beloved "you." The poem demands that I take a side.

Imagine one of the stanzas, the simplest to adjust with just three revisions—the removal of the phrase "I guess" (which isn't salvageable in third person) from the first line, and two changes in the second line, from "I've" to "He's" and from "myself" to "himself":

That's just life, both sides.
He's been foolish enough to find himself
panicked in the rummage of upstairs closets,
kitchen drawers, assembling another armload of shoe box,
rags, eye-dropper,
whole afternoons of anxious knots and bad news.

Where are our cameras? We are hovering close, to be sure, perhaps just a little above, or watching from the doorway. *Watching*: that's the crux. The nervous energy of the original—and thus the speed—is reduced because we are not *in* it or *of* it, but *outside* it. We tend to agree this father is foolish. We suddenly feel less sympathetic to his position. We consider remaining neutral.

In the end, who is "Hope Against Hope" intended to persuade? Not really us, the readers—though we do feel petitioned—but "you." *You* must

believe *me*, across time and water under the bridge and all the evidence
to the contrary. You must see my position, how I couldn't have raised you
any differently. So this poem wouldn't be this poem in third person. It
would lose its imperative, its reason to be.

. . .

Jaeger's first collection, *War on War* (1988), depicts a young man who sees
the Vietnam War casting its shadow over every coming-of-age ritual, from
Boy Scout campouts to P.E. class, who joins protest marches where he feels
out of place, who dodges the draft by moving to Europe. It tells the simulta-
neous story of soldiers on both sides in a series of persona poems, using that
"I" but varying the speaker, young men caught up in the ugliness of battle,
compromising themselves in the process. In contrast, the opening poem is
measured; this very young speaker is an innocent witness, not a participant.

LET'S HOPE THIS THING BLOWS OVER SOON

The Chinese, is all my father said
when my mother asked who we were fighting
with a nuclear sunshine on the snow
so immaculate it hurt my eyes.
Three cars ahead of us and I couldn't count
how many behind, all burning
headlights and flying colors on each antenna—
yellow and black of the first funeral I ever knew.
Why? my mother asked and my father shrugged.
Our attic full of souvenirs from the Allied invasion
twenty years old, but he had no recollection now.

A dead relative. In our congressional district
where cows outnumbered Republicans,
he was the first young man home in a box
from some battlefield whose name I couldn't recall.
Second cousin who took my hand years ago
as we toured his Holsteins, their stanchions locked
in a whitewashed barn larger
than my own backyard. *Watch your step,
watch your step,* I remembered him laughing,

then he shouldered me like a sack-of-potatoes
through the air of night, back into the living
room where our parents halted their gab, then guffawed
at the thick splash of manure under my shoes.

He died watching his step through a mine field,
though his coffin-face had forgotten,
eyebrows penciled in place, rouge
dusted on his cheeks and on his only
almost-human-looking hand. One empty black sleeve
on his dress uniform pressed and folded
neatly across his chest. I wasn't so brave
as to touch him, like most of my aunts who also
talked how handsome he had grown
and how just like the last war, other heroes
came home dead too. I wondered
where was that arm? Was it under water somewhere?
Might some barefoot kid harvesting rice
kick it loose and find it reaching after him nearby?

In the cemetery the sun exploded on new snow.
I followed in my father's footsteps, blinded,
careful not to stumble over bodies lying all around.
Then a short sermon to save us all
from frostbite. I let my father put the dead weight
of his arm on my shoulders. *Let's hope
this thing blows over soon*, he said,
and I knew what he was talking about,
with me in the ninth grade and a brother
old enough to drive. But I was curious
how below zero the bugler's mouthpiece
must have scorched his lips,
how the coffin slipped from its scaffold
into its concrete case with a sack-of-potatoes
thud, and when the ten-gun salute blasted the elms above,
how their icicles stabbed to the earth, shattering
the delicate safety of our lives. (*War* 3–4)

The startling image of the icicles stabbing the earth, the father and son "careful not to stumble over bodies," and the indelible sensory image of the "sack-of-potatoes / thud" all speak to a boy's fear (and his father's too) that the war could eventually claim *him*. There are clever line breaks and foreshadowing early in the poem: "then [my second cousin] shouldered me like a sack-of-potatoes / through the air of night, back into the living / room . . ." We see where that sack of potatoes originated; its reappearance at the poem's conclusion becomes more poignant. We admire the way a line break can deepen meaning: "back into the living / room" implies that the second cousin has become a dead man in the speaker's memory, that he has been revised into a ghost touring the old barn. We admire Jaeger's mindful word and image choices—"nuclear sunshine," "*Watch your step*," that read like clues of the war to come. In many ways this is a relentless poem, throwing warning after warning at this hapless, confused family, who is, after all, a stand-in for America, stumbling into the Vietnam War.

How does the first-person voice enhance and control this scene? We are asked to consider the soldier's funeral through a boy's eyes. Or more precisely, through the eyes of an adult looking back at his boyhood, who sends himself hints of what's to come through carefully chosen details. The boy is not so innocent he doesn't know that soldiers risk and sometimes lose their lives, but he is not quite able yet to read other clues—the dead weight of his father's arm, or the terrible truth that this war will *not* blow over soon. The speaker cannot quite awaken the boy to his own future, no matter how carefully he chooses his descriptions, until those icicles stab the ground.

The boy's mind is flexible, free to wander and wonder: what happened to the soldier's missing arm? "Might some barefoot kid harvesting rice / kick it loose and find it reaching after him nearby?" His thoughts rush to his innocent counterpart, half a world away, shocked and horrified as he discovers a piece of the same dead, broken man. A ninth-grade boy who cannot admit to his own horror can project it on a boy from a land "whose name I couldn't recall." And feel empathy. Isn't one of the primary necessities of warfare an enemy? Here at home as America's involvement in the war begins, even his parents are not sure who the enemy is or why we are fighting. None of it makes sense, especially this death, nor why the "delicate safety of our lives" must be shattered.

The boy is our surrogate. Our nation is confused. We have trouble reading the signs of an awful and protracted war to come. We don't quite accept these unfamiliar Vietnamese as our enemy. We are unprepared for death. We feel powerless to change our course. This is the power of the first-person voice to report truth.

. . .

Each generation of poets rails against the poetry establishment. The Modernists in the early twentieth century pushed against the hearts and flowers of the Romantics, found new forms, repudiated poems of childhood, and "made it new" with precise and surprising images. The mid-century Postmodernists reclaimed the old Romantic subjects by portraying them warts and all. Their techniques included a more natural voice (most often free verse), personal or "confessional" content, and a first-person speaker. The aim was authentic experience and an allegiance to truth, using the self as fodder. This was the prevailing tide when I started reading poetry in the early 1990s, and I found the waters welcoming. I didn't know poems could sound so natural, that poets could write about ordinary moments like pushing a cart down the grocery aisle or raking leaves. I started to believe for the first time that I could write poetry as well as read it, that my life experience could be fuel for art.

Not surprisingly, the tide turned again, and a new generation of poets began resisting the "I" and any sort of story that "I" might tell. Poet Matthew Zapruder writes, with a hint of irony, of the 1990s when

> . . . [e]veryone knew a poet had to relinquish the crutch of narrative to write true poetry and not its mere, sad cousin, lyrical prose. . . . [T]his rejection of narrative was also bound up in an idea about who had the "right" to speak. At all costs, we young poets wanted to avoid the possibility of being caught out as writers who took on, unintentionally or otherwise, oracular, superior stances in our poems that made it seem as though we thought we were better than our readers. (Zapruder)

Poets in the new century have gone to great lengths to subvert the narrative and avoid the "I." Critic Stephen Burt described the trigger for one recent and not atypical collection, *The Source*: "Noah Eli Gordon says he read 'only page 26' in 10,000-odd books from a public library in Denver, then took his favorite sentences and altered them so that they might fit together, changing some nouns to 'the Source'" (Burt). This resistance to first person came of real cracks in the prevailing style. Poets *have* used the "I" voice to make self-serving, "beautiful" observations about drives at sunset or hospice visits in order to appear more sensitive to beauty and truth than their readers. Poets *have* written about the personal ("This is from my journal . . .") with the misconception that *revealing* meant *interesting*. Poets *have* used the first person as a substitute for insight—mistakenly assuming that poetry of witness does not require poetic transformation—be it musical, metaphorical, or formal. The form appears to be no form at all, but is difficult to master.

. . .

Nineteen years passed between the publication of *Hope Against Hope* (1990) and Jaeger's third full-length collection, *Suddenly, Out of a Long Sleep* (2009), broken only by a *Greatest Hits 1983–2002* (2003) chapbook. In those intervening years, the first-person poem lost much of its favor with the establishment, and even Jaeger began to reevaluate the tools in his toolbox.

> I leaf through what I've written from thirty years ago and strain to recall who it was that wrote such things. . . . And twenty years ago . . . surely it was someone else signing my name. Ten years ago . . . another imposter still. It's like rummaging through an old shoe box of unlabeled photos. I should know these folks, but who the hell are they? . . . The person I am now . . . speaks a whole lot less loudly than these younger, reckless voices. (*Greatest Hits*)

Maturity, life experience, changing tastes and influences, a changing world—all factor into the way poetry changes along with its author. "I was looking for a way in which I might still make poems of the events of my everyday life," Jaeger explains, "but I wanted the poems to focus on something bigger than myself . . ." (Jaeger, correspondence). The result is poems more tranquil and philosophical, that seldom call upon the "I" to convey the heart-pumping visceral *now*; instead, the "I" serves as observer, everyman, a witness. And Jaeger uses second and third person more frequently, as in the expansive poem, "How He Cut Himself Shaving," which uses the "he" as a stand-in for "I." Many of these are poems recalling the world of Jaeger's youth, in which his family takes real or imagined roles. For the reader, it shouldn't matter if these poems rely less on facts and more on elaboration, but it gives Jaeger more freedom to explore the larger truth.

I'm interested in the title of Jaeger's most recent collection, *We* (2010). The pronoun "we" is, after all, first-person plural. Jaeger acknowledges that perspective continues to be an important factor in the way he shapes his poems:

> I've been experimenting with persona poems, "you" poems, poems which focus on the "other," and poems from a "we" perspective.[...] I'm obsessed with how people ("we") connect or fail to connect, and the complexities and emotions of all this coming together and falling or pulling apart. I'm hoping in my best poems, the "I" can still be me, but me in the background, and whatever happens inside the poem will be my experience, yes, but only as I represent common human experience. (Jaeger, correspondence)

In *We* (2010), the reader meets a town full of characters—Melissa Kwasny in her blurb calls it a "soul community"—and their foibles, their heartaches and nobility, and their familiar ugliness. The "I" is sometimes neighbor, nephew, father, customer, teacher, man in the passing car, man at the window. In Jaeger's mature voice, "I" is no longer the embodiment of irrepressible emotion. Jaeger's "I" drops the reader's guard with self-deprecating humor and an enticing subject in his poem, "Confessions."

CONFESSIONS

I once shoplifted
a tin of Vienna sausages.
Crouched in the aisle
as if to study the syllables
of preservatives, tore off the lid,
pulled out a wiener and sucked it down.

I've cheated on exams.
Made love to foldouts.
Walked my paper route in a snowstorm after dark,

so I could steal down a particular alley
where through her gauze curtains, a lady
lounged with her nightgown undone.

I've thrown sticks at stray dogs.
Ignored the cat scratching to come inside.
Even in the rain.
Sat for idle hours in front of the TV, and not two feet away
the philodendrons for lack of a glass of water
gasped and expired.

So many excuses I've concocted to get by.
Called in sick when I was not. Grabbed credit
for happy accidents I had no hand in.
Pointed fingers
to pin the innocent with crimes
unmistakably mine.

I have failed
to learn from grievous error.
Repeated gossip.
Invented gossip. Held hands
in a circle of friends to rejoice
over the misfortune of strangers.
Pushed over tombstones.
Danced the devil's jig.

Once, when I was barely old enough
to walk home on my own, I hid
behind an abandoned garage.
Counted sixteen windows.
Needed only four handfuls of stones
to break every one. (*We* 99–100)

"Confessions" strays from the typical "confessional" poem because Jaeger has created a universal speaker. Postmodern confessional poems flirt with the inappropriate: Robert Lowell, king of confessionals, famously excerpted his ex-wife's letters in *The Dolphin* (1973). Jaeger's earlier "I," as in the poem, "Hope Against Hope," often feels very close to the poet's identity, very particular. But this later-life "I" reads differently; Jaeger takes full advantage of the intimacy and energy that comes of divulged secrets but creates a "we" identity. He gets to have it both ways.

It's hard to resist a list of failings that rings true (an essential trait if the poem—and poet—are to be trusted) and familiar (important that the poem is full of confessions that are neither too small, and thus trivial, or too large, and thus frightening, but just right). The poem is at points as alive with particulars as a deeply personal poem like "Hope Against Hope," but then retreats from specificity too: I "[p]ointed fingers / to pin the innocent with crimes / unmistakably mine." We, the readers, are given license to insert a crime—how large or small, our choice.

If we imagine it in second person ("You've thrown sticks at stray dogs"), the poem takes on the uncomfortable voice of a voyeur. If in third person ("Walked his paper route in a snowstorm after dark, / so he could steal down a particular alley / where through her gauze curtains, a lady / lounged with her nightgown undone"), a distance has been inserted and as readers we excuse ourselves. We're off the hook and thus less drawn in, less implicated. What is a confession if not in first person? An accusation. First person is essential here, at the very core of the message, but it belongs to all of us. The iconic quality of these scenes, the evident joy that comes of distance and wisdom, the relief of never getting caught, of never needing to repeat mistakes—all come together in an immediately recognizable anthem for human frailty.

. . .

Twenty years ago, Lowell Jaeger's poems taught me how to find my life in a poem and how to make poems of my life. While the energy and emotional rawness of his first two books have mellowed into a more expansive and philosophical voice in his latest two, Jaeger continues to find power in the first person. The tide shifts, poets make it new, but the first-person lyric will remain an essential tool and the most reliable and direct route into the human experience.

WORKS CITED

Burt, Stephen, "Anxious and Paralyzed: On Spahr, Gordon, Moschovakis and Ossip." *The Nation* 23 Jan. 2011. 27–32. Print.

Jaeger, Lowell. *Greatest Hits: 1983–2002*. Johnstown: Pudding House Publications, 2003. Print.

————. *Hope Against Hope*. Logan: Utah State University Press, 1990. Print.

————. Personal interview. Message to the author. 19 Dec 2011. Email.

————. *Suddenly, Out of a Long Sleep*. Sausalito: Arctos Press, 2009. Print.

————. *War On War*. Logan: Utah State University Press, 1988. Print.

————. *We*. Charlotte: Main Street Rag Publishing, 2010. Print.

Jaeger, Lowell, ed. *New Poets of the American West: An Anthology of Poets from Eleven Western States*. Kalispell: Many Voices Press, 2010. Print.

Zapruder, Matthew. "Second Look: Revisiting W. S. Merwin's The Vixen." *American Poet: The Journal of the Academy of American Poets* 41 (Fall 2011): 25–29. Print.

PART 3 SOVEREIGNTIES

Photo by Brian Herbel

CHAPTER 8

Renegade Worlds in the
Poetry of James Welch

KATHRYN W. SHANLEY *(Missoula, Montana)*

James Welch shook my world in the early 1970s when his first novel, *Winter in the Blood* (1974), was published. At the time, I was working in Minneapolis as a registered nurse, and my younger brothers and sister had been assigned the novel in their (then-new) American Indian Studies classes at the University of North Dakota. Gripped by the novel's crisp, clean prose and elegiac tone, I was also stunned by how, for the first time in my life, I was reading something I understood as the first skin around me, a character whose inner life was not only familiar to me but deeply a part of me, a place I knew by heart, northeastern Montana. Having grown up Nakoda in Poplar, Montana, on the Fort Peck Reservation, a little farther east on Highway 2 from where the novel is set, I understood the novel's restlessness and despair. Although his poetry was unknown to me then, I would soon find Welch's *Riding the Earthboy 40* (1971; 2004), and in it would find the same power. Later, Welch stated that he moved from poetry to writing prose because he wanted to show something of the rich, interpersonal, philosophical culture of people along the Hi-Line (Highway 2) to people who thought of such places as blink-and-you-miss-it realities. The snapshot images Welch offers in his poetry remain as aesthetically powerful and historically rich as anything he wrote afterward, and while

I represent one end of a continuum of readers who find his work compelling, he strove for broad appeal.

In *Riding the Earthboy 40*, James Welch's only collection of poetry, he addresses the warring expectations placed on him as a Blackfeet (Pikuni) / Gros Ventre (Aaniiih)[1] writer during the 1960s and 1970s. At the same time he offers new and different historical perspectives on what has happened to American Indians in the so-called Indian Wars and how Native people lived before Euro-American encroachment into their homeland. In a variety of intense emotional registers, Welch imagines nineteenth-century Plains Indian life from the Native point of view as well as the way that history played out in modern Native peoples' lives. Welch often speaks through narrators who occupy renegade worlds. The personae he adopts survive by their creative wits and fluid movements "between two worlds," those who remains "Native" in an occupied land. For his personae, being "Native" or "Indian" means inhabiting vital interstitial spaces, not "caught" between worlds—interstitial spaces which are the stuff that holds worlds together across time and space. Welch's focus on the individual consciousness further grounds his aesthetics in speaking subjects rather than omniscient narrators, and to borrow Gayatri Spivak's term, they are subalterns.[2] In

....

1 The name "Aaniiih" (White Clay People) is the Gros Ventre people's name for themselves. They share the Fort Belknap Reservation with the Assiniboine people, who call themselves "Nakoda," which means allies. The people on the Fort Belknap Reservation have begun officially using their names for themselves. The Blackfeet people (on the U.S. side of the border with Canada) are part of a larger group known as the Blackfoot Confederacy. "Siksika," one of three branches in the Confederacy means "black foot"—the origin of which is not clear; the other two branches are the Blood (Kainah) and Piegan or Pikuni. The Blackfeet Nation in Montana refer to themselves also as "Niitsitapi," which means "the real people." The four groups that share use of the Blackfoot language are often referred to as the Blackfoot Confederacy: three reside in Canada. The U.S. government mistakenly referred to the Pikuni (the Siksika people on the U.S. side of the border) as "Blackfeet," and hence, the different designations. See the website for the Blackfeet Reservation, http:// tribalnations.mt.gov/blackfeet.asp.

2 Although "subaltern" may seem to be a fancy term for categories of people we simply all recognize as outsiders, the term (which became important in critical theory and postcolonial studies, first with Antonio Gramsci and then Gayatri Spivak) provides a way of discussing social groups who are excluded from the political discourse

other words, the powers they possess are the powers of the insignificant, the silenced or overlooked, and the objectized, yet Welch speaks not so much for them—for "the disinherited"—as he speaks with them, or from among their company. Their fates may not be his, but could have been and could be yet—he seems to know that by heart. Such knowledge, in my estimation, makes the perspectives of Welch's renegades both "Indian" in historically specific ways and universal in recognizably human ways.[3] A plain emotional truth screams to be heard: that they and their ways face erasure. Welch chooses poetry early in his career to capture the emotions of the voiceless that masquerade as cultural difference or backwardness and moves those emotions into realms of empathetic understandability, all the while leaving an incommensurable element of experience intact. In dreamlike conversations with the reader, the renegade personae speak from the grave, the open prairie, the church, and the bar.

The poems on which this essay will focus are, for the most part, taken from the second section of *Riding the Earthboy 40*, "The Renegade Wants Words," because that section contains the most accessible and historically grounded poems in the collection and because "renegade" captures the historical position of the author as well. Even though people who had the good fortune of knowing him would probably first describe Jim as mild-mannered and soft-spoken, his perspectives were consistently renegade. He avoided sharing autobiographical detail about his life, possibly because he wanted his work to stand on its own or because he would have had to translate himself and his experience across such a great divide of popular representations of American Indians. In the trajectory of Welch's work, these poems, particularly the renegade voices within them, represent

....

of a society. Because they are the voiceless, Spivak's question, "Can the Subaltern Speak?" attempts to capture the idea that key differences exist between how critics and writers give voice to subalterns, and how subalterns themselves would speak if they had the means to do so and the audience to hear them. The focus is on group identity more than on individual identity.

3 In my experience, Native people from reservations often favor the term "Indian," despite its dubious origins and colonial usage. For people outside the cultures, the term "Native American" works best. Throughout my career, I have been asked what term to use more often than anything else; I soon caught on. I often say: don't let terms hang you up such that little else gets said.

the most silenced aspects of Indian history. Beginning here allows for a perspective on Welch's visionary literary enterprise that denies nothing, does not allow sentimentality for his personae in their precariously situated moral dilemmas. The renegade who wants words wants to speak his piece in his own defense, and he rises out of erasure when his story is heard, regardless of whether he can ever be truly vindicated or known.

The term "renegade" takes on special meaning in Welch's work. Usually defined as someone who rejects his religion, cause, allegiance, or group, for another, "renegade" in the context of Welch's poems refers to individuals of a different sort—they are "renegade Indians," a common enough locution in Western films and pulp fiction. "Indians"—itself a somewhat derogatory moniker in mainstream culture—were called renegades in the nineteenth and early twentieth centuries when they thwarted white aims and stood in the way of western expansion. Yet, from an Indian point of view, they would more accurately be termed "resisters," since they turn against the Euro-American cultural values being imposed upon them, not necessarily against their own cultural values. The term becomes doubly ironic when one considers that "renegade Indians" contrast not with law-abiding "whites" but with those Indians who do comply with treaty obligations and Euro-American expectations. However suspect the origins and terms of those "agreements" may be or however flagrantly people of the settler-colonialist culture violate them, Indians are expected to comply. If they do not, they become renegades.

The title of the poem which names the *Earthboy* section, "The Renegade Wants Words," refers to an obscure historical happening in Zortman, Montana, a small gold mining town just across the southeastern boundary of the Fort Belknap Reservation. The poem captures something of the hundreds and hundreds of scenes in Hollywood Westerns where "renegades" are whooping it up, running around the circled wagon train, or otherwise threatening settlers—a form of resistance made to look doomed, if not ridiculous to the TV viewer.[4] Although the Indians who were hanged there probably did what they were accused of doing, in the previous century

....

4 In *American Indians and the American Imaginary* (2013), Pauline Turner Strong offers a comprehensive, yet cogent history of the representational issues and politics faced by Native American peoples across time.

Zortman had (and still has today) a reputation for hating Indians, however they behave. The difference between the cultural values of the hanged and those who did the hanging illustrates the irony and contradiction inherent in the term "renegade" when that term is applied to Indians. In an effort to explain their values and motivations, one of the hanged men speaks from the grave in defense of himself and his fellows:

> We died in Zortman on a Sunday
> in the square, beneath sky so blue
> the eagles spoke in foreign tongues.
> Our deeds were numbered: burning homes,
> stealing women, wine and gold. . . . (37)

The square referred to "is actually a square of bars with a notoriously awful jailhouse at one end. . . . The jail is actually a small box with no windows, no heat, and very little room, into which inmates are dumped somewhat like sardines every week-end" (Bryan 36). According to William L. Bryan, Jr., Zortman need not be covered by a blues blue sky to be considered sad. Blues sway us toward sorrows, and this renegade sings a song of truth.

Without apology or apparent self-consciousness or self-pity, the renegade tells of his people's ways. Implicitly he reveals how drastically their culture contrasts with that of the newcomers. Even the eagles are strangers who speak in "foreign tongues" in this "sky so blue"—a sky that leads them far from home. The "sky so blue" suggests the sorrow these Indians feel in a land that has become "foreign" to them. They are a people, the narrator tells us, who "mapped these plains with sticks / and flint, drove herds of bison wild / for meat and legend"—a people who move with the seasons, the "spring breakup" (37). They are a people who take care of their own, even "the hulking idiot" (37), if we take the phrase to mean poor relatives. We could also take it ironically to mean settlers who were assisted by Native people in various regions as they attempted to adjust to their new surroundings. The Native people in the poem are a people whose women (and presumably men) possess temperaments formed by the same forces that form the winter ice around them. By the account of the renegade persona who speaks, the hangman's revenge stems from a disdain for Indian culture as much as anything else: riding "naked across those burning hills" in the summer; burning "homes for heat" in the winter; and, perhaps most of all, painting their "bodies / in blood" (37). The warriors want to continue being who they are, to wage their war of resistance in the only way they know.

Being a warrior is a mark of great honor and responsibility to men of Plains Indian heritage. People of the Blackfeet Nation organized themselves into a dozen or more secret societies, "graded according to age, the whole constituting an association which was in part benevolent and helpful, and in part military" (Wissler 399).[5] The Aaniiih had similar societies (Cooper 436). The organization served as their educational system in which people learned age-appropriate knowledge and skills to make them into properly cultured adult members of their tribe. The renegades hanged at Zortman, members of the Blackfeet or the Aaniiih nations, may well have belonged to one of the secret societies who function as a police force within and avenging force for offenses against the people. Initiation and participation in the activities of such societies included the ritualistic painting of one's body red, green, blue, white, black, yellow, or a combination of colors, according to prescribed designs. Red, referred to as "the seventh color," the number seven being sacred to the people, identified its wearer as being of a particular society, depending on the design. Black-soldiers and the Horns of the Blood "wore no clothing (except breech cloth and moccasins) and [painted] their bodies red," the color of blood. The leader of the Kit-fox of the Piegan, the society "of all the societies . . . [that possessed] the strongest medicine," was also painted red. (Wissler 399–400). Hence, although Welch avoids specific and detailed ethnographic description of these men, "painted our bodies in blood" could well allude to a traditional practice arising from millennia of Plains living at the same time that it signifies the blood on the men's bodies from the killing of settlers.

The last stanza of the poem echoes the first, ending with a statement about the negation of the natives' rights as citizens, rights that signing treaties should have assured:

. . . Who can talk revenge?

....

5 Usually the age-graded societies of childhood were divided by four-year increments, guided by a similar contemporary mainstream educational concept leading to dividing children into kindergarten age, grade school, etc.

Were we wild for wanting men to listen
to the earth, to plant only by moons?

In Zortman on a Sunday we died.
No bells, no man in black
to tell us where we failed.
Makeshift hangman, our necks,
noon and the eagles—not one good word. (37)

These renegade Indians, not even treated as so-called common criminals, are even denied full participation in the Euro-American's hanging ritual. That they might "repent" ironically remains out of the question—it is as though the people hanging them recognize that the civil and spiritual laws the renegade Indians have violated do not apply to Indians. Renegade Indians do not qualify as citizens or, most likely, even as human beings; the law by which they are judged paradoxically also defines them as outside the law. The simplest thing is to eliminate them. The inevitability of their demise resonates in the words, "Our deeds were numbered," all their deeds. Still, the narrator gives them "a word" and a "good side"—"those times we fed the hulking idiot, / mapped these plains with sticks / and flint, drove herds of bison wild / for meat and legend" and "trust[ed] in stars" (37).

The hanging at Zortman on a Sunday afternoon represents a historical incident from a time when hanging was a regularly practiced law of land, when the West was "wild." It was a time when nameless Indians were killed for resisting Euro-American encroachment on their land and the imposition of alien cultural values upon their people. Though they had probably always been a territorial people, they encountered a very different enemy in the Euro-American—an enemy who felt entitled and empowered through Manifest Destiny to displace Indians from the land that they sought to claim for themselves.

The discovery of gold in the area had led to illegal mining in the late 1880s and early 1890s that the government hoped to curtail by buying the land from the Aaniiih and Nakoda nations. Although the tribal leaders were reluctant to sell the land, the government was able, with the help of George Bird Grinnell, Western historian and ethnographer, and others, to persuade them that, essentially, they had no real choice. Between 1900 and 1904, the land purchase of the Zortman-Landusky mines area proved a bargain indeed for the government,[6] becoming the largest industry in the state. Moreover, the profits continued rolling in: "Today the Zortman-Landusky is the largest low-grade heap leach gold mine in production in the Western world" (Bryan 36–37).

And as for their becoming like "white people" and hence being able to take care of themselves . . . ? The Native people's self-sufficiency actually declined from the point when they signed away more of their traditional hunting grounds onward. Welch lived on the Fort Belknap Reservation, home of his mother, and would have witnessed the decline and poverty up close. All the same, prosperity may not mean the same thing in different cultures. Marshall Sahlins argued, in the 1960s, that the hunter/gatherer society is probably the "original affluent society," in that they are societies in which the people's needs are easily met by what they have (Sahlins 96). From that standpoint, the renegades' people suffered staggering losses. Who indeed has the right to talk revenge?

Read in its doubled sense of time, then, the poem finally turns on the word "wild," the one word used consistently to describe renegade Indians, and two rhetorical questions: "Who can talk revenge? / Were we wild for wanting men to listen / to the earth, to plant only by moons?" (37). In asking those questions the narrator makes the renegades' silenced reasons for what they did understandable—the testimony (under the law) or confession (under the church) no one wants to hear because the renegades were believed to be "wild," primitive and, therefore, subhuman. The question of who has the right to speak of revenge becomes all the more ironic when one considers that the new inhabitants of that once-lovely valley have created a "foreign" environment through dredge mining. Therefore, when this hanged man questions who has the right to talk revenge and questions that he and his fellows should be called "wild" (untamed, barbarous), he has a legitimate argument. The so-called Indian renegades know a different cultural order, a different way of being civilized. They know enough "to plant only by moons" and to live in rhythm with their surroundings.

....

6 "Over a two-day period, Grinnell and Pollock were able to convince the Indians to sell a strip of land seven miles long and four miles wide, for $350,000. This small 'bite' out of the reservation was a steal for the U.S. Government" (Bryan 36).

Stealing wine, women and gold signifies a corrupt extension of the cultural practice of stealing horses, an act which brought status to Plains warriors; it could be the stuff which would earn one a new name. An appetite for gold therefore reflects a cultural corruption into the likeness of a Columbus, who is reputed to have declared to Queen Isabella in a letter in 1502: "Gold is a wonderful thing! Whoever owns it is lord of all he wants. With gold it is even possible to open for souls the way to paradise!" (qtd. in Johansen and Maestas 16). Besides making his patron and himself rich, Columbus and his crew were following the legal fiction known as the Doctrine of Discovery, a European pact that allowed that confiscating gold or other treasures was fine as long as an effort was also made to spread the Word of God to the infidels. On the Plains, the demand for gold, along with hides and furs, changed the Native political economy irrevocably, and led to unparalleled gold rush encroachment. Welch understands well the connotations "gold" carries.

The conflicting values of the hanged men and the men who hanged them hark back to a time when the land was not "foreign" to Natives. In "Thanksgiving at Snake Butte," Welch reaches retrospectively beyond the era of the Zortman renegade to find fragments of a past that is not primarily defined by cultural conflict and defeat. The poem suggestively and imaginatively "uncovers" an ancestral person and place, though its occasion is contemporary. It begins with a description of a present-day hunt:

> In time we rode that trail
> up the butte as far as time
> would let us. The answer to our time
> lay hidden in the long grasses
> on the top. . . . (36)

They seek game, just as their ancestors had, only now they carry rifles. They hear a noise, and their "horses balked, stiff-legged, / their nostrils flared at something unseen / gliding smoothly through brush away" (36). The competition between predator and prey continues more or less the same for all time. The repetition of the word "time" in the first few lines suggests that the poem is up to more than the telling of a hunting story, when the narrator rides into the foothills to discover a rock drawing, and in it, a hunter like and unlike himself.

> . . . Before us lay
> the smooth stones of our ancestors, the fish,
> the lizard, snake and bent-kneed
>
> bowman—etched by something crude,
> by a wandering race, driven by their names
> for time: its winds, its rain, its snow
> and the cold moon tugging at the crude figures
> in this, the season of their loss. (36)

Although the present-day hunters tote rifles instead of bows, arrows, and spears, the speaker intuits a connection between them and the rock drawings from another epoch. His journey thus becomes to him more than a pragmatic search for food, more than sport. He and the ancient hunter both possess a desire to record their own time and something of their individual lives within it. Just as the previous poem's narrator speaks for the renegades whose fierce cultural pride was not enough to prevent their extinction, Welch himself, as an artist in his day, seeks to record his experience and perception. The narrator speaks for his ancient ancestors, though the particulars of their lives are unknown to him. The "cold moon" tugs at "the crude figures," as if to vivify them magically, but they do not speak. They do not speak, but neither are they subalterns.

While the Aaniini and Blackfeet sides of history during the early contact period can possibly be reconstructed with some modest degree of historical accuracy, the rock painter's story cannot. Who they were and how they lived is subject to a wide range of speculations; however, Welch knows well the tribal belief in being tuned to the death and rebirth cycles of nature and the rituals through which blessing is sought within those cycles. Thanksgiving season, a good time to hunt because the animals have not yet adjusted to the bright white of fresh snow, also represents a time of communal celebration, prayer after harvest, and purification toward new beginnings. Thus, the rock-wall painting becomes something of a prayer by hunters seeking a blessing in "their names / for time: its winds, its rain, its snow . . . the season of their loss" (36). Plenty and loss, in the context of Native cultures, are bound inextricably together in the whole mystery of living. The title of the poem suggests a contrast between the time of the Pilgrims' first Thanksgiving, when some reciprocity between the indigenous peoples of America and the newcomers could be realized, the time of the ancient hunter and artist, and the time of the poet.

During a slack moment in another epoch, a hunter (like the narrator) pauses before the kill to consider his life and to mark it in stone. The narrator does not mean to and cannot resurrect the rock-painting culture of "a wandering race"; it is enough merely to connect with it, somehow. Perhaps the connection enables him to live in his own time and place. From "the season of their loss" he reaps a harvest of quiet possibility, sheds an ounce of his own grief. Exactly what "the season of their loss" means in their epoch cannot be ascertained, but the phrase suggests both that they experienced loss in their own terms and that they are lost to the poet. Nonetheless, a theme of human connection also carries the poem. We all know what it means to be hungry, to seek food.

In his search for a usable past, Welch, like numerous other poets, returns to the place of ancestors, but because he cannot even begin to recover it, he must imaginatively recreate it, all the while respecting what cannot be recovered. Like Pablo Neruda, the Chilean poet, who scales "The Heights of Macchu Picchu" in search of Incan ruins, Welch's narrators return in his own time to touch and be touched by the spirit of the ancestral person, the ancestral place. As the narrator of "Thanksgiving at Snake Butte" imagines the language of the "wandering race" with its different words for "time: its winds, its rain, its snow / and the cold moon" (36).

The paradoxical truth about "the season of their loss" makes for a mythological foundation which in turn becomes the season of the poet's gain—loss and gain being but different cycles of the same cold moon. The tribal worldview, even in its romanticized versions, offers a meaningful contrast to the Western tradition that has been forced upon American Indian peoples. For as Welch's narrator says in "Blackfeet, Blood and Piegan Hunters," connections with the tribal past are "faint" and require a "strong song" to make them something through which to survive; nevertheless, such connections do provide some inspirational sustenance.

> . . . Look away and we are gone.
> Look back. Tracks are there, a little faint,
> our song strong enough for headstrong hunters
> who look ahead to one more kill. (32)

Ultimately, Welch sees the limitations of "living" in the past, for he also says, "Let glory go the way of all sad things. / Children need a myth that tells them be alive" (32). The traces of the past he speaks of are too elusive, too flimsy to use as guides for living with the problems of contemporary Indian country—unemployment, poverty, alcoholism, and disease. Let there be no mistake about it: what Indians need is a genuine survivor's song.

Through the poet's imagination, "Thanksgiving at Snake Butte" inspires us to think of a time when a free people lived out their lives without the subjugation of reservation fences, boarding school assimilation policies, and theft of land and resources. Although their lives were no doubt complicated, even troubled by other concerns, at least we can be sure they lived beyond such terms as "renegade," because when they strove to preserve their tribal ways, they did not have to negate Euro-American ways to do so. "Thanksgiving at Snake Butte" also reflects a gratitude for the legacy represented by the rock drawings. By reclaiming ancient ways of being and giving, the poet becomes a renegade of sorts himself—one who rejects the settler culture, its religion, causes, and allegiances.

WORKS CITED

Bryan, Jr., William L. "The Great Gold Robbery of 1895." *Montana's Indians: Yesterday and Today*. Vol. 11. (Helena, MT: Montana Magazine, Inc., 1985). 36-37.

Cooper, John M. *The Gros Ventres of Montana, Part II: Religion and Ritual*. Ed. Regina Flannery. The Catholic University of America Anthropological Series No. 16. Washington, D.C.: Catholic University of America Press, 1957. Print.

Johansen, Bruce, and Roberto Maestas. *Wasi'chu: The Continuing Indian Wars*. New York: Monthly Review Press, 1979. Print.

Neruda, Pablo. *Selected Poems*. Ed. Nathaniel Tarn. Trans. Anthony Kerrigan, et al. 1970. New York: Dell Publishing, l972. Print.

Sahlins, Marshall. "The Original Affluent Society." *The Politics of Egalitarianism: Theory and Practice*. Ed. Jacqueline Solway. New York: Berghahn Books, 2006. 79-98. Print.

Strong, Pauline Turner. *American Indians and the American Imaginary: Cultural Representation Across the Centuries*. Boulder: Paradigm Publishers, 2013. Print.

Thackeray, William W. "'Crying for Pity' in *Winter in the Blood*." *Multi-Ethnic Literature of the United States* 7.l (Spring l980): 61–78. Print.

Welch, James. *Riding the Earthboy 40*. 1974. New York: Penguin Books, 2004. Print.

Wissler, Clark. "Societies and Dance Associations of the Blackfoot Indians." *Anthropological Papers of the American Museum of Natural History*, Vol. XI, Part IV. 357–460. Print.

CHAPTER 9

Written in the Hearts of Our People:
Three Native American Montana Poets

LOWELL JAEGER *(Bigfork, Montana)*

I

Recently, I stumbled across a poem, a clever poem, a risky poem.[1] The poem spoke in the imagined voice of a deer, from the imagined perspective of the deer. This poem was the proverbial deer-in-the-headlights poem, articulating for the reader what goes on in the deer's mind as he stares transfixed by the headlights of an approaching car. The poem begins:

Away in the eyefar
nightrise over the sapwood, and one likes
underhooves the heatfeel after sun flees, heat stays on this
smooth to the hoof hardpan . . . (37)

Words like "eyefar," "nightrise," and "heatfeel" signify the lingo of a primitive consciousness, a backward mindset, innocent of the world's complexities. The deer interprets the headlights as "moonrise mounding

....

1 "Collision" by Steven Heighton appeared in the Winter 2011 issue of *The Literary Review*. The poem was chosen by Mark Doty for the 2012 edition of *Best American Poetry*.

over groundswell," and, as expected, the deer gets run over by those twin moons which "come with a growling."

What's recognizable in this poem, despite its cleverness, is a limited cultural perspective, the mindset of Western civilization percolated through Judeo-Christian doctrines of the separateness of man and nature and the superiority ("dominion") of man over the natural world. The human who penned the poem is assuming the superior position of being able to interpret the deer's mind while the deer only dimly understands his demise.

By way of contrast, consider the poem, "Porcupine on the Highway," by Lois Red Elk, as it appears in her collection of poems, *Our Blood Remembers* (2011). Red Elk is a Montana Dakota/Lakota elder, and her take on the consciousness of roadkill is a far cry from the assumption that animals are backward or innocent of the world's complexities.

Red Elk's poem is a five-stanza dialogue between three characters: a Lakota named Amos, his sister, and a dead porcupine lying in the highway near where Sister's car has broken down. While Sister waits on the highway for Amos to come and repair her car, she stuffs the dead porcupine in her trunk. She doesn't pity the porcupine. She'll use the quills to "make Myrna a quilled bracelet and brother some armbands" (73).

The poet doesn't see her human world as separate from the porcupine's world, and the porcupine participates in conversation with humans, albeit a psychic/spiritual conversation. The porcupine is honored that people once read his bones and studied his entrails for health and weather. The porcupine gives its body "willingly" to the quill worker. All three of the characters are intimately involved with each other and with the events and consequences of events in the physical realm. Unlike the deer in the aforementioned poem, the porcupine's perspective (especially in death) may be broader, more far-sighted than the perspective of the humans. In Red Elk's world, Amos and Sister have no assumption of dominion over the porcupine, even though they are harvesting the quills. Sister, the quill worker, gathers the quills enthusiastically. There is no tragedy here, no imbalance of power. In this poem, the human and animal worlds are woven into one cloth. There is no separation.

I want to say that in Red Elk's poem there is a "harmony" between humans and nature, but that pushes me toward the slippery slope of my non-Indian, Judeo-Christian programming in which, if man is not separate from nature, then everything is peachy between them, like Eden before the Fall. I'm sure that's not it, either. The lure of Romantic Primitivism is a comfortable delusion of Judeo-Christian culture, the opposite of the assumption of man's dominion over the wild. Both are shortsighted. There's another wavelength somewhere between (or alternative to) these two extremes. Confined as we are by the boundaries of our own cultural worldview, we are like the man in Plato's cave who cannot fathom a workable reality beyond his shadow world. It's difficult for me, as a poet and as a reader, to glimpse an alternative wavelength outside my cultural mindset—even when I'm imagining how a deer thinks and what his thoughts might sound like.

Much has been written already about this alternative wavelength. University of Montana Professor William Bevis's *Ten Tough Trips* (1990) includes insightful chapters on the dilemmas readers face in attempting to cross the cultural/psychic gap between Indian and non-Indian cultures. Montana poet Roger Dunsmore's excellent essays in *Earth's Mind* (1997) also struggle heroically to unshackle readers' minds from their own cultural bondage. There's simply not space in this short essay to examine the thoughts of these authors thoroughly. Their concerns seem largely to be these: Native Tribalism vs. European Individualism. Native Spiritualism vs. European Materialism.

II

All poets are (knowingly or unknowingly) in the business of translating their respective cultures to the wider world. Poems are cultural artifacts, like designs painted on clay pots or the particular rhythms of a dance. As cultural translators, Native American poets are especially challenged; Native poets face cultural barriers surrounding what cannot be shared with persons outside the tribe. The "why" of these limits is not difficult to guess, given the long history of misinterpretation between Native cultures and invading European cultures and the devastating consequences of cultural imperialism. Also, as evidenced in the deer and porcupine poems discussed above, the chasm between the Native and non-Native mindsets may be an insurmountable leap. While some aspects of Native cultures simply cannot be broadcast, other aspects are so foreign to the non-Native ear as to remain invisible or verge on the incomprehensible. Furthermore, there are problems inherent in language itself; some words/phrases of Native American languages don't translate into English easily, if at all. So, too, concepts in Native American cosmologies and mythologies do not translate into English easily, if at all. English words or terms like "chief," "medicine man," and "great spirit" are approximate translations for Native American concepts with no exact English language equivalents. These words are a pidgin language that fails to convey the nuance and complexity of Native American thought.

New works by three Montana Native American poets offer readers a view of Indian culture, within the limits of what non-Indians are permitted to know and capable of understanding: *Put Sey (Good Enough)* (2008) by Victor A. Charlo, *Our Blood Remembers* (2011) by Lois Red Elk, and *Nakoda Sky People* (2012) by Minerva Allen. All three books have been published recently by Many Voices Press, a nonprofit press of Flathead Valley Community College in Kalispell, Montana. All three poets are tribal elders (now in their seventies) representing three distinct cultures: Charlo is Flathead Salish, Red Elk is Dakota/Lakota, and Allen is Assiniboine/ Nakoda. All three have been leaders on their respective reservations and have been active in teaching/preserving Native languages and traditions. All three are translators, writing poems to translate their tribal experiences to the world outside their tribes.

As translators, Charlo, Red Elk, and Allen face constraints put upon them by their Native cultures. There's a reluctance (inherent in the nature of tribal identity?) to speak about oneself as an individual. Recently, I asked two questions via e-mail of each of these three poets: "What do you want your reader to know/understand about YOU in your poems?" And, "What do you want your reader to know/understand about your CULTURE?" All three poets struggled with the first question. Lois Red Elk observed, "When I start to answer your first question, I immediately confuse myself with my culture." Minerva Allen stated plainly, "I really don't like talking about myself." Victor Charlo responded:

> In the non-Indian world, it seems I can say anything. In the Native world, there are things I can't talk about or say. So how do I reflect my world in my poetry, telling and not telling my story? This is what I grapple with. My poetry reflects the struggle to define myself while living in these two worlds.

This is in stark contrast to so many non-Indian poets of the last century, especially the confessional poets like Anne Sexton or Robert Lowell, who open their poems to the most intimate details of their personal lives and interactions with others.[2]

The second question seemed easier for these poets to answer, though their responses were qualified with various cautions. Red Elk wrote, "I love my culture, my spirituality. I believe both of these are dynamic, and I write about these with a careful and true eye because I have experienced the sustaining rewards of both." She continues:

> To translate and write honestly about culture and spirituality, I have to go to a pocket of spiritual tranquility where energy, prayers, and intensity come together and focus. To be in this place, I believe, is another plane of being that we Native people possess . . . . How I know this is listening to my elders pray in Dakota. Their prayers are like poetry.

Then, as a note of caution, Red Elk adds:

> I know when and where to draw the line about sharing traditional cultural information. I do not share any of the traditional sacred information with non-Natives. I share as much traditional information with young native people as I think they should know. I share extremely spiritual information or dreams with medicine men and women only.

Victor Charlo takes a similar stance:

> My landscape is my palette and these are the things I draw on for inspiration. The poems about people and places are remembrances about our culture and things that have happened to us, things that have weight of importance. These are the most important things in my life. This is what I write about.

Charlo adds his note of caution, similar to Red Elk's caution:

....

2   This is also in contrast to poems written by some Native American poets of a younger generation. Sherman Alexie's latest collection of poems, *Face* (2009), for instance, is especially self-involved, and most of the poems in that collection directly spotlight the poet himself.

There are different layers I have to myself, and ways any person protects himself (and those things sacred not to be discussed or revealed to a non-Native audience). So the question is—how deeply do I expose layer after layer?

Given these challenges in translating the Native American world to the surrounding world, how do Native poets like Charlo, Red Elk, and Allen proceed? Amidst what can't be said, what do these poets say? In poem after poem, all three of these poets express a twofold purpose: 1) Send a message to the outside world that Native cultures thrive; and 2) Pass along Native history, Native pride, and Native traditions to the younger generation of each of these poets' respective tribes.

III

In an introductory essay to her collection of poems, *Nakoda Sky People* (2012), Minerva Allen states directly, "We keep our history and culture alive by telling of our ancestors and legends to young people" (4). She tells of learning the Assiniboine way of life from her grandparents, and now she feels a duty to pass along what she knows. "When I go to sleep at night," Allen writes, "my prayer to the creator is to let me stay a little longer here on earth. I have unfinished business. I want to write and leave some good words for my people" (4). What does she want her reader (outside the tribe) to know/understand about her culture? Minerva Allen replies, "First of all it's letting people know how we are different." These thoughts are expressed beautifully in her short lyric poem, "Ashes":

> The ashes of our ancestors are sacred
> and their resting places are hallowed ground.
> Our religion is the traditions of our ancestors—
> dreams of our old men given to them
> in solemn hours of the night; and the visions
> of our medicine men. It is written
> in the hearts of our people. (58)

One of the most unusual and inventive poems in this collection is the poem "Seeing a Pow-Wow through the Eyes of a Friend," in which the poet enjoys watching her friend gain appreciation for the dance. This poem also exemplifies Allen's strategy to bridge the cultural gap by "letting other people know how we are different." She compares the pow-wow to a three-ring circus, a metaphor by which she communicates her culture to her non-Indian friend:

> a ring master controlling the kids and
> > the crowd.
> > Each event following into place
> as the evening flows; night passes through.
> > The beautiful colors flashing.
> > The quick steps of young girls.
> Each doing what has been done for
> > centuries
>
> . . . .
>
> > The pride which
> travels through one's being each
> > in his own way. (60)

The poems "Snake Man" and "Gumbo Lily" recount traditional stories. "Snake Man" is a legend in which a man eats a snake and becomes a snake himself, promising the rest of the tribe,

> Every time you come,
> leave me something to eat and I will
> lay across the big water for you to cross
> > on my back. (42)

The poem "Gumbo Lily" is the story of the origin of a plant by that name common in central Montana. These are examples of poems which pass along lasting traditions, educating younger generations. "Indian writers," Allen says, "might come from different eras, different places, different tribes, but we all have one thing in common—we are storytellers from a long way back and we will be heard for generations to come." Similarly, the poem "Ghost Dance" alludes to the aurora borealis. This poem may have sprung from a traditional tale, or it may be the invention of the poet. Either way, this poem is Minerva Allen's storytelling magic at its best:

> In the dark of the night

the stars up above
are our guide.

The moon is sleeping.
The ghost-lights dance
long streaks
from the earth to the sky
in the North.

Don't look my children.
It's the ghost dance.

Up North
the spirits are angry
and doing a war dance. (37)

Lois Red Elk's collection of poems, *Our Blood Remembers* (2011), also pursues the twofold purpose to acknowledge the resilience of her Native American culture and to participate in the continuation of that culture by passing along legends and traditions to younger generations. In her introductory essay, "Toward Sharing a Life," Red Elk wants the reader to know that her grandmothers are direct descendants of the "revered holy man," Sitting Bull. The opening lines of the title poem, "Our Blood Remembers," invoke a powerful image of the day Sitting Bull died:

The day the earth wept, a quiet wind covered the
lands weeping softly like elderly women, shawl
over bowed head. We all heard, remember? We were
all there. Our ancestral blood remembers the day
Sitting Bull, the chief of chiefs, was murdered. His
white horse quivered as grief shot up through the
crust of hard packed snow. (43)

Generations later, Red Elk unabashedly recounts Sitting Bull's influence still lingering in her bloodline. The title of her book, Red Elk says, was "given" to her one day as she was resting: "Just as I was awakening, I heard Sitting Bull say, 'Remember our blood.' I analyzed that to mean that I was to be a representative of our people and share the good ways of our nation."

The word "share" in the above statement is rich with meaning and at the same time purposefully ambiguous. The sharing that Red Elk wants to do with the outside world does not include the guarded mysteries and rituals of her tribe, but is more so that she sees herself as "representative" of her people. She insists that her culture be known and acknowledged in a fitting way: "I don't think it's necessary to share my deeply spiritual nighttime dreams with everyone," Red Elk writes, "I only share that with those who understand that part of my Lakota spirituality, and that would be the medicine men/women or interpreters." Again, there are limits as to what can be or should be spoken to outsiders, though there is also a lasting desire to "share the good ways of our nation."

In the title poem, Red Elk reminds the reader of Sitting Bull's words, "Let us put our minds together to see what life we will make for our children." In this direction, many of Red Elk's poems praise her Native traditions and contemporary tribal life with an eye on the twofold purpose to acknowledge her culture's lasting traditions while educating the children as a continuing thread of those traditions. She says in the poem, "Grandmother Praying," that she will "witness and celebrate abundant rewards / for a people reclaiming a birthright." This "reclaiming" is evident in the opening poem, "Blanket of Song and Culture," with news of a new child born into the security of the tribe and snuggled within the culture:

. . . Wrapped in the red blanket of song,
and culture, mother and father lifted their voices
and took the vow of the pierced ears ritual to teach
and raise their children in the good Lakota way. (7)

Red Elk enthusiastically and lovingly speaks out in praise of her people, and she is simultaneously unafraid to speak up in defense of what she cherishes. "For Thieves Only" is a poem that rails against the all-too-common Indian wannabe who claims Native American ancestry to falsely appropriate an insider's right to Native beliefs and traditions. Red Elk writes, "Don't tell me your great, great / grandmother is an Indian Princess!" (39). A few lines later she boldly stakes claim to her birthright as earned by her lasting commitments to her tribal way of life. "I paid the price," she says, "I am tradition. / I have survived." (39).

While some of Red Elk's poems, like "For Thieves Only," send a fierce, protective message to outsiders, other poems are more directly addressed to her own people, warning against self-destructive behaviors and chiding them for neglecting their tribal roots and obligations. "Hit by Hard Times" and "Images of What You Hate" are elegiac poems mourning the damages of alcohol, while "Tonight the Fists" bemoans the pains of domestic violence. The strongest of these poems on the difficulties of contemporary Native life is the poem, "Red Fire Ants," a poem directed to the younger generation in which "teen problems swarm the land / like red fire ants" who "gambled the food money," "snorted the diaper money," "drank up the tennis shoe money," and "toked up the utility bill money." (46). Again, the advice Red Elk offers is to return to traditional ways for spiritual sustenance:

> . . . hang on to the passing horses,
> they will teach you about companionship and commitment.
>
> Hang on to the low flying eagles, they will teach you about
> prayer and spiritual places. Hang on to the grazing black tail
>
> deer, they will teach you family responsibility. Hang on to
> stomping buffalo, they will teach you to live the beautiful
>
> way. Hang on to the diving red tail hawk, it will teach you
> to handle your problems immediately. (46)

It's worth noting the purposeful arrangement of the poems into four sections which flow full-circle from the past into the future. Section I, Dakod Wicohan (Dakota Culture), is largely praiseful poems of Dakota people and traditions. Section II, Woiyotiyetkiye (A Difficult Time), consists of poems warning against drugs and alcohol and cultural exploitation. Continuing around the circle, Section III, Ukiya (Returning), consists of poems that point forward from the hardships in Section II. Finally, Section IV, Iwahoiciya (We Promise), vows to preserve traditions and "walk courageously" into the future. Again, this organization expresses succinctly the overriding message of these poems: 1) Reader, please know that Lakota culture thrives; and 2) Children, please know we must embrace our heritage for our culture and traditions to persist into the future. "I suggest that my poems are a testament," Red Elk wrote in a recent e-mail, "that our ways have never died, that our spirit is triumphant because we will always keep and understand our identity as children of the earth . . . ."

Victor A. Charlo, through lineage, is a spiritual leader of the Flathead Salish. Unlike Red Elk and Allen, Charlo's parents chose not to raise him in traditional ways, and they preferred English to be spoken in the household rather than their tribal language. In early adulthood, Charlo attended a Jesuit seminary and was taught Latin, but after a time Charlo quit the seminary and returned home. He has been active ever since in tribal life, and he has encouraged his own children to practice their Native traditions and to learn the Salish language. Charlo roamed for a time with Montana poet Richard Hugo and some of Hugo's literary and drinking associates, which provided Charlo with important first lessons in poetic craft.

Despite all the outside influence in Charlo's early years, his poems are solidly in the same track as his contemporaries, Lois Red Elk and Minerva Allen: what sparks these poems is a call to the outside world to recognize and appreciate Indian culture, and also Charlo's duty to perpetuate the culture into future generations. The poet's daughter, April Charlo, wrote an introductory essay for *Put Sey (Good Enough)* in which she praises her father. "My dad is just a normal guy who loves his kids and his grandkids," April states, ". . . . a humble person. The only thing he brags about is the legacy of his children, and that is why you will hear him say, 'I do this for my children'" (9). April Charlo worked for the Native American Language Teacher Training Institute, relearning her native Salish tongue. She has translated several of her father's poems and accompanies her father at readings, reciting the poems in Salish as a demonstration of traditional ways continuing with the current generation.

Charlo's return later in life to his Native traditions has caused him trepidation in walking the line between wanting to write about his Native life and the limits of what, in respecting tribal customs, he is permitted to say. "Sometimes I feel as though I'm writing about things I'm not supposed to write about, in the traditional sense", Charlo wrote in his introductory essay to *Put Sey.* "There are a lot of things I was told I shouldn't write about, and so to compensate, I write around those things" (12). The idea of "writing around those things" is evident in the content of many of his poems. For instance, the poems, "Agnes" and "Agnes Again," are in praise of Agnes Vanderburg, an elder Salish woman who served as mentor to Charlo and others in teaching Salish language and traditions. Charlo depicts the traditional practice of Native customs through images of Agnes, rather than assuming this role for himself, and in this way he is "writing around" his obligations to not speak beyond the limits of propriety. In "Agnes," Charlo reverently speaks of Vanderburg's lessons, and questions his own rights to knowledge she offers: "Why did I learn to write? Why did I want to? / Is it worth the loss of your world going away?" (*Put Sey* 20). In "Agnes Again," Charlo also stays within the limits of what he is permitted to say by again "writing around" what Vanderburg teaches rather than articulating the teaching directly:

> She teaches so I won't forget.
> She sings sore-footed horse's song
> who says, "I'll be all right and we'll
> travel again." She digs bitterroot
> so that children and grandchildren
> will know how to use the root for better
> times. The song remains in my mind.
>
> I would travel with sore-footed horse as he sings
> of better times. We would run with the wind,
> catch stars when buffalo crowd clouds. (*Put Sey* 40)

On the other hand, Charlo's familiarity with non-Indian thought has put him in an unusual frame of mind in which at times his poems argue eloquently in opposition to the cosmological paradigms and imperialistic assumptions of non-Indian cultures. The poem "Cycles," for instance, pokes holes in the idea of non-Indian "linear thought." Here's the first stanza, in which he sets up his premise:

> We always come back
> to where we are. Some say non-Indians think
> in straight lines, linear thought, yet Einstein
> said parallel lines bend if they go far
> enough in space. So maybe there is no
> linear thought. (*Put Sey* 39)

This is less an attack on non-Native thought than it is a scaffolding for the second stanza in which Charlo talks about nonlinear reasoning of the tribal mind in which the future and the past are never separated. This is the poet's gift to non-Native readers, his lesson in opening non-Native minds to alternative wavelengths of cultural thought:

> What comes to mind when
> I think of the future is going home to old
> ways. Some think of the old way as going
> back. I don't. We move on the cycle
> and we do the same tasks
> again and again, only differently each time—
> live simply, care for family,
> relatives, when life is serious as meat.
> To live to hunt to live again,
> to live as the people:
> blood to bison. (*Put Sey* 39)

In the poem "Swift Current Time," Charlo takes on the likes of Heraclites, pushing western civilization's reverence for Greek thought to its breaking point in the modern world. Having just returned from his journey near the North Pole, Charlo is confused about time zones and asks a waitress "who tells us time never changes in Swift Current." This sets Charlo meditating on the question of what things change and what things do not:

> I think of my favorite Greek philosopher, Heraclites, his theory
> of the universe—the world is always in a state of flux —
> everything changing, nothing ever the same.
>
> I imagine him with two wet feet arguing
> that you can't put your foot in the same river twice. (*Put Sey* 28)

Charlo wonders if anything really changes, questioning Heraclites. On the radio he has heard news of Canadian police calling Native children "savages" after Halloween pranks. Charlo uses this news as a blow to Heraclites by showing how some things, namely prejudice and racism, maybe never change. Here's the final stanza:

> In car we tune to radio station that tells us
> Canadian police call native children savages after Halloween.
> I think sadly that this news doesn't make sense, and I wish

news of Heraclites' debate would come through cold,
north wind reporting that he has won with time,
has declared that all minds have changed,
that native children are sacred in all eyes
and that we are all travelers to Chief Mountain,
carriers of living water from Swift Current River
always moving, holy time. (*Put Sey* 28)

Readers of these three Native American Montana poets must consider that these poems are penned within the limits of what Minerva Allen, Lois Red Elk, and Victor Charlo can and cannot divulge of her/his culture. Some knowledge is protected within the tribe, guarded from the ears of outsiders for good reason—a five-hundred-year history of misinterpretation, cultural imperialism, and commercial exploitation. Then, too, even if the particulars of sacred ceremonies and traditions were made public, Native American cultural experience is nuanced in ways that may be impossible for non-Natives to fully realize and appreciate.

Each of these three Native American Montana poets has developed a strategy of her/his own to communicate with the world outside the tribe, while at the same time respecting the privacy and sacredness of things that cannot be told. What these three poets desire to communicate to the world is that "we are different," as Minerva Allen says, meaning she wants the world to know her tribal way of life is valid and thriving, and that she is rightfully proud of her heritage. Then, too, each of these three poets is addressing the world within the tribe as well as the world outside. For tribal traditions to endure they must be passed on to succeeding generations. In the same manner which Lois Red Elk describes herself as "representative" for her people, each of these poets, as tribal elders, sees herself/himself as educator/guide to their tribes' children. In this regard, these poems might be seen as the glowing embers nomadic tribes carried—bundled safely—to kindle again the same fire, but in a different time and place. These poets are the carriers of that fire.

Lastly, these three collections of poems are a precious record of cultural persistence and resiliency. In the midst of overwhelming destruction and pain, Native American cultures do thrive, and these three poets are the voices of that triumph. The poems of Victor Charlo, Lois Red Elk, and

Minerva Allen are artifacts of particular cultures, a record for all time of how it was here and now. These poems are inestimably precious because the human lives depicted are so much like other lives everywhere and at the same time so rare. Still, culture is coded in much more than what words alone, even poetry, can convey. The larger truths—as Minerva Allen reminds us—are "written in the hearts of our people."

WORKS CITED

Allen, Minerva. *Nakoda Sky People*. Ed. Lowell Jaeger. Kalispell: Many Voices Press, 2012. Print.

————. "Re: How Long Can We Keep This Living Song Alive?" Message to the author. 15 Apr. 2011. Email.

Bevis, William W. *Ten Tough Trips*. Seattle: University of Washington Press, 1990. Print.

Charlo, April. "Victor A. Charlo Is My Dad: An Introduction to the Man." *Put Sey (Good Enough)*. By Victor A. Charlo. Kalispell: Many Voices Press, 2008. 6–9. Print.

Charlo, Victor A. *Put Sey (Good Enough)*. Kalispell: Many Voices Press, 2008. Print.

————. "Re: How Long Can We Keep This Living Song Alive?" Message to the author. 15 Apr. 2011. E-mail.

Dunsmore, Roger. *Earth's Mind: Essays in Native Literature*. Albuquerque: University of New Mexico Press, 1997. Print.

Red Elk, Lois. *Our Blood Remembers*. Kalispell: Many Voices Press, 2011. Print.

————. "Re: How Long Can We Keep This Living Song Alive?" Message to the author. 15 Apr. 2011. E-mail.

CHAPTER 10

"Through the Monster's Mouth": Contemporary Indigenous Poetry and Land Rights on the Flathead Reservation

DAVID L. MOORE *(Missoula, Montana)*

Contemporary Indigenous poetry of the Flathead Reservation speaks of land and law, of love and pain, of culture and history unique to this beautiful place, yet woven with the stories of America. Rhythms of thought and expression in the reservation communities move through three accomplished writers of very different sensibilities. Victor Charlo, Jennifer Finley, and Heather Cahoon are deeply connected with Salish[1] families and histories of their home. Vic Charlo, poet, playwright, and hereditary chief of the Bitterroot Salish nation, earned degrees from the University of Montana and Gonzaga University, and has taught at Two Eagle River School and Kicking Horse Job Corps. Jennifer Finley, poet, playwright, and journalist, earned degrees from Eastern New Mexico University, Northern Arizona University, and the University of Washington, and has taught in numerous locations, including Salish Kootenai College. Heather Cahoon, poet

....

1   See Salish-Pend d'Oreille Culture Committee, *The Salish People and the Lewis and Clark Expedition* (xiii), for a discussion of variations and appropriate spellings of Salish/Selish.

and historian, earned degrees from the University of Montana where she teaches in the Department of Native American Studies. They each approach the beauty and pain in their poetry from many different life experiences and perspectives, but this essay looks at two fundamental and inextricable values that unite their poems—kinship and land. We will see how both of these values work in their lines, linking the aesthetic and ethical, the poetic and the political. We will look closely at how the poetry grows out of and reinvigorates the language and life of the people. Through their linkages of art and community and history, of language and the ground itself, we may begin to read and understand the life and potency in these poems.

Bypassing generalizations about Indigenous harmony with nature, we can read those two indivisible values, land and kinship, in the political language of other tribal members as well in the poets, especially as they work through tribal institutions in their quest to manage the land and resources that are home for these poems and these people. Since one interpretation of the ancient Salish word for themselves, roughly transliterated as "sqwelix," means "flesh of the land," the tribal identity is indeed built on this kinship with the land, and it plays out in newspapers as well as poetry. (Another linguistic interpretation translates as "strong people.") Thus a literary focus on kinship and land illuminates dynamics in the expression, how the poems function. One peculiar story, with its archetypal politics, serves as representative ground for the poems: a conflict over the National Bison Range. With that history in addition to more ancient tribal stories as context, we may see how the poems speak to and from the body politic of the nation.

Questions of tribal survivance crystalize in this quiet but prolonged drama on the edge of the news. The leadership of the Confederated Salish and Kootenai Tribes has been striving for over a century to reclaim management of the National Bison Range on their own reservation. As controversies swirl around that claim, the artists and poets of the reservation express ancient and urgent concerns that fit the conceptual map of the tribal government's strategies. Efforts to establish their management of the Bison Range furnish a classic case for legal and cultural questions of Indigenous sovereignty within a nation state, a crucial though larger topic than this paper can address.

Let's look at how the language of the poetry by members of that community resonates with the language of the politics, both based in tribal sovereignty. "That night the sun set behind the Bison Range / and turned the remaining reservation sky // the colors of a rainbow trout (Cahoon 37). Even when a Salish poet and scholar such as Heather Cahoon invokes sunsets in these lines from her poem, "Skyward," her self-expression carries the additional weight of history, politics, and economics surrounding tribal sovereignty under the "reservation sky." The words of American Indian poets are layered with history and so are necessarily political. A setting sun echoes with historical loss. The Bison Range, as Cahoon invokes it, resonates with historical struggle. Her verbal adjective, "remaining," reverberates with losses on the reservation as well. Even the lovely "colors of a rainbow trout" invoke a context of invasive history, as that species of fish is not indigenous to these waters.

Similarly, when poet and playwright Vic Charlo writes a poem in the spirit of a traditional invocation, the historical context drums through the text, as in these lines concluding a short poem entitled "Buffalo": "We will know forever / Buffalo on the edge of life / Buffalo on the edge of life" (16). The repeated "edge of life" refers both to existential mortality and to historical annihilation of the "Buffalo," repeated to reaffirm the persistence of that life against that history. Immediately in such a rhythmic affirmation, the voice of Charlo, as a traditional chief of his tribe, links the life of the buffalo to the persistence and resilience of the Salish people against that history. "We will know forever" our kinship on the land.

The historical dynamics of colonialism and resistance weave in like manner through the poems of Jennifer Finley (previously published as Jennifer Greene). For instance, in "I Take My Home," she writes in the last two stanzas,

My home is in me
like the smell of cold
lake water in my skin,
my lungs
wherever I go.

Wherever I go,
my grandfather's hands,
plum colored and strong,
are touching mine. (*What I Keep* 6)

Like Charlo's affirmations on "the edge of life," or like Cahoon's close observations of "the remaining reservation sky," Finley confirms generational connections between the land, the people, and the changes "[w]herever I go."

Let's look a little closer at their peopled land. Comprising more than half the Flathead Reservation of the Confederated Salish & Kootenai Tribes in Montana, the Mission and Jocko Valleys are a spectacularly beautiful agricultural area, about thirty miles long, bordered on the east by the snow-capped peaks of the Mission Range in the Northern Rocky Mountains. Flathead Lake on the north end of the Mission Valley is the largest freshwater body of water west of the Mississippi River, and remains one of the geological jewels of North America.

In the hills at the south end of the Mission Valley, the National Bison Range was carved out of the reservation, without full tribal consent, by the federal government in 1908 and is now one of the oldest wildlife refuges in the nation. Today the National Bison Range serves as the central point for bison research in the United States. The 18,500 acres of the range are part of a Wildlife Refuge Complex that includes native Palouse prairie and mountainous forests, as well as extensive wetlands. In addition to the professionally managed herd of 350 to 500 bison, the land supports elk, deer, pronghorn, black bears, coyotes, ground squirrels, eagles, hawks, meadowlarks, bluebirds, ducks, and geese, among many other residents and visitors, including two-hundred other species of birds, and, annually, 250,000 humans with their approximately 80,000 to 100,000 cars and RVs.

Currently, the Bison Range is administered under the Interior Department by the U.S. Fish and Wildlife Service, with contested levels of co-management by the Tribes, as part of the National Wildlife Refuge System. Noting this legal—or historically illegal—arrangement is important for this study, as the National Bison Range encapsulates the intense layers of political pressure bearing on the life of every individual on this reservation. Those crosscurrents play out in cross-cultural expression by politicians, civil servants, and poets alike.

While the Confederated Salish and Kootenai Tribes have been working to take over management of the Bison Range since it was annexed from their treaty land in 1908, a familiar pattern of increasing intrusion by non-Indian institutions and individuals has complicated the exchange. (The tribes, including the Pend d'Oreille or Kalispell, cousins of the Salish, were confederated on this reservation in Northwestern Montana by the Hellgate Treaty of 1855.) Under legislation in the 1990s updating the Indian Self-Determination Act of 1975, the tribes have been negotiating for renewed sovereignty in the form of management over that resource (along with other natural resources, plus their own administration of health, education, welfare, and housing). This is a Native nation with an exemplary record of natural resource management, having established the first tribal wilderness area in the country in the early 1980s, and having administered a pristine air quality program, among numerous other professional activities on behalf of the environment. As tribal member Terry Tanner explained in a recent newspaper article about the Mission Mountains Wilderness, "'We just celebrated its 30th anniversary last month,' Tanner told the group of [Indigenous] visitors from as far away as Nepal and Brazil. 'For a long time, white people have been telling indigenous people how to manage their lands. Indigenous people have to have their voices heard'" (Chaney, "International foresters"). Embedded in these simple words, "how to manage their lands," are cultural values of kinship on and with that land, as well as the history of resistance against political forces that would deny that right of kinship and responsibility.

In spite of the Tribes' record of successful, professional resource management, there are doubters inside and outside of the federal government who question both the ability and the right of the Tribes to manage the National Bison Range. We must read the doubters in a specific context: the long history in federal Indian policy of the discourse of "competence" or "incompetence" of Native Americans to manage their own affairs on the land. As Thomas Biolsi explains the larger history, "The reservation system of the late nineteenth and early twentieth centuries was based on the congressionally authorized and judicially sanctioned status of wardship [for Native Americans] applied with considerable administrative discretion. Wardship was founded on the assumption of Indian incompetence to function effectively in the market economy of the wider American society" (119). Competence and incompetence were decided by white administrators of the Office of Indian Affairs, later the Bureau of Indian Affairs, by a set of racialized criteria, a system that persisted for decades and that extended beyond the "Indian New Deal" of the 1930s. As Biolsi explains, "What was termed incompetence was rooted in the essentialized characteristics of most Indians presumed in the colonial gaze" (119). Such terminology reified the colonial power structure. The generational legacies of this institutional racism implicated Indian lives continent-wide on every level, from psychological to economic. Biolsi continues, "Allotment, substantial sums of money, and some personal property were held in trust for individual Indians unless or until they were deemed competent. This wardship system was ultimately rooted in law enacted by Congress. . . . Wardship entailed a complex set of formal and informal character appraisals that were applied to Lakota [and other tribal] persons, on the basis of which administrative decisions on individual cases were made" (119–20). The interpenetrating presence of federal and local "trustees" of Indian trust lands is second only in intimacy and intrusion to the equally widespread and concentrated discretion of teachers and administrators, both parochial and secular, in Indian boarding schools. Biolsi explains some of the effects: "The authorities' record keeping and their self-righteous, patronizing, racist, and invidious character appraisals of individual Lakota [and other tribal members] were not just matters of 'discourse' understood as purely representational. . . . [O]ne must also consider the materiality of the state's actual and fictive creation of individuals. The files and appraisals had serious, practical consequences for people. . . . Access to this money depended on how one's character was perceived by the bureaucrats" (123).

Although less overt today because of its racist overtones, that familiar discourse of incompetence has met Indigenous efforts to manage the Range since the beginning of the last century, following the much longer patterns of colonialism. With considerable restraint, the Native American participants in these negotiations rarely invoke this pattern explicitly, only gesturing to it in their public remarks. It is these kinds of gestures that link the political language with the poetical.

The poetry generally lets that legacy of oppression echo as context for the imagery, narrative, and music of the text. Like Coyote emerging through the monster's mouth, these storytellers often let the drama encircle their words silently, without explicitly making the point. However, here are lines from a prose poem by Finley that are relatively explicit about racial pressures:

> I look at my reservation filled with drive-thru coffee shops, t-shirt shops and school lunch rooms filled with white tables where white teachers don't see Indian students who pray for justice, and I see my old self. On my reservation, tribal members make up less than twenty percent of the population. (*What Lasts* 43)

So much history is packed in these lines. The catalogued details of modern, non-Indian cultural domination in "coffee shops, t-shirt shops and school lunch rooms" becomes explicitly racialized "with white tables where white teachers don't see." The justice that "Indian students pray for" is historically specific where "tribal members make up less than twenty percent" of "my reservation." Few non-Indians know what so many Indians know: that the 1887 Dawes Allotment Act broke up the tribal land base into individual plots. Then on the Flathead, as on so many reservations nationwide, the 1910 Homestead Act opened up "surplus" allotments on the reservation to non-Indian settlers, whose descendants now make up eighty percent of the population. Finley stands in witness of this injustice: "I look at my reservation . . ."

A less direct allusion to the racial history arises in lines from Charlo's poem "Pattee Canyon Run, 1976":

> We, Bitterroot Salish, ride here to escape new enemy,
> quick meat our interest now as then.
> Steep slope chides us windless and crazy
> yet I can feel trail in old smoke and breeze. (23)

Charlo alludes to the ancient history of conflict with the Blackfeet. That old enemy tribe used to ambush Charlo's Salish ancestors in what is now called Hellgate Canyon at the northeast corner of the Missoula Valley, so his tribe would travel instead through what is now called Pattee Canyon at the southeast corner of Missoula. Today, they have to elude the "new enemy": white settler culture that would restrict tribal hunting—against treaty agreements—on ancestral hunting grounds beyond the reservation. Such an alienating context imbues the lines, even as they affirm kinship with the land where they ride to hunt "quick meat," both quick with vitality and close to the reservation.

That close relation to the land and its populations remains the value, even against changing enemies. On this ground of kinship, the familiar Euro-American dichotomy of nature-versus-culture quite dissolves. As historian Robert Bigart explains, "The economic history of the Salish-speaking tribes of the Flathead Indian Reservation pirouettes on buffalo. . . . The buffalo were also integral to the economic changes engulfing the Salish during the nineteenth century" (1). Bigart introduces oral histories from Salish elders, one of whom, Dominic Michell, recounts the logic of kinship:

> . . . Then, too, before the good Fathers came, our Indians believed the buffalo was a very strong spirit power, and was a good friend to Indians who protected the herds.
> "Now, you can see why the buffalo was so important to my people—the Indians. It was food, shelter, clothing and religion. It must be protected by tribal laws, some of which must be very strict." (Whealdon et al. 23–24)

This fundamental cultural value is the basis of the Confederated Salish & Kootenai Tribes' claim to manage the National Bison Range. Where an ancient tribal story recounts a pledge by Sun Buffalo Cow, "I will be meat for my Salish" (Whealdon et al. 25–26), the modern-day tribal government chooses to reciprocate with the bison and the land by taking care of the National Bison Range. Such ancient and intimate connection with a game animal currently "administered" in Montana under the Department of Livestock, is, of course, seen by certain non-Indian federal employees as naïve and passé to the extreme, as mere nostalgic fables of "the vanishing Indian." Opposition on the part of governmental wildlife managers and others resisting Indian oversight of the National Bison Range cannot help but reflect the old pattern of denial of tribal sovereignty by settler colonialism.

Resistance to tribal management thus plays too neatly into historical precedent, though now "the Indian wars" are mostly played out in the courts. For example, one of the national organizations active in disrupting earlier tribal participation in management of the National Bison Range has struck in the courts. In April 2009, the Blue Goose Alliance, an organization linked to Public Employees for Environmental Responsibility (PEER), sued the Interior Department over tribal co-management of the National Bison Range. Their suit raised a central legal question over definition of "inherently federal" functions in the administration of lands.[2]

PEER's litigation was in opposition to an agreement worked out through "intense negotiations" between the tribes and the federal government after an earlier break, as explained in this excerpt from the *Missoulian* newspaper. It reads like a dramatic script, a short narrative in the longer history that the poets reflect in briefer moments.

> The new agreement was signed 1 1/2 years after the FWS abruptly canceled a previous agreement and locked tribal employees out of the Bison Range as a bitter feud broke out between the two sides.
>
> The Fish and Wildlife Service accused the tribes of failing to perform some of their duties properly and neglecting others altogether, and said tribal employees created a hostile work environment—charges the tribes strongly denied.
>
> Tribal employees, meantime, accused the agency of deliberately sabotaging their work in a turf war designed to return the tribal jobs to federal employees, while the FWS insisted it had gone the extra mile to help the tribes succeed.
>
> With this new agreement, the CSKT will assume a substantive role in managing mission-critical programs at the Bison Range. . . .
>
> Calling it a "historic opportunity," James Steele Jr. pledged Thursday that the Confederated Salish and Kootenai Tribes will make the most of a new funding agreement that will return some responsibilities at the National Bison Range to the tribes.
>
> Steele, CSKT chairman, and H. Dale Hall, director of the U.S. Fish and Wildlife Service, signed the agreement at a late-morning ceremony in Washington, D.C. (Devlin, "National Bison Range")

Even certain phrases filtered through this newspaper account are alive with the value of kinship on the land: "return some responsibilities at the National Bison Range to the tribes" combines words that resonate

....

2 The language of "inherently federal responsibilities" had been amended to the Indian Self-Determination Act in 1994 by Sen. John McCain (AZ) at the request of the International Association of State Fish and Wildlife Agencies.

with kinship values. In this historical context, "responsibilities" embodies the reciprocal system of exchange between tribal culture and the land. Similarly, the historical resonance in the verb "return" assumes the prior "responsibilities" of the tribes—spanning millennia before any negotiations with the federal government. Further, such an agreement, built on the land, codified an aspect of what is called "government-to-government relations" in a certain parallel relation to more interpersonal kinship. On that vital principle of reciprocal sovereignty, a balance of power seemed visible to the participants, but not to PEER.[3]

Thus we may see the oppositional political context, described in the newspaper, as a language-shadow beside the dynamics of resistance and affirmation in the poetry. Against the polemics of current events, there is something both solid and elusive in these three poets, a unique Salish characteristic in a steady silence that simplifies and amplifies the sounds and images. It acknowledges confidence in something larger than the words, an Indigenous confidence in the ground, the land, and the people's place there.[4] What it is exactly may remain ineffable, like the constant presence of nature in language, the presence of language in nature. Yet the core confidence in each of these poets is as firm as these mountains.

Paradoxically, Charlo writes with such confidence in this excerpt from a poem entitled "Uneasy with Montana,"

....

3   Recently, the courts agreed with the Tribes, finding no basis for PEER's complaints against the Tribes. On April 7, 2011, the *Missoulian* newspaper posted the news:

> . . . On almost a point-by-point basis, the Office of Inspector General of the Department of Interior found no merit in allegations long made against the tribes by Public Employees for Environmental Responsibility, which had called for the independent review.

CSKT Chairman E.T. "Bud" Moran called the inspector general's report "both gratifying and unsurprising."

"The report proves what most of us in Montana already know," Moran went on. "PEER's allegations concerning tribal performance at the Bison Range are just wrong." (Devlin, "Federal Bison Range review finds no merit")

4   See the CS&KT publication, *Bull Trout's Gift: A Salish Story about the Value of Reciprocity*, for discussion of the fundamental Salish cultural quality of confidence with the land.

I should follow buffalo on this aimless
Monday in Missoula. We finally find them
in U.C. Bookstore, along with others waiting in arm.

I look for different ways to be as I hunt truth
over other shoulders, knowing I'm not right,
my life, an excuse of bow and scrape.
Go back . . . (36)

The gap, the silence, across the period on the page between "aimless /
Monday in Missoula" and "We finally find them" understates volumes of
history, charged with longing. "[B]uffalo" remains the heart's desire, to "*Go
back*." Charlo's silence ironically sets the disciplined, traditional buffalo hunt
for survival into a casual literary shopping spree. However surrounded, the
affirmative presence of cultural identity evoked in the words and silences of
this poem is an expression of the presence of tribal sovereignty that never
left the land, nor the National Bison Range. The poetry resonates with life
and death, and something more that survives the cycles.

Tony Incashola, Director of the Salish-Pend d'Oreille Culture Com-
mittee, speaks to that something more even than life and death. During
a recent biannual gathering at the Medicine Tree, which today is only a
tall stump, beside Highway 93 up the Bitterroot River south of Missoula,
Incashola explained,

> "It teaches about our way of life and our values...This tree and area
> are part of our landmarks that teach us the dos and don'ts of life. . . ."
>   And the ancestors have been watching over their offspring for a long,
> long, time. "We've been here for quite awhile. Time for us here began
> after the last Ice Age," Incashola said. "Think about what life was like
> 500 years ago. There was no such thing as the Wild West. Our people
> were here taking care of the land and each other. There is nothing wild
> about that. Think about our ancestors' pain when they were denied the
> rights to live their lives their own way." (Azure 2)

Since its death in the last generation, the Medicine Tree still stands, now
embodying both death and somehow life in its cultural radiance. Readers
might think that the death of a sacred pine tree would bode ill for a cultural
sense of strength and resilience, but if "Time for us began after the last Ice

Age," the death of one tree is only a small part of a much bigger cultural and natural cycle of time and space. "This area is a sacred place." Neither life nor death triumphs, as elder and language instructor Pat Pierre said during the same event, with "the laws that are written in our hearts—the law of who we are and what we must do to maintain our ways" (Azure 2). As Incashola expresses this larger view, "There was a time when I thought 60, 70, 80 years was a long time but it's not. It is very important that we don't waste time and don't lose our ways" (Azure 8). Like so much in Salish cultural traditions, it is bigger than life and death. It is the Medicine Tree.

The land of those stories can simply stand—silently—as presence inside and beyond this history and this myth and this poetry: the Medicine Tree up the Bitterroot River; the Ravalli canyon and the Jocko Valley up on the rez. The poetry and tribal stories survive and emerge from the monster of history. The poems speak precisely and do the storytelling work to show the ways that the tree and the land and the ancient stories remain in the cycles. The urban and reservation pain in Charlo, Cahoon, and Finley's poems is one of the ways their poems refocus on that silent tribal confidence.

Such Indigenous expression can actually participate in those larger cycles of time on the land affirmed by Incashola. As Simon J. Ortiz, Acoma writer and scholar, explains, "Language, when it is regarded not only as expression but is realized as experience as well, works in and *is* of that manner. Language is perception of experience as well as expression" (237). The language itself becomes an experience—and since experience stands, like a stump, beyond the ability of language to encompass it, Ortiz here points to this elusive dynamic I'm reading in these poets. Their expression gets at the inexpressible; they animate something that persists, even beyond life, that is not measured by life and death.

For example, Cahoon writes both lyrically and unsentimentally about what animates her mixed-blood experience, another de facto unity beyond oppositional history. In her poem, "Blonde," she describes driving as a child with her dad across the November reservation as, "He is telling me stories / of children with black hair and brown eyes" (Cahoon 24). Because of her own blonde features she feels a sense of exclusion, yet she finds release and even resolution in the larger natural cycles, through these concluding lines.

It is November and the dying grasses on the prairie
are the same color as my hair. If I wanted I could

lie down in them and disappear, I could escape
the angry wind. But I don't, I know the land and I
would blend together into one and then no one
would ever know I had existed. So I stand. (Cahoon 24)

Where "dying grasses" equals "the same color as my hair," she might
need to "escape / the angry wind" of history, as her mixed blood might
war inside her. The oppositional dialectic that plays out so tediously in
the Bison Range controversy is intimately familiar inside so many Native
families like hers. However, like the vibrant silence in Charlo's uneasy
poem, Cahoon expresses and experiences a quietly transformational leap
between the sentences: "I could escape / the angry wind. But I don't."
Instead of escape hers is a humble and forthright, vertical affirmation where
she claims her place, "and then no one / would ever know I had existed.
So I stand." There's another leap before the final three-word sentence.
The emotional and spiritual logic of the affirmation of kinship in and on
the land is clear: because "I know the land and I / would blend together
into one." Like the tribe stepping up to manage the bison, Cahoon's own
complexities of loss and survivance interweave so intricately here that
positive and negative categories of imagery and feeling no longer apply.
Something else stands, something unassuming but as powerful as the
land itself that "I know."

Janice Gould, a Maidu poet, has written of a healing process in Indig-
enous poetry, and we can read it in Cahoon, Charlo, and Finley's work.

We respond to pain and suffering by seeking a healing, a healing that
cannot be completed in the human world but must be completed by
understanding our ties to the spirit world.

American Indian poetry tries to remind us of this truth about healing
because Indian writers are reminded of it when they look back at their
own tribe's or another tribe's oral tradition....Language is a vehicle of
ceremony. But it is not through poetry—or ceremony—that healing
takes place. These are only forms and languages that aid in setting the
conditions for healing. Healing takes place through the spirit, through
love and compassion, which are qualities of the spirit. The American
Indian poets I admire most are those whose work seems infused with—
informed by—this spirit. (Rader and Gould 11)

Gould's spiritual manifesto sets a standard, but she also is describing a transformational dynamic in the poetry as ceremony, as "forms and languages that aid in setting the conditions for healing." By telling the truth, by detailing the rotations of loss, this particular poetry inside this particular history, can evoke Gould's "qualities of the spirit" as part of the experience of language itself. Expression becomes synonymous with compassion.

Let's look at this dynamic in another poem by Cahoon, "Winter at Ninepipes," here in its brief entirety. She is describing one of the richest wetlands in western Montana, an extended part of the Bison Range wildlife refuge.

> Winter burns these willows dry
> and cottonwoods turn stone.
> Grass is white and fences freeze
> in bone-hard postures.
> Wire sags in frozen glory,
> refusing to fall down.
> Winter strengthens some.
> Dry wind sends snow whirling
> across frozen lakes, stinging
> harshly all objects in its path.
> Russian olives near the shore
> grip their bark, a fight
> they lose by spring.
> Graveyards on the ground.
> Snow outlasts the brightest days,
> bitter wind runs wild in sky,
> winter settles in. (Cahoon 48)

For all the wintry imagery, the poem resonates—between the words, in the silences—with life, precisely in the heart of struggle. "Winter burns." One cannot help but be reminded how the buffalo, *Bison bison*, evolved to survive by facing forward into North American winter storms, unlike *Bovinae bos*, the nonindigenous cattle who huddle and freeze to death with their backsides to the wind. Thus where "Snow outlasts the brightest days" and "winter settles in," barbed "Wire sags in frozen glory, / refusing to fall down. / Winter strengthens some." Here is a clear evocation of strength through the cycles. Where "fences freeze / in bone-hard postures" and "cottonwoods turn stone," the seemingly stark completion of death achieves its descriptive drama in the silent dialectic of lost images from spring and summer and fall, now silenced as "bitter wind runs wild in sky." Something stands amid these images beyond life and death on the land, and the writing brings that something off the page.

We may read these values of grounded kinship in another personal lyric, this one a love poem by Jennifer Finley to her husband. Here are some selections of her imagery and music.

> You were the first man I wanted
> to love repeatedly. . . .
>
> It's hard to know when you're 20 and beautiful
> and strong that loss and birth are lovers. . . .
>
> It's so sad houses last longer than people
> and become orphans until they crumble or
> burn back into dust or get adopted by someone
> else to live inside. You and I are still together
> after all these years, and we do not look the
> same.
>
> . . . and it's a fact that everything dies
> and how maybe everything that dies will someday come back.
>   (15–16)

The term "repeatedly," in its vivid polysyllables, offers the very rhythm of youthful desire that she expresses here, setting up a contrast with age and "sad houses." Then she glances modestly at the ineffable theme where "loss and birth are lovers," where death and life are not the whole story. She offers "maybe" with quiet humility in her interrogative claim that "everything that dies will someday come back." As the earlier narrative of the poem had jumped among memories in their relationship, from Martha's Vineyard and the sands of Atlantic beaches to "Montana, far away from the ocean," to memories of Bruce Springsteen lyrics and their own "three kids who have hands like you / and eyes like me," the juxtapositions of geography and history and family again evoke that larger something of both "loss and birth." Abundance, like a buffalo spirit, seems to be "what lasts."

Another of Finley's poems, "Beach Stone," addresses these cycles directly, as in these concluding lines from the point of view of a stone "glossy black / with one white stripe down my center":

> Once, I slept near a red apple,
> sour, unpicked, fallen. We were lost
> in a pile of cracking leaves until a black
> bear ate it. I loved the bear. He died
> and melted with the warming snow
> back into the grass.
>
> I miss the sound of his breath
> and the sound of claws on bark. (*What Lasts* 56)

The poet's longing, through the stone, evokes the sound of the breath of a bear dying in the leaves. That sound persists in the poem; a presence looms in the experience of the language.

Norma C. Wilson contextualizes such expression: "Contemporary Native poetry has its roots in the land, in the oral tradition, and in history. . . . Native references to traditional oral literature and to the land are more than literary allusions—they embody life and spirit, a vision of the sacred" (ix). The voice in Finley's poem, which begins, "My world is silent. / I'm ancient beyond words," transcends time in its close experience of the land, "the sound of claws on bark."

As Simon J. Ortiz puts it, "Language is more than just a functional mechanism. It is a spiritual energy that is available to all. It includes all of us and is not exclusively in the power of human beings—we are part of that power as human beings" (240). Ortiz suggests that animate forces populate not only the world described in language, but the language and the poetry itself. Charlo and Cahoon and Finley here are committed to engaging energetically with diverse lives, actively seeking intimate understanding across lines of difference between and among human communities and more-than-human communities. Their poetry is about that dialogue, just as the efforts of their tribal administrators are about dialogue between and among humans and bison. They transform present history into Indigenous presence. This particular set of Salish poets lives with and shares with us Ortiz's power, "a spiritual energy." They draw on the power of poetry to affirm their own and their people's and the buffalo's presence on the land.

WORKS CITED

Azure, B. L. "Medicine Tree trip recharges the spirit and affirms the links to the homeland." *Char-Koosta News* [Pablo, MT] 15 September 2011: 2, 8. Print.

Backus, Perry. "FWS pulls National Bison Range pact." *Missoulian* [Missoula, MT] 12 December 2006. Web. 13 March 2011.

Biolsi, Thomas. "The Birth of the Reservation: Making the Modern Individual Among the Lakota." *American Nations: Encounters in Indian Country 1850 to the Present*. Eds. Frederick E. Hoxie, Peter C. Mancall, and James H. Merrell. New York: Routledge, 2001. 111–40. Print.

Bigart, Robert. Introduction. *"I Will Be Meat for My Salish": The Buffalo and the Montana Writers Project Interviews on the Flathead Indian Reservation*. By Bon I. Whealdon, et al. Ed. Robert Bigart. Co-publishers: Pablo: Salish Kootenai College Press; Helena: Montana Historical Society Press, 2001. 1–18. Print.

Cahoon, Heather. *Elk Thirst: Poems*. Missoula: University of Montana, 2005. Print.

———. "For Better or For Worse: Flathead Indian Reservation Governance & Sovereignty." Diss. University of Montana, 2005. Print.

Chaney, Rob. "International foresters visit Flathead Reservation to study tribes' example." *Missoulian* [Missoula, MT] 27 July 2012. Web. 27 July 2012.

Charlo, Victor A. *Put Sey (Good Enough)*. Ed. Roger Dunsmore. Kalispell: Many Voices Press, 2008. Print.

Confederated Salish & Kootenai Tribes. *Bull Trout's Gift: A Salish Story about the Value of Reciprocity*. Lincoln: Nebraska University Press, 2011. Print.

Deloria, Vine, Jr., and Clifford M. Lytle. *The Nations Within: The Past and Future of American Indian Sovereignty*. Austin: University of Texas Press, 1984. Print.

Devlin, Vince. "Federal Bison Range review finds no merit to allegations against CSKT." *Missoulian* [Missoula, MT] 7 April 2011. Web. 19 July 2012.

———. "National Bison Range: CSKT, FWS sign pact." *Missoulian* [Missoula, MT] 20 June 2008. Web. 19 July 2012.

Finley, Jennifer K. [see Jennifer K. Greene]

Greene, Jennifer K. *What I Keep*. Greenfield Center, NY: Greenfield Review Press, 1999. Print.

———. *What Lasts*. Kanona, NY: FootHills Publishing, 2010. Print.

Ortiz, Simon J. "Song/Poetry and Language–Expression and Perception." Eds. Dean Rader and Janice Gould. *Speak to Me Words: Essays on Contemporary American Indian Poetry*. Tucson: The University of Arizona Press, 2003. 235–46. Print.

Rader, Dean, and Janice Gould. "Introduction: Generations and Emanations." Eds. Dean Rader and Janice Gould. *Speak to Me Words: Essays on Contemporary American Indian Poetry*. Tucson: The University of Arizona Press, 2003. 3–20. Print.

Salish-Pend d'Oreille Culture Committee, Elders Cultural Advisory Council, and Confederated Salish and Kootenai Tribes. *The Salish People and the Lewis and Clark Expedition*. Lincoln: University of Nebraska Press, 2008. Print.

Swaney, Kim. "Bison and Tribes left in the cold: Fish and Wildlife Service terminates negotiations." *Char-Koosta News* [Pablo, MT] 14 December 2006. Web. 17 June 2011.

USFWS *National Bison Range – Montana*. Inherently Federal Management of National public lands, 2007. Web. 13 March 2011.

Whealdon, Bon I., et al. *The Buffalo and the Montana Writers Project Interviews on the Flathead Indian Reservation*. Ed. Robert Bigart. Co-publishers: Pablo: Salish Kootenai College Press; Helena: Montana Historical Society Press, 2001. Print.

Wilson, Norma C. *The Nature of Native American Poetry*. Albuquerque: University of New Mexico Press, 2001. Print.

PART 4   LAST? BEST? PLACE?

Photo by Brian Herbel

CHAPTER 11

"No Shepherd of a Child's Surmises": J. V. Cunningham as a Montana Poet

TIMOTHY STEELE *(Los Angeles, California)*

J. V. Cunningham's readers may be disconcerted to see his poetry treated in a regional context. Cunningham's poems are not in the least provincial. They address perennial issues in human experience—love, friendship, marriage, and mortality—and draw deeply, if unobtrusively, on the Anglo-American poetic tradition represented by such writers as William Shakespeare, John Donne, Ben Jonson, Jonathan Swift, Walter Savage Landor, Emily Dickinson, Edwin Arlington Robinson, Robert Frost, and Louise Bogan. Further, Cunningham is one of the best epigrammatists in the English language. His skill and range in the genre are such that his only peers are Jonson, Robert Herrick, and Landor. In addition, Cunningham is a master metrician. Though he lived in an age when most poets cultivated free verse, he explored and enriched the resources of conventional versification. His individually distinctive management of his craft connects us with an art of rhythmically organized speech that began millennia ago in places like China, India, Egypt, and Greece and that persists, albeit in a marginalized condition, down to our day.

Yet Cunningham spent his most formative years in Billings, Montana, and he always considered himself a native of the state. More than four decades after he had last lived in it, he introduced a lecture at Mount

Holyoke College on Dickinson by saying apologetically, "I am a renegade Irish Catholic from the plains of Montana. . . . Consequently, I speak without authority on a nineteenth-century New England spinster" (*The Collected Essays* 353). On another occasion, commenting in the third person on his own writing, he referred to "his early life on the Montana plains," noting that "he found that the patterns of his deepest feelings were most often clothed in the landscapes of that time" (*The Collected Essays* 414). He came from a family who, as he put it, "were all construction people and railroaders" ("Interview" 2) and who had laid the track and served the trains that crossed the Great Plains, deserts, and mountains from Council Bluffs, Iowa, to the Pacific Ocean; and many of his poems depict the austere beauties of the American West and its lonely open spaces. As cosmopolitan as he became in spirit and intellect—in addition to composing poems, Cunningham wrote brilliant and entertaining essays on such varied subjects as the Roman poet Statius, Shakespearean tragedy, and the poetry of Wallace Stevens—he always stayed connected to his youthful experiences in Montana.

CUNNINGHAM'S LIFE

Cunningham was born in Cumberland, Maryland, on August 23, 1911. He was the second of four children—three boys and a girl—of working-class Irish-Catholic parents. In the mid-teens, his father, a steam-shovel operator who worked for the railroads, moved the family to Billings. In 1923, at the insistence of Cunningham's mother, who was concerned about obtaining the best possible education for her children, the family moved to Denver. There Cunningham enrolled in the Jesuit-run Regis High School and took a rigorous curriculum that included four years of Latin and two of Greek. Having skipped two grades in the schools in Billings, he graduated in 1927, at age fifteen. The year before, however, Cunningham's father had been killed while working in California on the San Pedro harbor. His steam shovel had toppled over on an incline and crushed him. After his father's death, financial constraints apparently prevented Cunningham at that time from continuing his academic studies, except for a semester at St. Mary's College in Kansas.

In his late teens, Cunningham worked as a copyboy for the *Denver Morning Post* and then as a "runner"—a messenger/office boy—for Otis and Company, the largest brokerage house on the Denver Stock Exchange. And in 1929, while he was working for Otis, there occurred what he termed "the dominant experience of my life" ("Interview" 6). On October 29—Black Tuesday—the market crashed. "The day had a finality, inarguable, absolute," Cunningham recollected later, "though in fact the day seemed not to end. The ticker tape ran on past midnight Mountain Time, we slept a few hours in office chairs, and were back at work at 8 a.m." (Cunningham, "Commencement" 13-14)· Scarcely less traumatic was the aftermath of the crash. Cunningham particularly recalled the suicides of two of its victims:

> One [was] in the large lobby of the Equitable Building, filled with people. I'd come back from a run, paused a moment before going into the office, and casually looked across the lobby, all the way across. A man put a gun to his temple, and you heard the shot. Perhaps a day or two later, I was in the corridor, waiting for a call, when a body landed on the skylight within ten or fifteen feet of where I was standing. ("Interview" 6)

Cunningham soon found himself, like so many others, unemployed. With his older brother Tom, he set off on a year of wandering through the Southwest, trying to eke out a living by freelance writing for trade journals of the day—business magazines, such as *Dry Goods Economist*, and *The American Lumberman*. This work was even less profitable than it sounds. Cunningham and his brother made little money and were intermittently homeless. There was, as Cunningham said of this period, "a good deal of starving involved" ("Interview" 11).

In 1931, Cunningham wrote from temporary lodgings in Tucson to the poet Yvor Winters, then a graduate student and instructor at Stanford University. Cunningham had earlier corresponded with Winters about poetry, and on this occasion he explained his plight to Winters and asked "if it was possible to go to college and stay alive" ("Interview" 10). Writing this letter proved to be a life-changing act. Winters immediately wrote back, urging Cunningham to come to California. When he arrived, Winters and his wife, Janet Lewis, put him up in a cottage/shed behind their house, and Cunningham gradually recovered the physical and psychic health that his itinerant existence had undermined. He enrolled at Stanford, majoring in classics as an undergraduate and eventually receiving a doctorate in English[1]. Thereafter, Cunningham held a series of teaching posts at the Universities of Hawaii, Chicago, Harvard, and Virginia. In 1953, he was hired by Brandeis University, where he taught until his retirement in 1980. If he felt deep personal debts to such individuals as Winters and Morris Rosenfeld (the owner of a bookstore in Denver who encouraged the teen-aged Cunningham's interest in modern literature), he felt a great professional affection for Brandeis. Not long before his death, he commented on the irony of an Irish-Catholic Westerner's finding a home in an institution created principally by the energies of the Jewish community on the East Coast.

One other biographical fact deserves mention, especially in connection with Cunningham's Montana background. He was a dedicated smoker. The Canadian writer, Barbara Hodgson, once observed in conversation about Joni Mitchell that the singer-songwriter's having smoked from an early age was probably simply a result of her having grown up in Alberta and Saskatchewan. "It's a prairie thing," Hodgson said. Perhaps Cunningham's youth in the same Northern Plains region contributed to his lifelong passion for tobacco. In any case, he wrote a graceful and touching (if not exactly politically correct) epigram entitled "Night-piece" about enjoying cigarettes of an evening in the company of his wife:

> Three matches in a folder, you and me.
> I sit and smoke, and now there's only two,
> And one, and none: a small finality
> In a continuing world, a thing to do.
> And you, fast at your book, whose fingers keep
> Its single place as you sift down to sleep. (*The Poems* 63)

....

1 The title of Cunningham's doctoral dissertation is "Tragic Effect and Tragic Process in Some Plays of Shakespeare, and Their Background in the Literary and Ethical Theory of Classical Antiquity and the Middle Ages." Cunningham subsequently cut down and rearranged the dissertation and published it as *Woe or Wonder: The Emotional Effect of Shakespearean Tragedy* (1951).

Eventually, however, the cigarettes caught up with Cunningham. In his later years, he suffered from emphysema, and he died of heart failure, brought on by the disease and by a hip fracture, on March 30, 1985, at Marlborough Hospital in Marlborough, Massachusetts.

CUNNINGHAM AND THE PLAIN STYLE

Cunningham's style is at odds with assumptions we commonly entertain about poetic speech. Many of us share the view set forth by *The Random House Dictionary of the English Language* (2nd. ed.) when it speaks of "Poetry" as "lofty thought or impassioned feeling expressed in imaginative words." We expect that the diction of poetry will differ markedly from that of prose. We expect that the language of poems will be more figurative or more sensory. And we anticipate that poetry will feature, in association with its unusual verbal properties, obvious emotional urgency. Cunningham's poems, however, have little ornament, and his mature verse, far from sounding unconventional, impresses instead by its colloquial freshness and clarity. Further, though Cunningham's poems are serious, they are also clever and, often, unabashedly humorous.

Cunningham, in brief, writes in "the plain style." This term refers to one of the three "modes of speech" (*genera dicendi*) in which young writers and orators received instruction in the ancient Greco-Roman schools of rhetoric and which are discussed in detail by such authors and educators as Cicero and Quintilian. The other two styles are the middle (or pleasant) and the high (or grand). The most important point to make here about the plain style is that our English adjective gives but a poor sense of the original terms for and intentions of the style. In Greek, the words denoting the plain style are *ischnos,* meaning "lean, spare," and, less frequently, *leptos,* meaning "fine, light, delicate." Though Roman writers introduce a wider range of terms for the style, the nearest Latin equivalent to *ischnos* and *leptos* is *subtilis;* and it is with this term that Cicero and Quintilian most often refer to the plain style. *Subtilis* derives from *subtexo* ("to weave beneath, to connect, to join") and means "subtle, discriminating, finely woven." Cunningham himself alludes to the word's etymological associations when he describes his own plain style as being "crisscrossed and webbed with subtlety and distinctions" (*The Collected Essays* 408). In other words, the plain style aims at nimble sophistication.[2]

An early admiration for certain poems of Swift, Landor, and Robinson, all of whom write with impressive directness and cogency, first drew Cunningham to the plain style ("Interview" 14). This development was reinforced at Stanford, where, with the Renaissance scholar, W. D. Briggs, Cunningham studied the poetry of Ben Jonson, arguably the most various and effective practitioner of the plain style in English; and from his work in Classics, Cunningham acquired a deep appreciation of the ancient rhetorical tradition mentioned above. Finally, his youth in Montana and in the American West may also have affected the formation of his stylistic preferences. The hardscrabble conditions in which he grew up, plus his experience of dire want during the Great Depression, left him with a keen appreciation for essential matters in life and literature and a distaste for unnecessary embellishment or superfluous decoration.

In view of Cunningham's concern with the plain style, it is natural that he developed an interest in the epigram, for it is a type of poetry singularly well suited to the style. Epigrams are by definition short, witty poems. Indeed, the etymology of the word indicates the condensed quality of poems in the genre. *Epigramma* means "inscription" in Greek, and in classical times many epigrams were literally inscribed on public monuments to address or commemorate important civic events. A case in point is Simonides's distich for the Spartans who perished defending the pass at Thermopylae against Xerxes's huge invading Persian army:

Go tell the Spartans, thou that passest by,
That here, obedient to their laws, we lie.
(Trans. William Lisle Bowles)

....

2   For the ancient writers alluded to this paragraph, I have consulted the following editions: Aristotle, *The Poetics*, "Longinus," *On the Sublime*, Demetrius, *On Style*, ed. and trans. by W. Hamilton Fyfe and W. Rhys Roberts (LCL, Cambridge, MA: Harvard University Press, 1932); Cicero, *Brutus* and *Orator*, ed. and trans. by G. L. Hendrickson and H. M. Hubbell (LCL, Cambridge, MA: Harvard University Press, 1971); Quintilian, *Institutio Oratoria*, ed. and trans. by H. E. Butler, 4 vols. (LCL, Cambridge, MA: Harvard University Press, 1920).

If we associate the epigram with "wit," we should think of that quality in terms of dexterous compactness rather than in terms of any particular tone or subject. As Simonides's poem illustrates, epigrams can be serious, even at their most clever. This point is relevant to Cunningham's epigrams, which range from low naughtiness,

> Lip was a man who used his head.
> He used it when he went to bed
> With his friend's wife, and with his friend,
> With either sex at either end. (*The Poems* 55)

to criticism of social hypocrisy,

> This is my curse. Pompous, I pray
> That you believe the things you say
> And that you live them, day by day. (*The Poems* 46)

to broader yet equally trenchant satire,

> This Humanist whom no beliefs constrained
> Grew so broad-minded he was scatter-brained. (*The Poems* 45)

to poignant reflection on the human condition,

> Life flows to death as rivers to the sea,
> And life is fresh and death is salt to me. (*The Poems* 56)

In his poem, "On Doctor Drink," Cunningham says, "I like the trivial, vulgar and exalted" (*The Poems* 59), and this might serve as a motto for his epigrams. Their register of subjects and tones includes the humble and the lofty, and everything in between.

As well as epigrams, Cunningham wrote fine poems in more familiar lyric veins. These share, with the epigrams, concentration of statement and rigor of thought, but are richer in sensory detail and more discursive in argument. "The Dogdays" exemplifies this latter aspect of Cunningham's work. The title refers to the sultriest and unhealthiest period in summer, a time traditionally associated with the appearance in the evening sky of Sirius, the Dog Star. The poem itself appears to deal with a love that failed.

> The morning changes in the sun
> As though the hush were insecure,

And love, so perilously begun,
Could never in the noon endure,

The noon of unachieved intent,
Grown hazy with unshadowed light,
Where changing is subservient
To hope no longer, nor delight.

Nothing alive will stir for hours,
Dispassion will leave love unsaid,
While through the window masked with flowers
A lone wasp staggers from the dead.

Watch now, bereft of coming days,
The wasp in the darkened chamber fly,
Whirring ever in an airy maze,
Lost in the light he entered by. (*The Poems* 4–5)

Cunningham opens his poem by speaking of the early stages of day—morning—and of the early stages of a romantic relationship. However, the relationship is risky—it is "perilously begun"—and it may lack sufficient strength or grounding to endure the full light of noon and experience. Indeed, with the striking phrase that starts the second stanza—"[t]he noon of unachieved intent"—Cunningham indicates the aspirations or expectations of the original feeling have not been sustained or realized. Life and change go on. But no longer are they accompanied or guided by "hope" or "delight." In the third stanza, love itself has evidently succumbed to an enervation that does not permit positive action and communication. And at the end of the stanza, Cunningham introduces a wasp that, stunned by the season's heat and light, flies into a room in which it will be "bereft of coming days." It will, that is, die.

The image of the wasp deserves special praise. Not only is the image striking on its own terms, it also masterfully serves the theme, by rendering conceptual articulation of it unnecessary. Cunningham does not have to tell us that when love goes wrong its light blinds and confuses rather than illuminates. He does not have to speak of the desolation and emotional paralysis we feel when an experience that initially promised to lead us outward to a richer life leads us instead into a baffling labyrinth—"an airy maze"—of disappointment and despair. The image says everything.

Like all of Cunningham's poetry, "The Dogdays" is powerfully distilled, but it is also more oblique and (what may seem a paradox in view of the obliquity) more imagistic than the work with which he is customarily identified. Cunningham also employs this more richly detailed style in his fifteen-poem verse narrative *To What Strangers, What Welcome* (1964). And we see the style in one of the two poems he wrote explicitly about Montana, poems to which we shall now turn.

CUNNINGHAM AND MONTANA

Cunningham addresses Montana most memorably in "Montana Pastoral," which he wrote in 1941, and "Montana Fifty Years Ago," which dates from 1966–1967. As its title indicates, "Montana Pastoral" situates itself in the long tradition of pastoral poetry initiated by such ancient Greek and Roman poets as Theocritus and Virgil. Pastoral verse typically praises the salutary charms and benefits of rural life. The bucolic world of Cunningham's poem, however, is hardly cheering or nourishing. Nature is not a kindly mother who lavishes grapes and apples on happy harvesters, nor do shepherds pasture sheep and pipe amorous ditties to local nymphs. Instead, Cunningham evokes a harsh and menacing landscape:

> I am no shepherd of a child's surmises.
> I have seen fear where the coiled serpent rises,
>
> Thirst where the grasses burn in early May
> And thistle, mustard, and the wild oat stay.
>
> There is dust in this air. I saw in the heat
> Grasshoppers busy in the threshing wheat.
>
> So to this hour. Through the warm dusk I drove
> To blizzards sifting on the hissing stove,
>
> And found no images of pastoral will,
> But fear, thirst, hunger, and this huddled chill. (*The Poems* 17)

Some years after writing this poem, Cunningham described it as "a curt autobiography . . . in which the details of fear, thirst, hunger, and the desperation of this huddled chill were hardly a just summary of his first twenty years but rather an epigrammatic presentation of the salient motives those years communicated to his later life" (*The Collected Essays* 418). One can see what Cunningham means when he characterizes the poem as "curt" and "epigrammatic." Though "Montana Pastoral" is not an epigram, its argument is compact, as is its form, which consists of five tightly managed iambic pentameter couplets. The poet announces at the outset that he is without illusions—he is "no shepherd of a child's surmises"—the reason being, he goes on to explain, that experience has schooled him in privation. The serpent has taught him fear. The weedy drought-ridden land has taught him thirst. He has learned hunger from the uncertain harvests, periodically destroyed as they are on the Great Plains by grasshopper plagues. The blizzard has instructed him in his vulnerability to the cold. (According to Cunningham, the poem's details derive largely from springs and summers that he spent as a boy on a dry-land ranch owned by one of Cunningham's father's friends "thirty-six miles from Billings, over the rimrock in the Wheat Basin country" ["Interview" 3]; however, the "huddled chill" came from a later experience. In the fall or early winter of 1930, when he and his brother Tom were driving south from Denver to Santa Fe, they "ran into a sudden blizzard and stayed for some days at a little cabin just short of the top of Raton Pass, just north of the New Mexico border" ["Interview" 9].)[3]

Overall, "Montana Pastoral" reads like a compressed version of John Steinbeck's *Grapes of Wrath* (1939). As the Joads do, Cunningham experiences an environment that can be hostile even in the best of times. By the end of the poem, he finds himself on the road, and though he does not name the vehicle he drives, it is probably no more reliable than the Joads' Hudson truck. Economic disaster has engulfed the nation, and personal calamities have befallen him.

Though "Montana Fifty Years Ago" draws on impressions of the same dry-land ranch that inspired much of "Montana Pastoral," this later poem,

....

3   For a fine discussion of "Montana Pastoral" in relation to the pastoral tradition, see Steven Shankman, "J. V. Cunningham's 'Montana Pastoral' and the Pastoral Tradition," in Shankman's *In Search of the Classic: Reconsidering the Greco-Roman Tradition, Homer to Valéry and Beyond* (University Park: Pennsylvania State University Press, 1994), 205–13.

Cunningham related once, "is an attempt to summarize not so much my own experience, but to put into form the kind of situation out at the ranch" ("Interview" 4).

Gaunt kept house with her child for the old man,
Met at the train, dust-driven as the sink
She came to, the child white as the alkali.
To the West distant mountains, the Big Lake
To the Northeast. Dead trees and almost dead
In the front yard, the front door locked and nailed,
A handpump in the sink. Outside, a land
Of gophers, cottontails, and rattlesnakes,
In good years of alfalfa, oats, and wheat.
Root cellar, blacksmith shop, milk house, and barn,
Granary, corral. An old *World Almanac*
To thumb at night, the child coughing, the lamp smoked,
The chores done. So he came to her one night,
To the front room, now bedroom, and moved in.
Nothing was said, nothing was ever said.
And then the child died and she disappeared.
This was Montana fifty years ago. (*The Poems* 93)

If we juxtapose this poem with "Montana Pastoral," we notice several things immediately. For one thing, "Montana Fifty Years Ago" is not spoken in the first person; rather, it is narrated impersonally. For another thing, the poem does not rhyme but is in blank verse—unrhymed iambic pentameter. (At the risk of indulging in overly sensitive reading, we might note that the verse features some interestingly expressive prosodic variations. For instance, the trochaic first and third feet in the line, "Nothing was said, nothing was ever said," suggest the emphatic, unbreachable taciturnity of the people described.) For yet another thing, the details of the poem are more numerous and more specifically rendered than those in "Montana Pastoral." To take an obvious example, the "serpent[s]" of that poem are "rattlesnakes" in "Montana Fifty Years Ago." Similarly, in the latter poem, Cunningham communicates a sense of drought not by referring generally to parched grasses but by mentioning the dead and near dead trees in the front yard of the ranch and by speaking of the dusty sink and hand pump in the house. So, too, "Montana Fifty Years Ago" gives us an ampler feeling of daily life than the earlier poem does. The poet enumerates the routines that occupy the characters from dawn to dark—the caring for crops and livestock, the rounds of chores. He provides as well a fuller sense of place by referring to the outbuildings and areas around the house; and he indicates its cultural isolation by indicating that the only reading material is an old *World Almanac*. And whereas "Montana Pastoral" has only one person in it, the narrator of "Montana Fifty Years Ago" depicts a drama involving three people, the gaunt housekeeper, her employer and (eventual) lover, and the sickly, coughing child whose death ends both the poem and the relationship between the couple.

Another striking difference between the poems concerns their methods of presentation. "Montana Pastoral" is deductive. As was noted previously, the poem moves from a general statement to particular observations that derive from and support the statement. In contrast, "Montana Fifty Years Ago" is inductive. It begins and develops by means of the presentation of particulars and, at the end, draws a general conclusion from them: "This was Montana fifty years ago."

Moreover, if "Montana Pastoral" is definitive and summary, "Montana Fifty Years Ago" treats its subject reticently. The narrator does not pretend to know all that lies behind what he describes. Like Robinson, who in his great study of domestic passion, "Eros Turannos," suggests it is folly to imagine "the story of a house / Were told, or ever could be," Cunningham evokes a milieu and a tragedy that occurs within it. But he recognizes, just as Robinson does, that he cannot know the whole truth.

The different times and conditions in which Cunningham composed the two poems account for some of the differences between them. "Montana Pastoral" is a young person's work. Cunningham is discussing experiences that are still raw and recent. If he speaks with blunt authority, it is because his topic is his life, in all its painful immediacy. However, the Cunningham who writes "Montana Fifty Years Ago" is twenty-five years older and sees things from a more mature perspective, which is not to say that the later poem is necessarily better, but which is to note that it expresses a self that has survived critical trials and rites of passage and is now more flexibly observant than the wounded young self of "Montana Pastoral" was. Similarly, in the later poem Cunningham views Montana through a wider lens. However unprepossessing or forbidding the ranch seems, Cunningham regards its inhabitants with empathic interest and communicates something universal in their circumstances and sorrows. Critics frequently say—and rightly so—that Cunningham's poetry impresses us through its exactitude and intelligence. But as "Montana Fifty Years Ago" demonstrates, Cunningham's poems can also move us by their quiet, heartfelt acknowledgment that our insight is limited and that we sometimes experience feelings or witness events whose significance eludes definition.

Whether writing of Montana or the world beyond, Cunningham was one of the finest poets in English in the twentieth century. He was as well one of the most original, though his originality is not of a type we readily recognize today. Rather than breaking with tradition, he modulates, enriches, and transforms it from within. If we give Cunningham short shrift in our current anthologies and surveys of our nation's verse, it is because he is so bracingly accomplished in his chosen métier and so independent of our narrow fashions. Contemporary critical neglect notwithstanding, his work will always have readers. It is by turns funny, insightful, intellectually stimulating, and moving, and its style is rock solid.

Not long after Cunningham died, X. J. Kennedy wrote a "Terse Elegy for J. V. Cunningham," in which he spoke of Cunningham's having

> . . . penned with patient skill and lore immense,
> Prodigious mind, keen ear, rare common sense,
> Only those words he could crush down no more
> Like matter pressured to a dwarf star's core. (113)

And Kennedy added:

> Let eyes unborn wake one day to esteem
> His steady, baleful, solitary gleam. (113)

In the meantime, may living eyes look to Cunningham's poems for their wit, thoughtfulness, and generosity, and for their love for the state of his birth and for the country and planet of which it is part.

WORKS CITED

Cunningham, J. V. Interview with Timothy Steele. "An Interview with J. V. Cunningham." *The Iowa Review* 15.3 (Fall 1985): 1–24. Print.

———. *The Collected Essays of J. V. Cunningham.* Chicago: The Swallow Press, 1976. Print.

———. "Commencement Address, Lawrence University, June 11, 1978." *Folio* XVII (Spring 1980): Print.

———. *The Poems of J. V. Cunningham.* Ed. Timothy Steele. Athens: The Swallow Press/ Ohio University Press, 1997. Print.

———. *Woe or Wonder: The Emotional Effect of Shakespearean Tragedy.* Denver: The University of Denver Press, 1951. A Revision of "Tragic Effect and Tragic Process in Some Plays of Shakespeare, and Their Background in the Literary and Ethical Theory of Classical Antiquity and the Middle Ages." Diss. Stanford University, 1945. Print.

Kennedy, X. J. *In a Prominent Bar in Secaucus: New and Selected Poems, 1955–2007.* Baltimore: The Johns Hopkins University Press, 2007. Print.

CHAPTER 12

Ed Lahey: Underground Poet

DAVID ABRAMS *(Butte, Montana)*

I stand at the edge of the Alice Pit, a dry, abandoned hole in the hill above Butte. Someone with high hopes once dug here, the first open pit mine in Butte. Someone with mineral lust once scooped away the soil, ears ringing with the bells of a thousand cash registers. The Alice only lasted five years before shutting down, the failed dreams blowing away in the wind that knifes its way from Walkerville down to Butte. Now it's been reclaimed, a bowl of green, terraced like the seats in a football stadium.

I linger at the lip of the hole on a late April day. The wind at my back wants to push me into the pit, tumble me down the green scar of earth.

I've come here as a sort of personal eulogy to Butte's unofficial poet laureate who, I just learned, has died in an assisted-living home up in Missoula. Staring at a hole in the ground seems a fitting tribute to Ed Lahey. His, after all, was the voice of the miner—one in a long tradition of writers in Montana who made mining central to their work. Men like novelist Myron Brinig who described Butte as "a gaudy scramble of races and creeds" (35) in his autobiographical novel *Singermann* (1919). In "The Idealist," published in *The Last Best Place: A Montana Anthology* (1988), Butte poet Berton Braley unapologetically defends his mining town against its detractors:

Ugly and bleak? Well, maybe,
  But my eyes have learned to find

The beauty of truth, not substance,

The beauty that lies behind. (458)

Lahey also scratched beneath the copper-rich surface of Butte, but what he found was less beautiful than Braley's greeting-card vision.

Lahey's poem "The Beauty and the Beast," from his collection, *Birds of a Feather* (2005), growls in my ear as I stare at the Alice: "empty as a starling's song . . . / a small acidic lake / above the wounded town" (61). Lahey was keenly attuned to the sensitivity of Butte. Despite their reputation for living in a rough-and-tumble town, residents of the Mining City rarely stop thinking about these lakes of poison, poised to tip and spill across the already-wounded town (fittingly renamed "Poisonville" by Dashiell Hammett in his private-eye novel *Red Harvest* [1929]). Those lines from "The Beauty and the Beast" serve as both lament and warning.

Lahey was an artist who found commonplace beauty in the wreckage of a town like Butte. Read his poems closely and you'll discover a man torn between celebrating the town's decadent past and wryly, ruefully mourning what it has become.

Look, for instance, at one of his most celebrated poems, "The Ballad of the Board of Trade Bar." The bar is gone now—a parking lot next to the old city hall marks its place like a missing tooth in a mouth that used to smile—but for the space of Lahey's poem, it comes alive again with the kind of verbal energy typical of his other work.

"The Ballad of the Board of Trade Bar" centers around a prostitute named Coal Oil Belle who "was a red lamp legend / in a brown town" (21). Each night as the shift-change whistle echoed around town (aurally illustrated in Lahey's internal rhyme), Belle could be found "behind a smelter stack" (21), plying her trade.

Belle is literally a colorful figure in Lahey's "brown town"; the color red is mentioned twice and then there's the silver-lined coffin in which she's buried. In his poem, Lahey buries her "beneath a smoking torch" (22)—which could refer to the lovelorn torch her customers still carry for her, but more tellingly points to the smoldering smelter stacks of the dozens of mines dotting Butte's landscape. "In a town of misery," Lahey writes, "one needs sentimental history" (21).

He saves his most bitter sentiment for the final stanza where Belle gets the last laugh. There she is in her silver coffin, "ten pounds of bone" (22) residing in the mineral-rich earth for which Butte was known. "[W]hen the whistles blow," Lahey supposes, "her earless sockets listen" and her hips still move in sexual rhythm "to the pocket sound / of a lover's jingle" (22). It's a marvelous marriage of earthy sexuality and criticism of the crass materialism (silver coins jingling in a pocket) that was rampant in Butte.

Lahey had an unmistakable love/hate relationship with his hometown. It is, as he writes in "Deep Bells," a "city of tired miners" (93). It is also a city of "mystic mountains, blue sky, that / furls around the town, still as hesitant air" (93). Butte is ugly, Butte is beautiful, and it works its way into your soul like coal dust into the seams of your palms. It is a stoic place, "a place of private / struggle" (93).

Ed Lahey had a voice deep as dynamite. At his readings, he hardly needed a microphone, his words rumbling out of his 6'5" frame—grizzly bear dimensions—and setting the chairs to buzzing. He filled a room with his voice, his demeanor, his words.

I once heard someone say, "When I listened to him read, it was like hearing the resonance of the earth." And yet, he never rose as large as he should have on Montana's literary map.

After Lahey died on April 27, 2011—two days before I walked to the edge of the Alice Pit—it took more than a week for his obituary to appear in the local Butte newspaper, and even then his passing didn't so much as raise a ripple on the toxic waters of the city's Berkeley Pit ("twenty billion gallons and rising" (147), he writes in his poem "A Note From the Third World"). Lahey, the son of a miner and a former worker in Butte's Swiss-cheese network of mines, struggled for popular recognition during his life and, it seems, even after death.

By contrast, there was a much louder and more public mourning two hours up the interstate in Missoula where some of Lahey's closest friends—mostly writers and artists—reeled in shock and sadness at news of his death. He'd been ill for quite some time—a broken man at the end of what even he called a heartbreak life—but still it was hard to believe he was gone.

"He had the most beautiful and large soul and it spilled over into our lives," said Sheryl Noethe, Montana's poet laureate.

Lahey wrote raw-nerve poems of blue-collar life, but his work went largely unchampioned by that very laboring class. He often stands in the shadow of his contemporary and mentor, Richard Hugo, but the two poets share similar themes in the concentration of their work: the dim drink-stained bar, the bruised knuckles from a fistfight, the comfort of a prostitute's bed.

Lahey's poem "In My Three Act Dream" describes how comfort is sought in drink ("good corn bourbon / smoking my liver") and women ("my green-eyed girl with the apple breasts") (19). In Lahey's Butte, prostitutes like Coal Oil Belle earn their wages behind smelter stacks, offering themselves under the neon blaze of Butte's uptown district, debasing themselves for underground men, but when the end comes they're buried in $2,000 engraved coffins lined with silver.

In its glory days, above-ground Butte was a bustling hive of commerce and culture with a peak population of 100,000 in the early 1900s, making it the largest city between Minneapolis and Seattle. Bars and brothels thrived, restaurants never closed, and Charlie Chaplin and Sarah Bernhardt lit up the theater stages. But below the surface, it was a dark dank world where timbers groaned, the ground shuddered, compressors moaned, drills chattered, and a miner's cough was full of "silicotic glitter" ("A Letter to the Editor") (17). The bipolar city was rough and the poet tumbled with the best of them.

"The town has grown into my nervous system," Lahey told a reporter in 2005. "Sometimes I feel like a hostage in a war, but I am glad, too" ("A Poet's Life"). The wind at the Alice Pit stabs me in the back and I head down off the hill to my house on the Flats where I open the paper (the *Missoula* paper) and read Lahey's obituary in that day's edition.

MISSOULA – Edward Thomas Lahey was born in Butte on July 8, 1936, to Edward and Frances Lahey, and grew up in a successful and colorful mining family, the youngest of two. He died on Wednesday, April 27, 2011, in Missoula. . . . After achieving a Master of Arts in English from the University of Montana, Ed went on to teach American literature (and was a member of Richard Hugo's poetry workshop). He left teaching in the late 1960s, and devoted the remainder of his life to his work. His first book of poetry, *The Blind Horses*, won the first Montana Arts Council First Book Award in 1979. Clark City Press published a complete collection of Ed's poetry, "Birds of a Feather" in 2005. In 2008, he received the Montana Arts Council Governor's Arts award for his lifetime work. Later in 2008, his semi-fictional memoir, "The Thin Air Gang" was published. ("Obituary")

I read how he grew up in a house on Aluminum Street, not far from the Travona Mine; how he went to work as a teenager and got paid $10 a day to crawl into manganese gondola cars with a five-pound sledge and clear out the dusty residue; how he would later sit in the Silver Dollar Saloon and read his poems to the half-stoned (and, no doubt, sometimes all-stoned) patrons—poems which sang like theme songs from a jukebox, songs about labor and corporate greed and the cynicism of easy, early death.

Mines are merciless and so were the mining companies who poisoned the Richest Hill on Earth while also lining their corporate pockets with copper. Lahey burned with anger at the way Butte workers were treated and that boiled over into his stanzas. In one of my favorite poems, "A Different Price," he writes:

Topside,
a bull gear caught Haggerty's hand,
slick iron on a wet day.
I heard him speak to it.
"Whoa," he said.
It cut his hand off anyway. (14)

The mine doesn't care. It has callous disregard for its workers. They are meat in its machine. Lahey knew this, he lived it, and he wrote sympathetically of those who were caught in the cogs—both literal and metaphoric. As his poem "In My Three Act Dream" tells us, "payday's just a shack / at the edge of the great pit's lip" (19).

Lahey saw his hometown from the inside out. His work is as landscape-centric as Hugo's, but with a rougher, more bitter edge. In "Sacajawea," the skies over Butte are full of clouds "of white so pure / cotton would not compare," but Lahey's personal sky is "empty as a dead / wolf's lair" (112). There is no optimism to be found here where the only light comes from a burning cigarette. "Isn't change so certain, hope / is just a side of despair?" (112). The Mining City is a place of doused dreams, of faltered visions: "Who but fools say faith out loud / in days like these in Butte?" (112).

In "Rack 'Em Up," Lahey writes of looking "straight into the face of rock" and running the drill with "nothing but stamina to urge me on" (148) past his aching shoulders in the tunnels four-hundred feet below the uptown sidewalks. But what did it gain him or the rest of the world? In the end, he writes,

> . . . none of it
> made a damn bit of difference
> except to teach me we have nothing
> or damned little to say. (149)

Butte and its mines were never more alive than they are in what is perhaps Lahey's most famous poem, "The Blind Horses," in which an old man dying in a hospital bed tells the poet he is still haunted by the memory of the mules who worked the mines in the late nineteenth century. Back then, before animal cruelty laws were on the books, mules were wrapped in canvas bags with hoods placed over their heads; then they were lowered down the shaft into the mines. They wouldn't resurface for another five years. Barring injury, illness or a suspension of mine operations, the mules stayed underground, kept in stone barns and working eight-hour shifts pulling railcars loaded with six tons of ore. Eventually, they forgot about the eye-dazzle of sun, the green bite of grass. In "The Blind Horses," we read of the four-legged laborers put to work in mines like the Lexington, "tunnel-blind from lack of light" (12) and rubbing the timbered tunnels clean as they haul copper the color of peacocks. The old man in the hospital bed tells Lahey he remembers a fire in 1898 when horses burned up in green flame, hoofbeats ringing against the granite walls. The poem ends with this unforgettable line: "'I hear them breathing, Ed'" (12).

A few weeks after Lahey's death, his friend and fellow poet Mark Gibbons sent me a message on Facebook which said, in part, "Ed Lahey's poems breathe and moan and sweat and sing. You'd have loved Ed if you love his poems. Read them and know him."

It's true, Lahey's effectiveness as a poet is the blatant personal nature of his work; he was a writer who turned himself inside out and spread it on the page. He didn't hide behind clever artifice or, as Gibbons said, "literary mumbo-jumbo." To read Ed was to know Ed.

But yet, I wondered, why didn't Butte seem to know Ed? Is it because he didn't toe the line with sentimentality for the Company? Or is it because he was an artist in a town not easily given to the frilly and flowery?

For a son of a miner who owed his family security to digging for pay, he seemed to find plenty of fault with Butte's historic livelihood. The first words of the first poem ("The Orphan Girl Prospect") in *Birds of a Feather* (2005) place us center-map in Lahey's geography: "Deep in mined-out waste" (1). And the first line of "Contract Miners" speaks to man muscling the rocky strata beneath Butte: "Underground we fought the earth together" (15). In "No Pick or Shovel," he's even more explicit in his contempt for the waste tailings of Butte:

I was born there. Mining exhausts
a town. The rich take the riches.
The poor are left with "The Hill."
Barren granite, empty as a rock bee's nest,
a dead stone honeycomb. (150)

Lahey's miners have gumbo on their boots and dull dynamite headaches. Their work is hard and endless. He writes in "Contributor's Note" of ". . . the gopher crews / who mucked around / the goddamn clock" (46).

In the end, the Anaconda Copper Mining Company abandons Butte to its fate and Lahey muses on the betrayal in "After the Copper Mines Failed."

The Company pulled out
to write The Hill operation off
as a tax loss,
and city fathers spoke
of sentimental history
instead of evil. (137)

In that poem, arson kills uptown Butte, whose buildings burn "like candles on a cake" (137). Tourists stroll the streets "like actors on / a vacant movie set" (138). Miners grow mean in bars, "muttering to one another / of explosive rounds that would go / with a sexual shudder" (138).

Lahey suffered no fools—in life as in his art—and would be the first to rebuke political correctness. To some, he seemed a grouchy throwback to an era gone by. In his poem "oldpoet.gone," Gibbons wrote of his friend: "He's a telegram/stopped in an on-line world" (qtd. in "Western Lives").

This seems a fitting description of the poet, stubborn as the orneriest Butte citizen, reluctant to get caught up in the sweep of the Internet, social media, or any other new-fangled gewgaws carried on the bandwagon. I won't say Lahey is "stuck in time," but nostalgia is central to his work and he seems to hold fast to the notion that the old ways were better. The good old days are gone and all we're left with are reminders like jukeboxes, oil stoves, and sodden wool coats.

In "Winter Runoff," there are equal parts sentiment and misery inside the bar: "The juke box is silent / waiting out the final days of winter" (111). The oil-drum stove glows with stolen company coal, melting snow runs through ancient drain pipes and

> Men with gnarled and knotted
> hands clump arthritic knees,
> steam rises from bulky coats
> soaking in a pool of heat.
> Slush trickles down the eaves. (111)

If it's sentiment you seek, just look at what Lahey does with the ground itself, anthropomorphizing it with a sensual danger in "Elegy in a Mine Yard" with this stanza:

> on Taboo Hill where hoist drums
> rust and slant toward glory holes
> that gape like hungry mouths
> of stone giants banged wide
> by lust. (36)

In "A Note From the Third World," he writes wistfully of Butte: "I wait for the town I came from / to die inside" (147). People here are salt of the earth, but they are also, in a sense, killed by the earth, the soil and rock they've spent their lives and generations of lives, digging and scouring and raping. They are beholden to the ground and they are also betrayed by that same earth which has withered their lungs and forced them into the indignity of walking through Walmart trailed by an oxygen tank on wheels.

In the end, Lahey could not remain in Butte—for whatever reason (health, family, work)—and his departure is a memorable event, a red-letter day in his head. He writes about it in several poems, describing how he goes to the Greyhound bus station on Harrison Avenue, literal baggage in hand, emotional baggage on his heart. Fittingly, the final poem in the collection *Birds of a Feather* (2005) is called "Cardboard Suitcase." In that flimsy valise, he packs all his memories of his hardscrabble past, the miserable sweating hours underground, the empty hours of drink, the bitter prostitutes, the reversals of fortune. He even brings up the ghost of Frank Little, the union labor leader lynched in 1917 and widely mourned by miners who suspected the Company was behind the attack.

> I headed for the station
> It was time to leave.
> I had worn out my welcome.
> For me the town was dead.
> I packed my cardboard suitcase.
>
> Butte was over.
> The miners had all died out.
> What was left did not suit me,
> but I knew it would not end.
>
> Frank Little's memory would
> hang on like death. I would
> never be anywhere but from there.
> A town to toast.
>
> In my memory,
> Butte was a mythic place,
> where forty-eight head frames
> were pulling ore from shafts,
> shive wheels turning in the sun. (180)

Cardboard memories in hand, Lahey left Butte and moved to Missoula, returning only for the occasional visit. What was left for him here? Butte had dried up, the streets empty, lined by arson-gutted buildings, the once-bright neon signs now flickering intermittently. They paved the Board of Trade Bar and put up a parking lot.

At the end of his life, Lahey writes, he wandered around Missoula, seeing himself in shop windows. He was a man without a pick or shovel in the poem by that same name:

I see myself high in a gallus frame
close to a shiv wheel
that doesn't turn. Brakes locked.
I am closed down. No ore.

I have a ghost town inside,
vibrant memories of a life. (150)

Ed Lahey was a prominent voice of the underground, one in a long line of miner-poets, but now those shafts were sealed, the pockets of the earth flooded with groundwater. To paraphrase the old man in "The Blind Horses," he could hear the earth breathing and it was unsettling.

WORKS CITED

Devlin, Vince. "A Poet's Life." *Missoulian* [Missoula, MT] 23 Oct. 2005. Web. 5 May 2011.

Kittredge, William, and Annick Smith, eds. *The Last Best Place: A Montana Anthology.* Helena: Montana Historical Society Press, 1988. Print.

Lahey, Ed. *Birds of a Feather: The Complete Poems of Ed Lahey.* Livingston: Clark City Press, 2005. Print.

"Edward Thomas Lahey Obituary." *Missoulian* [Missoula, MT] 8 May 2011. Web. 11 May 2011.

Scott, Tristan. "Western Lives: Poet Ed Lahey gracefully wrote of grit." *Missoulian* [Missoula, MT] 9 May 2011. Web. 13 May 2011.

CHAPTER 13

"Montana blue, the vanishing point": U.S. Indian Autonomy in M. L. Smoker's *Another Attempt at Rescue*

CAREY R. VOELLER *(Glendale, South Carolina)*

In 1988, editors William Kittredge and Annick Smith published *The Last Best Place: A Montana Anthology*. The collection—clocking in at over 1,000 pages—contains over 230 accounts ranging from fiction to poetry to remembrances to introductory essays written by authors such as James Welch, Kittredge, Mary Clearman Blew, and William Bevis, among others. The title resonated with both Montanans and non-Montanans so much that it eventually culminated in a legal battle between a Las Vegas businessman, David Lipson, who wished to market and trademark the term for a number of his businesses, and Montana Senators Conrad Burns (Republican) and Max Baucus (Democrat), who fought against Lipson's attempted privatization of "The Last Best Place" (Robbins "In Montana"). In the end (or at the beginning), Kittredge himself coined the phrase. Indeed, there is magic and mystique in the title.

For some, "The Last Best Place" refers to the vast, natural beauty of Montana—a paradise yet untainted by modernity, urbanity, and industrial capitalism. Even before Kittredge, Norman Maclean, in *A River Runs through It* (1976), romanticized Montana, fly fishing, and the Missouri

177

and Big Blackfoot rivers. Tragedy mars the novella, but the book helps contribute to the Edenic mythos of Montana. Richard Hugo, one of Montana's most famous twentieth-century poets, wrote about hard living and hard drinking in many of his poems, but he also mythologized the state as remote, isolated, and occasionally untouched by human progress. In "Driving Montana," he writes:

> You are lost
> in miles of land without people, without
> one fear of being found, in the dash
> of rabbits, soar of antelope, swirl
> merge and clatter of streams. (*Making Certain* 204)

And Hollywood films such as *A River Runs through It* (1992), *Legends of the Fall* (1994), and *The Horse Whisperer* (1998) have presented Montana as a place of struggle but more often as one of beauty, love, close families and friends, and on and on. While indeed all of these factors are true for some people of the state, there is also another side to the mythology of "The Last Best Place."

For other residents, Montana—like any place—is often far from perfect, not wholly a paradise. M. L. Smoker's first collection of poems, *Another Attempt at Rescue* (2005), individually speaks to personal experiences in Montana and to her young adult life on the Fort Peck Indian Reservation. A graduate of the MFA program in Poetry at the University of Montana and now Director of Indian Education at Montana Office of Public Instruction in Helena, Smoker is an enrolled member of both Sioux and Assiniboine tribes. She makes it clear that:

> I definitely am not a spokesperson for my tribe. I am very proud of that affiliation and my heritage, however my stories, my interactions, my poetry are but one thread in an entire fabric…Many people from my reservation and of my tribe have VERY different experiences from me… My collection was very much about my personal journey, connecting and reconnecting with who I am. (Smoker, "Re: Essay Comments")

Analyzing her "personal journey" in a small sampling of poems, I will argue that Smoker individually complicates the rosy (and often literary/ cinematic) mythos of Montana as "The Last Best Place." Through her own struggles and experiences, Smoker provides a fuller depiction of the state and most importantly shows the presence, endurance, survival, and success of American Indians.

RESERVATION LIFE

As with many contemporary American Indian authors, a central subject of Smoker's poetry is life on the reservation. Sometimes this depiction reflects bleakness; at other times it is "beautiful," as she states, "a place full of memory and meaning . . . an incredible landscape, a home I wouldn't exchange for anything" (Smoker, "Re: Essay Comments"). In "Another Attempt at Rescue," we see a combination of both bleakness and beauty. Smoker begins with an epigraph, "*March 20, 2003.*" The poem then opens with:

> The time is important here—not because this
> has been a long winter or because it is my first
> at home since childhood—but because there is so much
> else to be unsure of. We are on the brink of an invasion.

Smoker returns to the reservation but casts Montana against a larger international backdrop: the 2003 war in Iraq under President George W. Bush. Yet, for much of the first stanza, Smoker ignores the war, focusing instead on family and how she "paid a cousin twenty dollars / to shovel the walk. He and two of his buddies, / still smelling of an all-nighter, arrived at 7 am." Later, Smoker notices their "ungloved hands" and "winter made me feel / selfish and unsure. This ground seems unsure / of itself for its own reasons." The repetition of "unsure" seems less in relation to Operation Iraqi Freedom and more in regards to herself and her position at home. As she notices the "ungloved hands" of her cousin and his friends and feels "selfish," she chastises herself for her unawareness of the actual living conditions of her family. As I see it, the "ungloved hands" work as the most important subject in this stanza. First, they reflect the unstable conditions of Sioux/Assiniboine poverty, both in a lack of suitable clothing ("hands" unprotected during harsh Montana winters) and in a psychological movement toward self-destructive behavior. Secondly, the "ungloved hands" help prepare Smoker to find her certainty and emerging political voice in the remainder of the poem.

The subject of war continues in the second stanza. She states, "When I first began to write poems / I was laying claim to battle." The "battle" began "with a death," that of her mother. Smoker continues, "I have still not yet learned to write of war. / I have friends who speak out—as is necessary—." In the shadow of the Iraq invasion, she cannot find how to "write" or "speak." But then Smoker's "war" and her ability to "speak out" emerges:

> But I am from *this* place and a great deal
> has been going wrong for some time now.
> The two young Indian boys who almost drowned
> last night in the fast-rising creek near school
> are casualties in any case.
> There have been too many just like them
> and I have no way to fix these things. (Smoker, *Another Attempt*
> 44–45; italics in original)

A couple of key factors emerge here. First, "*this* place" takes priority over the international and political context. And, in "*this* place," where things have "been going wrong for some time now," there are Indian "casualties" in addition to the loss of U.S. soldiers overseas. Here Smoker finds a way "to write of war," but it is a war in Montana. Though she can now "write" of the "casualties" she witnesses on the reservation, she cannot "fix these things." She has attained some degree of power through poetry, but her physical ability to create actual change results in helplessness. Yet, we also see beauty and hope in the sense that Indians have survived and that they move onward: "But I will not regret that those boys made it home, / or that the cousins used the money at the bar." But beauty, pride, and hope still tangle with economic realities at the poem's end: "Still, there are no lights on this street. / Still, there is so much mud outside / that we carry it indoors with us" (Smoker, *Another Attempt* 45). "Another Attempt at Rescue" illustrates Montana's own "casualties." At the same time, it celebrates and loves home for the fact that family and Indians still endure.

Another example that depicts reservation life in Montana is "Seven Days Is Never Enough." This poem contains nine stanzas; the first begins with the title "monday" and the last begins with "tuesday" of the following week. Even the poem's title, juxtaposed against the number of stanzas, presents a sense of frustration in Big Sky country—and we see a textual affirmation of this at the poem's end. In the third stanza, "wednesday," Smoker writes, "my nephew storms into the room / he craves more than pepsi these days / so i hand him a seven-up" (*Another Attempt* 20). If alcohol is what her nephew "craves," Smoker refuses to deconstruct popular stereotypes about some American Indians when it comes to reservation life; instead, she—many times in her poetry—acknowledges and confronts subjects of addiction and dependence. But she tries to "fix" this problem by giving her nephew "a seven-up." Momentarily, we see a sense of control, unlike in "Another Attempt at Rescue" where Smoker states, "I have no way to fix these things."

But the ability to "fix" soon passes. In the same stanza, she continues, "so we drive down to the river / and guess what belongs to who / as the trash floats by" (*Another Attempt* 21). On the one hand, we witness happiness in Smoker spending time with a family member, much like her happiness regarding the two boys who survive their near drowning or nephews spending their money. On the other hand, "trash floats by" in the river—human progress and carelessness mars Montana's idyllic landscape. Smoker may be able to control the choice of her nephew's beverages, but she, in the larger natural world, cannot control or "fix" the polluted river before her. Smoker states, "…there are beautiful and amazing aspects about my home . . . I think it is an incredible landscape"(Smoker, "Re: Essay Comments"). But her image of (presumably) the Missouri serves as a stark contrast to Maclean, who often depicts the Blackfoot and other rivers as crystalline. In the novel *A River Runs through It*, rivers often flow peacefully, laden with sun, "big-grained vapor" (Maclean 20), "quiet, shady water" (Maclean 90), and giant Rainbow and Brown trout—but never are they clogged with "trash." Clearly, Smoker's representation of the Missouri, in this instance, appears quite different from Maclean's representation of the Blackfoot (and Robert Redford's, who directed the film adaptation of *A River Runs through It*): in the decades between Maclean's tale and Smoker's poem, modernity and its detritus have found their way into Montana's watersheds.

At the end of the novella, Maclean reflects on the death of his younger brother. He writes, "I am haunted by waters" (Maclean 104). Yet, even amid his personal losses, Maclean textually presents himself as an individual, who (perhaps because of his status as white and male) still embodies freedom, who can choose to ". . . fish the big waters alone, although some friends think I shouldn't" (Maclean 104). Smoker, conversely, ends her poem haunted not only by a polluted river but also by a sense of powerlessness and helplessness. As does Maclean, she reflects on a family member—in her case, a sister, who she calls, "but the line is dead." Smoker then continues:

> should i ask what the lesson
> is here
> should i roll on the ground
> for the secret message
> that says
> your life will never change
> your life will never change (*Another Attempt* 23).

Here, as a female and/or as an individual Indian, there seems no ready-made freedom. The poem, written entirely in lower-case letters and without punctuation, resists conventional norms (as does much modern poetry), but it also helps visually contribute to the lack of an established empowerment; we might read politically into her use of the lower-case "i" compared to Maclean's capitalized "I" or Richard Hugo's "I" in almost all of his Montana poetry. "Seven Days Is Never Enough" and "Another Attempt at Rescue" are poems that indeed find happiness in small yet important places, but they also complicate Montana as "The Last Best Place."

THE ASSINIBOINE LANGUAGE

For almost any American Indian, preserving the native tongue is crucial in connecting with the ancestral past as well as the present and future. When that language begins to disappear, so does the individual Indian and so does a lingual connection to and for the collective tribe. How could something so important as one's own language vanish? This theme is nowhere more apparent than in "Casualties." The poem's title is a recurring word for Smoker: "the two young Indian boys who almost drowned" in "Another Attempt at Rescue" are also termed "casualties." Again, loss goes beyond American soldiers; it also includes young Indian boys and languages.

Smoker begins "Casualties" with an epigraph from Michael Krauss: ". . . *linguistic diversity also forms a system necessary to our survival as human beings.*" With this quotation, she makes it clear that the loss of her language results in the loss of herself and humanity. She opens the poem with a positive image: "The sun has broken through." But the sunniness vanishes; a shadow emerges, as "today my words are dying out." The large space between "words" and "are" forces us to see a gap, an invitation to imagine a word or words that *might've* been written down. Smoker goes on: "Still as I tell of   stillness / of a very word / as ( )   as it leaves this world." The parentheses suggest two readings: either the word's definition hangs on by a dangling thread, a set of parentheses attempting to prevent its escape, or the word and its definition have already disappeared. After noting that "*My grandmother was told that the only way to survive was / to forget*," Smoker chastises herself:

Where   were you?
   Where were
you? Speaking of myself,
for   my own neglect: too often
I was nowhere to be found.
   I will not lie.
   I heard the ruin in each Assiniboine voice. (34)

Once more, the blank spaces above indicate "the vanishing," as Smoker calls it; her language disappears into history, all the while as she chastises herself for her own vanishing. She continues: "Hold   me   accountable / because I have not done my part /   to stay alive." Unlike the other poems, where Smoker seems up against governmental and environmental conditions that frustrate her, or that occasionally deem her powerless, here she admits that she indeed possessed control over her contemporary and historical legacy.

But language is not only verbal, it is also corporeal. Smoker goes on, detailing a new casualty and loss:

   There are a great many parts of my own
body that are gone:

where hands
belong there is one lost syllable.
And how a tooth might sound—
its absence
   a falling. (*Another Attempt* 34–35; italics in original)

Here she introduces amputation or disability as a sort of third term between the physical body and its verbal and aural meanings. When even "one… syllable" is "lost," the original Assiniboine language and the "abled" (completely intact) body of Smoker's speaker disappears, instead rewritten into a language and "disabled" body via modern standardized English. In the poem's closing lines, she states, "   I have let go   of one too many. / *I have never known where or how /   to begin*" (Smoker, *Another Attempt* 35; italics in original). As with her other poems, "Casualties" elicits a lack of frustration over personal and familial unawareness (or awareness). In the end, "Casualties" seems to cast Montana as a place where languages—and thus bodies—disappear. At the same time, beyond the language of both "Seven Days Is Never Enough" and "Casualties," Smoker herself embodies the presence and endurance of modern American Indians. In her case, she received two college degrees from Pepperdine University and the University of Montana, published a collection of poems, went into teaching and administration back home at a high school on the Fort Peck Reservation, currently works as a state legislator, and just recently gave birth to her first child. Her success story is only one of many American Indian success stories—in Montana and across the United States.

LOSING FAMILY

Another kind of loss—family—serves as the final subject I will discuss in *Another Attempt at Rescue* (2005). Smoker often intricately interweaves the death of her mother with Montana's landscape. This connection between family and place puts her in line with authors such as Maclean and Hugo. Yet Smoker's relationship between Montana and her mother is so central to her poetry that, in the end, it arguably receives much more attention than either Maclean or Hugo give it. One example of this occurs in the poem "Borrowing Blue." Smoker addresses this poem to an unnamed friend, an artist: "I'm not the painter here. I leave that to you…" But then she ruminates on the color blue, eventually mentioning that blue reminds her of ". . . the beaded moccasins and belt I danced in / before my mother died." Smoker continues:

My grandmother had made these for her as a child—
spelling out in blue beads on blue beads

each of our names, our collective history
in an invisible pattern only we could recognize.
Not the blue of Montana sky either,
not that at all, but the pulse of lake water lapping
at your ankles, the temperature rising
as a storm gathers on the plains.

In the above, Smoker brings together the loss of her mother with her grandmother and "our collective history." The loss of one family member points to the loss of other relatives. Later in the stanza, she toys with the color blue, as it operates "Not [as] the blue of Montana sky either." Smoker essentially acknowledges that Montana *can* indeed fit the blue "Big Sky" stereotype, but in this context it does *not*. Rather, she shifts our attention away from one natural element (air/sky) to another element (water). The lake appears blue, but it is blue threatened by "temperature" (or fire, a third element), perhaps representative of personal anger or sadness. And then we return to an image of the sky, yet one foreboding and frightening; thunderheads form over the "plains." Montana, family, sky, blue, water, fire, and loss all come together.

Smoker continues with this multitude of subjects. To the artist, she sadly states, "(We will never stop missing them, will we, / the parent each of us has lost.)." Smoker goes on to write that, if she were to look at her friend's paintings, ". . . I have no idea what I would see." Here again, there is inability to "fix these things," even when it comes to viewing a painting. But she imagines what she'd *like* to see—and in doing so, she tries to rewrite the fate of her mother:

I like to think there would be some kind of end
to the blue, a visual end to what is never
adequate: blue flame, blue bead, blue ovary,
blue lung. See how easily we fail? (55)

Here she would like sadness (feeling "blue) to end. To "think" of or see "a visual end" to "blue" (sadness) might help ease frustration over "what is never / adequate: blue flame, blue bead, blue ovary, / blue lung." In other words, Smoker wants what is impossible in the present moment. To move the color blue beyond sadness and frustration leads to familial happiness—a time before illness and hospital beds and death. But, as in many of her poems, the moment of control slips away, for she asks, "See how easily we fail?"

And thus the reality and impossibility take us to the end. In the final lines, Smoker states, "So yes, let's call it Montana blue, the vanishing point." As with "casualties," "vanishing" serves as a repeated and important word. She concludes the poem with:

> How can you take back
> the kind of blue you've been dreaming of—trust
> it will make something unhappen—
> if it is the same blue you're made of? (Smoker, *Another Attempt*
>   55–56)

As Smoker surrenders to the reality and inability to rid herself of sadness and "make something unhappen," blue happiness vanishes. Montana, as "The Last Best Place," is simultaneously the ending place—it is sometimes, sadly, "the vanishing point." But, in this poem and others, Smoker brings her mother back from beyond. She lives (and lives again), in different manifestations, textually throughout the collection—so we might also see many poems (and thus Montana) as an "appearing point."

CONCLUSION

The subjects and themes I have explored here are only a few of many in *Another Attempt at Rescue* (2005). The entire collection of poems does not exclusively focus on frustration, loss, despair, helplessness, or sadness. Many of Smoker's other poems are quite the opposite. For example, in "The Feed," we see her spending time with cousins while "aunties" (*Another Attempt* 47) joke in the kitchen as they prepare food. In "Can You Feel the Native American in Me," Smoker and her friend Lara laugh at a "white girl" after the woman dents "Lara's blue Celica" with the door of her boyfriend's truck; Lara gets "out to kick the girl's ass but they / sped out of the Town Pump's parking lot too fast." Afterward, on the way to see family, "we're bumping Tupac" (*Another Attempt* 58). There are many moments of lightheartedness, of references to popular culture, toughness, goofiness, and plain happiness at simply being alive. And this brings me back to an important point, one that Smoker also emphasizes: Indians still remain in Montana; they live and go about their lives. As I have already mentioned, Smoker is one example. And she says it best when she does speak for others:

> ... [W]e are still here, despite all efforts in the past to ensure our defeat and removal. American Indian populations continue to increase in our state. We are state legislators, doctors, poets, teachers. We have our cultures, our ceremonies. We have held so much intact, under great duress at times in the past. (Smoker, "Re: Essay Comments")

In this way, it seems the idea (or some aspect) of "The Last Best Place" still exists for Indians, perhaps in ways different from the typical representations. And Indian views necessarily complicate this often-romanticized slogan, just as does a good portion of *Another Attempt at Rescue* (2005). Again, Smoker says it best, and I close with her words: "... it was always our first place. And it is very important that the entire story of our landscape and the people who inhabit it be told" (Smoker, "Re: Essay Comments").

WORKS CITED

Hugo, Richard. "Driving Montana." *Making Certain It Goes On: The Collected Poems of Richard Hugo*. New York: W.W. Norton & Company, 1984. 204. Print.

Maclean, Norman. *A River Runs Through It and Other Stories*. Chicago: University of Chicago Press, 1976. Print.

Robbins, Jim. "In Montana, a Popular Expression Is Taken Off the Endangered List." *New YorkTimes* 17 August 2008. Web. 2 March 2012.

Smoker, M. L. *Another Attempt at Rescue*. Brooklyn: Hanging Loose Press, 2005. Print.

———. "Re: Essay Comments." Message to the author. 25 Feb. 2012. E-mail.

CHAPTER 14

Madeline DeFrees's Montana Renaissance

JOCELYN SILER *(Missoula, Montana)*

I first met Madeline DeFrees in 1975 when she was my professor in the MFA program at the University of Montana. Just two years before, after spending thirty-eight years as Sister Mary Gilbert of the Order of the Holy Names of Mary and Jesus, she had been permanently dispensed of her religious vows. Many of the poems she wrote at that time, as well as many of her conversations, were charged with the fear and wonder precipitated by the recent sea change in her life. Madeline's wonder was twofold: she expressed wonder at the future that opened before her, at the possibilities for personal and artistic freedom; however, there was also an astonishment at the past, a deep amazement that she had actually lived so many years under such constraint.

Amazement is still very much evident in Madeline's poetry. It's as if once she had put aside the claustrophobic certainty of life as a Roman Catholic nun she became permanently astonished by the possibilities opened by intellectual and creative exploration. The poems she writes as a nonagenarian are every bit as fresh and urgent as the ones she wrote when newly out of the convent.

DeFrees was brought up to be a nun. When her devout mother lost her first child, a girl, in infancy, she made a promise that if she was gifted with a second daughter she would do everything in her power to assure the girl entered the convent. Raised in Hillsboro, Oregon, DeFrees was sent to parochial school and then to high school at the all-girls St. Mary's Academy in Portland, which was run by the Order of the Holy Names of Mary and Jesus. When she graduated from high school at sixteen, she immediately became a postulant in the Holy Names herself. In her memoir about her religious calling, *The Springs of Silence* (1953), DeFrees reveals that she was so private about her vocation that she didn't tell her senior-prom date that she planned to enter the convent when she graduated (*Springs* 54).

DeFrees was raised in a working class family, and even though she was deemed "the smart one" of her siblings, no one in her family had gone to college, and there was no expectation that she would go. However, her entrance into the teaching order of the Holy Names reversed that expectation, and as a nun she earned a BA in English at Marylhurst College (now Marylhurst University) and an MA in journalism at the University of Oregon. DeFrees taught grade school and high school before taking her first college teaching position at Holy Names College (now Holy Names Music Center) in Spokane in 1950.

Throughout her time as a nun, DeFrees was writing. "Everyone wrote poems in the novitiate," Madeline said in an interview in 2009. "And I would just look around and think the difference between them and me is that they'll quit, and I won't" (DeFrees, *KUOW*).

Although while she was a nun she published a memoir about her religious calling and her first volume of verse, *From the Darkroom* (1964), life in the convent forced DeFrees into a state of artistic asceticism. Her order practiced a vow of silence. She couldn't read her poems aloud as she composed them. "We went everywhere in twos. So, if I was the companion to go to the dentist, I would put an old envelope in my pocket. . . . I learned to carry a whole stanza in my head, and to revise it without writing anything down. I just followed the swish of black serge beside me and worked on this poem. Then, when we got to the dentist, I wrote down the stanza, and that cleared my head for the next one" (DeFrees, *KUOW*).

DeFrees was torn between her desire to express herself fully in writing and her duty to be obedient to her religious vows. Everything she published had to be approved by Roman Catholic Church censors. "As a writer, what I was supposed to do was write these addresses; jubilee addresses, or verses for a Christmas card" (DeFrees, *KUOW*). Instead, her poetry was sophisticated and passionate: "On the sandy point the seeker may conquer the obdurate sea. / And learn from her ravished innocence the one humility." A Church censor changed DeFrees's "ravished innocence" to "sparkling innocence" (DeFrees, *KUOW*).

When asked what she wrote about during those years in the convent, Madeline replied "Oh, I was writing about trees. There were trees in every poem. That was a safe image. . . . I wanted to be like the tree, rooted and moving, both" (DeFrees, *KUOW*). Rooted in her religious calling, yet growing as a poet.

And she did continue to develop as a poet. Despite her obedience to Church censors, DeFrees gained an increasing reputation as a poet. She studied poetry with Karl Shapiro, and with John Berryman and Robert Fitzgerald. Her work was included in anthologies. She traveled and gave readings and developed professional friendships with other poets and writers, including Richard Hugo, who was then teaching at the University of Montana.

Constrained as the years in the convent may have been, the stillness of the unornamented life suited DeFrees's private nature and allowed her to practice the powers of seeing and contemplating with which she had been naturally gifted. DeFrees's self-declared major influences, Emily Dickinson and Gerard Manley Hopkins, had also lived lives of private withdrawal that allowed for concentrated, passionate artistic exploration.

"Requiem Mass: Convent Cemetery," DeFrees's favorite poem from her first book of poetry, *From the Darkroom* (1964), published when she was still a nun, describes the spareness of the ascetic life and the ultimate reward it offers glimmers of. However, it also underscores the essential loneliness she experienced within the convent.

> The shaft of their Gregorian cuts clean:
> through the domed summer, through the bare brightness,
> through the long shadows of the sycamores arching
> over white crosses where the bones moulder
> under the levelling loam.

The poem opens at the very beginning of the funeral mass, with the ancient call and response of the Introit sung by two groups of Sisters as the priest processes to the site of the service. The liturgical song of the nuns—the appropriate psalm for the day—"cuts clean" through to the very heart of what matters to the speaker in the poem. The mass is being celebrated not inside a church, but outside in the open air of the convent cemetery. This first stanza moves from the high, distant generality of the "domed summer" down through layers of increasing particularity. We are pulled by the chanting of the nuns from the brilliant but inscrutable "bare brightness" of the heavens through tree branches and their shadows to the grave markers and under the markers to the bones of the dead. The movement toward particularity emphasizes the nuns who have died and who now lie "under the levelling loam." "Levelling" is, of course, a reference to mortality. However, the word levelling also introduces the major theme of the poem—and of the Requiem Mass itself: that the Sisters who lie in the convent cemetery have been made, in death, radically equal and whole in that they are reconciled and one with God.

> Life shrinks to a pair of names
> (born into one, the other worn with the veil)
> and a single date, her entrance to eternity:
> May eight, February three, March ten, and then
> four digits, juggled a bit by time
> in the wry manner of a clock's ticking
> and a calendar's cancelled sheet.

Life in the world is inconsequential; it "shrinks to a pair of names." The only dates worth putting on the grave markers are the dates of the nuns' second births into eternity. Time is also inconsequential. It is, after all, only a human construct. In the light of the eternal, time is amusing, something to be "wry" about.

> All the fierce drama,
> too big for Broadway and Hollywood
> to frame in footlights or celluloid,
> told without glamour on a wedge of stone,
> cut from its context: the common life, inviolably alone,
> each in the same alphabet as the next,
> save for the abstract language of moss and lichen
> on the cold concrete.

The speaker emphasizes the equality of the women in the eyes of God. As full as the dead Sisters' lives may have been, the religious life pares them down to what really matters: the date they enter into eternity "told without glamour on a wedge of stone." There are echoes of Dickinson in this stanza. Think of "Safe in their Alabaster Chambers" (1861): "Diadems—drop—and Doges—surrender— / Soundless as dots—on a Disc of Snow—" (100). In eternity, what we were in life falls away. However, unlike Dickinson, the speaker here supplies no images of the afterlife, suggesting that although life in the world is inconsequential, life after death is as inscrutable as the "bare brightness" of the sky in the first stanza.

> Sparrows divide the stillness; we repeat,
> *Unto Thy faithful … life is changed …*
> He will not let them fall. Veiled heads bow low,
> calling Him out of silence with the priest,
> calling Him with the bells to come:
> *Absolve, Domine.*

The opening image of sparrows in flight recalls the Holy Spirit evoking the presence of God. The poem then shifts to fragments from the Roman Catholic Requiem Prayer, which guarantees life after death to the faithful. The inclusion of the prayer suggests that the discipline of the religious life is efficacious: prayer and ritual bring one closer to God. However, the fragmentary nature of the prayer's presentation undercuts a final communion with the divine, and in the grammar of the poem, God remains aloof. He is called upon to come out of a formless silence and entreated to forgive, but the stanza leaves it at that.

> Changed life, not taken; or taken, kept—
> bold word, transcending sunlight and the probing root
> that cracks the footstone where our Sisters lie.
> Dark hides the ways they travelled by,
> these solitary, single hearts, quickened by the same Love
> in a million guises.

The Requiem Prayer is referenced once more: life doesn't end; it is "kept." The "probing root . . . cracks" the tomb of death and announces the resurrection of the body. Then the poem makes a subtle turn. Although the lives of the nuns who lie in the convent cemetery are unknown to us, they are "single (as in singular) hearts," made alive in faith by the love of God and united and glorified with God after death. "[T]he same Love / in a million guises" references Hopkins's "Christ plays in ten thousand places, / Lovely in limbs, and lovely in eyes not his" (51).

> Disguises, rather, for we seldom see
> from above the tombstones. Only now and then
> between the Introit and the last Amen,
> here in the cemetery,
> we look and gauge our place and look away. (*From* 20–21)

In the poem's final stanza, the speaker reinforces the shadowy quality of life on earth, and suggests full being and sight in eternity. We see God only in glimpses "above the tombstones," much like St. Paul in Corinthians: "For now we see in a mirror dimly, but then face to face. Now I know in part; then I shall understand fully, even as I have been fully understood" (1 Corinthians 13.12).

However, finally, the sense and the tone of the stanza, and of the poem, are closer to the desolation of T. S. Eliot's "The Hollow Men" than they are to St. Paul's eschatological hopefulness. The individuals in both poems wear "disguises"; they gather at a verge of an underworld; they see only in stolen glimpses and look away; their prayer is fragmentary. As in many of the poems from DeFrees's first book, the speaker is distant, and the individuals who people the landscape are fragmented, disembodied, and indistinguishable. The priest is merely a voice the Sisters call out in concert with; the nuns are faceless "[v]eiled heads," and mouldering bones; rather than bringing the nuns into community, the collective life of the convent leaves them "inviolably alone."

. . .

As devout and intelligent as DeFrees was about her faith, she nonetheless experienced constant tension between her desire for artistic freedom and the requirements imposed on her by her vow of religious obedience.

> . . . I lived for a long time in terror of some kind of mental breakdown. The poems were, in a sense, my lifeline because they provided a measure

of release for my feelings. At the same time they compounded the problems because I felt guilty about my absolute need for writing[.]" (DeFrees, *Massachusetts Review* 265)

The poem that follows was first published in 1966, a year after the end of the Vatican II Conference, and a year before DeFrees was granted permission to step out of the religious and into the secular sphere to take a position teaching at the University of Montana. The 1960s were a time of unprecedented liberalism in the Roman Catholic Church. For a time, the repressive lid had been lifted. In a dramatic shift from her earlier poems, in "Orthopedic," DeFrees's authorial "I" is fully present, struggling to reconcile her desire for freedom with her religious vow of obedience. In its desperate plea for divine grace, DeFrees's poem is reminiscent in tone of John Donne's holy sonnet, "Batter my heart, three-person'd God" (285).

ORTHOPEDIC

Many times in dreams I awake
in a hospital bed, my foot or hand
remote on a plaster cross overhead,
suspended beyond my control
where extremities join in rivets of pain. (*When Sky Lets Go* 30)

In recurring dreams the speaker wakes into a state of agonizing, dismembered crucifixion. The speaker's limbs are distant, and the cross to which they are pinned is made of "plaster," the cheap material of a hypocritical, false saint. Furthermore, the speaker's hands and feet, which should be instruments of creativity and volitional movement are "beyond (her) control" and only cause pain.

A wave from the sterile brain goes out:
O lost among women, reclaim
your inheritance of nerve and bone,
rein in your disobedient members and observe
today's fast for tomorrow's famine.
Where you have been will carry you. (*When Sky Lets Go* 30)

Although the speaker's brain enjoins her to apply her will to control her arms and legs and make them obey, brain, body, and will are fragmented.

The brain is "sterile," and the advice it offers to "observe / today's fast for tomorrow's famine" makes no logical sense, and suggests there is no possibility for nourishment within the world of the poem. Nevertheless, the stanza ends with a hope that the speaker's past experiences will aid in her healing.

> All the world appears ambidextrous.
> Slight of hand and fleet of foot
> acrobats and dancers move to music,
> pirouette on a dime, or hand-over-hand
> mount ropes to the improbable top
> while I clump, heavy-handed, on club feet,
> a lump of deactivated matter,
> or black blob on a stick. (*When Sky Lets Go* 30)

The speaker decries her crippled, impotent state. From her perspective, all other creatures move through the world with extraordinary facility. She alone is lifeless and without volition. The penultimate image in the stanza is a backwards version of God's creation of Adam in Genesis: the "breath of life" has been removed from the speaker to make her a "lump of deactivated matter." The final image references both the sterility of DeFrees's life as a nun and, once again, the paralyzed shadow figures of Eliot's "The Hollow Men."

> Nevertheless, if the amoeba
> from one cell can make two
> this low life, with a little luck, may renew
> these alien extensions cemented
> and strung up there; grace lighten
> these limbs that languish like spare parts
> and fuse them with my salvaged self
> beyond the wrench and crush of each day's
> anguish on my high white shelf. (*When Sky Lets Go* 30)

Despite the poem's tone of unleavened despair in its first stanzas, the final stanza makes a radical tonal shift. The stanza is divided into two precise halves. In the first half, the speaker expresses some hope that even her "low life" might remake itself. The second half takes the form of a prayer, entreating grace to "fuse" her fragmented brain, body, and will and make her whole.

. . .

It was the years DeFrees spent in Missoula, writing within a community of other writers that loosened her ties with her order and with the Catholic Church. "When I went to Montana," DeFrees said, "I realized trees just didn't pack it. I began writing things much bolder" (DeFrees, *KUOW*). In 1973, six years after taking the teaching position in Missoula, Madeline DeFrees followed her poetic exploration out of the Order of the Holy Names of Mary and Jesus and fully into the world of artistic freedom.

The Madeline DeFrees I first met in 1975 was buzzing with intellectual and poetic energy. Her workshops were electric, and conversations with her often seemed to begin *in medias res* with some idea she'd been pursuing. In *"Psalm for a New Nun"* DeFrees expresses both her psychological intensity at that time and her astonishment at the widening possibilities of life beyond the convent.

> *My life was rescued like a bird from the fowlers' snare.*
> It comes back singing tonight in my loosened hair
>
> as I bend to the mirror in this contracted room
> lit by the electric music of the comb.
>
> With hair cropped close as a boy's, contained in a coif,
> the years made me forget what I had cut off.
>
> Now the glass cannot compass my dark halo
> and the frame censors the dense life it cannot follow.
>
> Like strength restored in the temple this sweetness wells
> quietly into tissues of abandoned cells;
>
> better by as much as it is better to be
> a woman, I feel this gradual urgency
>
> till the comb snaps, the mirror widens, and the walls recede.
> With head uncovered I am no longer afraid.

Broken is the snare and I am freed.
My help is in the name of the Lord who made
heaven and earth. Yes, earth. (*When Sky Lets Go* 50; italics in
   original)

The poem begins with a passage from Psalm 124, a song of thanksgiving for
the Israelites' divine deliverance from mortal danger. Although the poem
is written in a psalmic form, after the opening quote, it segues immediately
into the sensuality of the poem's scene. The speaker bends before a mirror
symbolic of imagination and truth. All that was suppressed in DeFrees's
earlier poems is fully present here. Rather than being fragmented, the
speaker's body has been restored in marvelous joyous triumph, and she
inhabits it. Life in the world is not shadowy and insubstantial; it is "dense,"
and it crackles with energy. The speaker is not one of many insubstantial
Sisters; she is *a* woman, and it is good to be just that.

The speaker's activity before the mirror—her pursuit of truth through
practicing her art—reaches a crisis and cannot be contained. In the final
stanza, the poem returns to the psalm, acknowledging divine interven-
tion. However, the Lord is being thanked not just for creating heaven.
Ultimately, the promise in the world of the poem is not beyond the grave,
but here, on "Yes, earth."

. . .

In 1979, DeFrees left the University of Montana to take a job at the Uni-
versity of Massachusetts-Amherst, where she directed the MFA program
from 1980 to 1983. She remained in Amherst until her retirement in 1985.
However, she has continued to teach and publish. In all, she has published
eight volumes of poetry. Her latest book, *Spectral Waves* (2006) was pub-
lished by Copper Canyon Press.

In the forty years since DeFrees left the convent she has stayed rooted
in the sensuality that swelled "quietly into . . . abandoned cells" in those
early days of astonishment. She has also continued to be amazed by the
possibilities of artistic freedom. Her most recent work is reminiscent of
Shelley and Wallace Stevens in that it combines the sharply seen detail
of material existence with a powerful homage to the transformational
powers of the imagination.

Lodged in a bony orbit in the skull, the eye
is slower than the hand
and more inclined to doubt in spite of
what the old saw claims: *Seeing is believing.*
This was not the case with skeptic
Thomas, who put his unbelieving hand
into the Master's wounded side ("Two Poems")

Although the poem is entitled "*The Eye*," the eye's ancillary position is imme-
diately emphasized by its personification as a dweller—it's "lodged"—in
the skull. In addition, the eye is "slower than the hand" and "more inclined
to doubt." DeFrees is slyly introducing the major theme of the poem: the
dynamic relationship between the senses, represented by the eye, and the
artistic imagination, represented by the hand. Although the powers of the
senses are remarkable, ultimately, it is the artistic imagination that orders
and transforms what the senses merely apprehend.

and only then
declared his faith. I trust the eye; it winnows
wheat from chaff. And in the furnace, separates
true metal from slag. An eye for minimal
upheaval proves a mode of second
sight: the anthill army's small
earthmoving crew. ("Two Poems")

DeFrees illustrates the notion that the senses aren't always sufficient
with the story of the Apostle Thomas from the Gospel of John. However,
although the senses may not be sufficient, they are necessary: the speaker
trusts the eye, and goes on to give examples as evidence for that trust. The
last example, the minutia of the anthill, playfully proposes that our first
view of things might be superficial, and that there are myriad levels that
will open to us if we would only look more deeply.

Wrought-iron handrails
filigreed with spider-cloth, sequined with dew.
Half-open clematis against

a chain-link fence, their creamy lemon
shading into white. Blue-black sky
swept clean with brushwork in the evening
light and winter-bare japonica's faint
flush of green before the leaves come out. ("Two Poems")

This delicately beautiful stanza is an illustration of what Stevens called
the "activity" that is reality (110–11): what has been literally seen is then
transformed by its interaction with the seer's imagination and put into
words in the form of a poem. Shelley put it this way in his poem, "Mont
Blanc":

My own, my human mind, which passively
Now renders and receives fast influencings,
Holding an unremitting interchange
With the clear universe of things around[.] (348)

In contrast to the abstract "domed summer" of "Requiem Mass, Convent
Cemetery," the particularity of these lines celebrates the speaker's aston-
ishment at material existence itself. DeFrees is subtly and sweetly forcing
us into the resonant beauty of a single moment of seeing.

Because the eyes are windows on the soul, wise
men close the curtain. Hoard rivers of bright
color. When words arrive with hearts
pinned to their sleeve, the brave will plunge
the writing hand into the right-brain
wound to draw out blood and water
the doubter can believe. ("Two Poems")

However, seeing is not where the poem ends. Although the eye is acknowl-
edged as being marvelous, in the end, it remains for the activity of the
artistic imagination, and specifically, for poets, to make believers out of
skeptics. DeFrees's "wise men" are much like Shelley's ". . . wise, and great,
and good, [who] / Interpret, or make felt, or deeply feel" (348). The wise
men of this stanza are "brave" in all the vibrant senses of the word: wild
and fierce, as well as courageous and gallant. They are also creatures of
the very "earth" DeFrees threw her lot in with when she wrote "Psalm for

a New Nun." The final image in "The Eye" emphasizes the earthly nature of the mind; it is corporeal, made of "blood and water," the elements of bodily life.

. . .

I last saw Madeline four years ago when she came to Missoula to give a reading at the University of Montana. We met for lunch, and although I hadn't seen her in a quarter of a century, her intellectual intensity was undimmed. If anything, being 89-years-old seemed to have made her intellectually sharper, and it had certainly increased her urgency. We talked about—what else—poetry, about its function and its necessity.

Directly afterwards, I had to go to a political event at which I'd agreed to speak. When I got to the event I was still very much under the thrall of our conversation. Madeline's ideas and intensity were still with me, so much so that I had to find a quiet space to recalibrate and come down out of the sublime into the ordinary. In an interview on Seattle Public Radio in 2009 the urgent Madeline I know expressed her relationship with her craft in this way: "Dick Hugo used to say it wasn't the person who could write the best double sestina, but it was the person who needed to write. I think I have that need" (DeFrees, KUOW).

WORKS CITED

DeFrees, Madeline. Interview with Carol Ann Russell. "An Interview with Madeline DeFrees." *Massachusetts Review* 23.2 (Summer 1982): 265–69. Print.
———. Interview with Marcie Sillman. KUOW. KUOW, 2009. Web. 29 January 2013.
———. (as Sister Mary Gilbert). *From the Darkroom*. Indianapolis: The Bobbs-Merrill Co., 1964. Print.
———. "Two Poems." *Image* 41 (Winter 2003–2004): 78–79. Web. 14 October 2013.
———. *When Sky Lets Go*. New York: George Braziller, Inc., 1978. Print.
Dickinson, Emily. "Safe in their Alabaster Chambers." *The Complete Poems of Emily Dickinson*. Ed. Thomas H. Johnson. Boston: Little, Brown and Company, 1960. 100. Print.
Donne, John. "Batter my heart, three-person'd God." *Complete Poetry and Selected Prose*. Ed. John Hayward. London: The Nonesuch Press, 1962. 285. Print.

Hopkins, Gerard Manley. "As kingfishers catch fire, dragonflies draw flame." *Poems and Prose of Gerard Manley Hopkins*. Ed. W. H. Gardner. Harmondsworth: Penguin Books, Ltd., 1963. 51. Print.

Shelley, Percy Bysshe. "Mont Blanc." *The Complete Poetical Works of Percy Bysshe Shelley*. Ed. George Edward Woodberry. Boston: Houghton Mifflin Company, 1901. 347–49. Print.

Stevens, Wallace. "Reality Is an Activity of the Most August Imagination." *Opus Posthumous*. Ed. Samuel French Morse. New York: Alfred A. Knopf, 1957. 110–11. Print.

The Holy Bible: New Revised Standard Version. New York: Oxford University Press, 2006. Print.

PART 5   HUGO REVISIONED

Photo by Brian Herbel

CHAPTER 15

The Dixon Bards

DAVID W. GILCREST *(Missoula, Montana)*

I was of three minds,
Like a tree
In which there are three blackbirds.
—Wallace Stevens, "Thirteen Ways of Looking at a Blackbird"

EAST OF PARADISE

In this essay I would like to offer a meditation on perception, memory, and
the imagination in Montana poetry. Such an inquiry necessarily evokes
an essential mystery, the capacity of language, of art more generally, to
connect us to the land, our world, each other, even as it inevitably distorts
what we see and understand, even as it gets in the way. Thus we begin in
paradox, and, as it turns out, a little east of Paradise, along Hwy 200 and
the Flathead River.

A set of poems triggered by the same place will be my focus. It is a rare
privilege to be able to read together poems that share a common genesis,
especially when the poets involved include those whose work is rightfully
regarded by many as synonymous with Montana literature.

The poems under consideration here demonstrate the power of desire
and the play of imaginative vision thrown into productive relief in poems
that are ostensibly "about" the same place. As one of our poets, Richard

Hugo, has argued, the process whereby particular subjects are necessarily transformed *in their writing* is the single virtue of poetic treatment. The initial subject, in this case a town in Western Montana, may be the *raison d'être* of the poem, but in itself it can only lead the poet and reader to "the real or generated subject, which the poem comes to say or mean" (Hugo 4). Each poem bears the indelible imprint of the poet's sensibilities, a kind of psychological and aesthetic signature. In this sense, the poem's subject serves as a kind of projection screen for the poet's creative associations. Much of the work and pleasure of reading poetry like this involves tracing those associations.

While it is true that each poem here represents a transaction between the poet and a place, it is equally true that, between the lines, these poems are in dialogue with one another. In the case of the first three poets we will consider, the poems are literally the result of shared experience and conversation. The fourth poem is an explicit response to the first three. Taken together, these poems offer an illuminating record of creative influence encompassing place, poets, and their poetry.

THREE GUYS WALK INTO A BAR

"The story is legendary. It begins like an old joke: 'Three guys go into a bar,' and people tell it again and again" (McCue 88). So writes Frances McCue in her wonderful book, *The Car That Brought You Here Still Runs* (2010). It is the winter of 1969–1970, a few months before the shooting of students at Kent State University and the deaths of Janis Joplin and Jimi Hendrix. The country is on edge thanks to the metastasizing war in Vietnam and waves of political violence and urban rioting. The "three guys" who walk into the bar include Hugo, at the time the director of the University of Montana's Creative Writing Program, James Welch, a former student of Hugo's on the verge of his own very distinguished writing career, and J. D. Reed, then a graduate student in creative writing at the university. The bar is in Dixon, Montana, where the Flathead River turns west before joining the Clark Fork west of Perma.

As the story goes, the three men stopped at the Dixon Bar for refreshment and conversation after spending the day together ice fishing. Under the beneficent influence of a number of rounds, the trio decided to write individual poems about the bar to be published together. And so it came to pass that readers of *The New Yorker* opened up the October 10, 1970, issue to find three poems published side-by-side on page 48 entitled "The Only Bar in Dixon."[1]

The publication of the three poems, coupled with the literary achievements of all three writers, served to put the Dixon Bar on Montana's literary map. Roughly speaking, the Dixon Bar is to Montana poetry more or less what New York City's Algonquin Hotel is to fans of Dorothy Parker, and what Tintern Abbey is to British Romanticists. Creative writing students, and other enthusiasts, trek to Dixon with some regularity, pilgrims to the shrine. Rumors regarding the Dixon Bar abound.

FOUR GUYS WALK INTO A BAR

Like most legends, the story of the Dixon Bards takes some liberties with reality. For example, it turns out that there were in fact four members of the expedition that day. Dwight Yates, another graduate student who was working on a masters' thesis on Nabokov at the University of Montana, recalls the day in some detail:

> Dick and Jim and I drove south in Dick's yellow Buick convertible toward the Bitterroot to pick up J.D. Reed who emerged wearing maybe a $1000 of Eddie Bauer and packing almost that in fishing equipment [. . .] I really can't remember the lake, but of course it was up north so that returning that afternoon, Dixon was the likely stop. Here I have to stretch, but I think there was a pool table, Tammy and Johnny and the other guy who sang about behind closed doors on the box, jars of jerky, maybe pickled eggs, and that woman tending bar. I think a couple of us played pool while Dick nursed his drink and sponged ambiance. And then we were done and back out in the bright light slanting off the snow

....

1 The story has been recounted variously by a number of writers, including Kim Stafford ("At the Only Bar in Dixon" in *James Welch*. Ed. Ron McFarland. Lewiston, ID: Confluence Press, 1986) and Vince Devlin ("One bar, two weeks, three poets, one title" in the *Missoulian* March 10, 2002). McCue's book prompted a slew of writers to revisit the story, including Michael Moore ("Poetry of place: Following Richard Hugo reveals truths, real and imagined" in the *Missoulian* May 3, 2010) and Azita Osanloo ("Triggering towns: McCue thoughtfully traces Hugo's path" in the *Missoula Independent*, May 13, 2010).

and into the yellow Buick convertible. "Gee," Dick said, addressing Jim and J.D. who were in back, "let's all do a poem about that bar, maybe get them published somewhere together." Maybe some resistance from the back seat. "This is an assignment. Your teacher has spoken." (Yates)

Yates's first-person account challenges some of the lore surrounding the legend (and some of the details deployed by the poets). As Yates tells the story, there is no mention of the quartet running into any Indians that day. According to Yates, the idea for the poetic hat trick was rooted in Hugo's challenge to the younger poets in the group (Yates, as a literature student with a bias toward fiction, was not included in the challenge). And while Welch would later describe the placement of the poems in *The New Yorker* in an interview with Don Lee as "a fluke," (194) it's clear from Yates's account that Reed's connection at that magazine increased the odds at least marginally.[2]

Hugo's own response to the assignment begins with a calm recognition, or declaration, of belonging:

THE ONLY BAR IN DIXON

Home. Home. I knew it entering.
Green cheap plaster and the stores
across the street toward the river
failed. One Indian depressed
on Thunderbird. Another buying
Thunderbird to go. This air
is fat with gangsters I imagine
on the run. If they ran here
they would be running from
imaginary cars. No one cares
about the wanted posters
in the brand new concrete block P.O.

This is home because some people
go to Perma and come back

....

2 Yates recalls Reed saying "he knew someone at *The New Yorker*," perhaps Howard Moss, who "could get them in the door."

from Perma saying Perma
is no fun. To revive, you take 382
to Hot Springs, your life savings
ready for a choice of bars, your hotel
glamorous with neon up the hill.
Is home because the Jocko
dies into the Flathead. Home because
the Flathead goes home north northwest.

I want home full of grim permission.
You can go as out of business here
as rivers or the railroad station.
I knew it entering.
      Five bourbons
and I'm in some other home.

    ("Three Poems on the Same Theme" 48)

With the two-beat repetition of "Home," a kind of verbal talisman, Hugo
seems to savor his surroundings, the familiar wonder of it all. But before
the poem risks lapsing into some kind of sentimental domesticity, Hugo
insists on grit, sketching a town down on its heels:

Green cheap plaster and the stores
across the street toward the river
failed. One Indian depressed
on Thunderbird. Another buying
Thunderbird to go.

Here, Hugo trades in cliché, in stereotype: a Montana reservation bar and
its drunken Indians. Or is this realism, the poet as cultural anthropologist?
If this is "Home," are these Indians cousins, brothers, or merely local color?
    The tone of the poem changes abruptly in the next lines as Hugo swerves
into fantasy:

      This air
is fat with gangsters I imagine
on the run. If they ran here
they would be running from

imaginary cars. No one cares
about the wanted posters
in the brand new concrete block P.O.

Hugo's evocation of "gangsters" is extremely odd, literally out of place (not to mention time) in a part of the country more accustomed to "outlaws" and "vigilantes." And the image of these imaginary gangsters "running from / imaginary cars" is also strangely metonymic. Like the paranoid gangsters, the reader struggles to fill the seats of the imaginary cars with imaginary G-Men, or some such. Of course, Hugo's flight of fancy here is meant in part to further his psychological portrait of Dixon. In the Dixon of his imagination there is indifference toward, or tolerance of, men on the lam: "No one cares / about the wanted posters / in the brand new concrete block P.O." The "brand new concrete block P.O." stands in stark contrast to the rest of Dixon with its "Green cheap plaster" and failed stores. As a symbol of governmental authority, as well as law and order (thus the wanted posters), the post office fails to command respect and loyalty in this place, an attitude Hugo subtly underscores by referring to it by the colloquially abbreviated "P.O." Gangsters, it appears, need worry only about their own shadows.

In the lines that follow Hugo ironizes the sense of home and belonging with which he begins the poem:

This is home because some people
go to Perma and come back
from Perma saying Perma
is no fun.

Here, Hugo considers how it is (at least) "some" residents come to regard Dixon as home, not by virtue of its own endearing qualities, but only because Perma, the next town down the road, "is no fun." This is a joke, perhaps, but one that communicates the weary pathos of limited horizons and even more limited expectations to be found in parts of America, rural or otherwise.

Hugo goes on to write:

To revive, you take 382
to Hot Springs, your life savings

ready for a choice of bars, your hotel
glamorous with neon up the hill.

Who needs revival? Hugo transforms the ultimately disappointed "some people" who journey to Perma looking for fun into a "you" that includes and encompasses the reader and, arguably, the poet himself. Having pinned your hopes on a trip to Perma, you now know better, and the neon lights of Hot Springs beckon. Hugo understands the shape of desire. Our need directs us elsewhere, whether to Perma, or Hot Springs, or to a bottle of Thunderbird. And to live again (*re+viva*) we turn our backs on home, at least until our "life savings" run out. Here, home is a deep gravity well and escape to an unlikely dream.

Hugo's dark revision of home continues in the final lines of the poem. Dixon (or the Dixon Bar itself, the syntax is fluid to the point of obscurity) "Is home because the Jocko / dies into the Flathead." The life of the Jocko River ends at Dixon, its unique character absorbed and obliterated by the larger Flathead River. Just as the Flathead is itself destined to die into other bodies of water, the Clark Fork near Paradise, the Columbia, ultimately the Pacific Ocean: "Home because / the Flathead goes home north northwest." "I want home full of grim permission," confesses the speaker. But what kind of permission is this? As children we bridle against the dictates of our parents, the constraints of home. We imagine a life of freedom, pursuing our passions, fulfilling our desires. But Hugo's "grim permission" anticipates an ultimate dissatisfaction. "You can go as out of business here / as rivers or the railroad station." If this is home, it is as home to failure and death as it is to life and liberty. Perhaps more so.

"I knew it entering," recalls Hugo, in a concluding refrain that now sounds rueful. "Five bourbons / and I'm in some other home." The insistent metaphor of home, writes Frances McCue, serves only to underscore "the insatiability of the speaker's longing for a place to belong" (94). Have the five bourbons transported Hugo into this new home of the Dixon Bar, grim permission self-administered? Or has the Dixon Bar, and its promise of home, simply dissolved, another iteration of Perma and Hot Springs, of desire and its inevitable disappointments? "It's a melancholic wish-come-true," writes McCue, "because the 'other home' is an alcoholic haze, a false peace earned through drinking" (94). We are reminded of Dorothy's mantra at the end of *The Wizard of Oz* (1939), "There's no place like home." For Dorothy, this is a statement of faith in the virtues of her domestic life back in Kansas, purchased through harrowing experience. Hugo's poem reflects a darker, ultimately tragic truth embedded in the cliché. Not only are we unlikely to discover a more ideal home for ourselves, try as we might, we may also discover we can't return to the home we left behind.

Although sharing the same title, Welch's contribution operates in a very different emotional register. The pronoun "I" appears five times in Hugo's lyrical poem, and not at all in Welch's, a fact that signals the latter's more pronounced concern with larger social and historical contexts:

THE ONLY BAR IN DIXON

These Indians once imitated life.
Whatever made them warm
they called wine, song or sleep,
a lucky number on the tribal roll.

Now the stores have gone the gray
of this November sky. Cars
whistle past, chrome wind, knowing
something lethal in the dust.

A man could build a reputation here.
Take that redhead at the bar—
she knows we're thugs, killers
on a fishing trip with luck.

No luck. No room for those
sensitive enough to know they're beat.
Even the Flathead turns away,
a river thick with bodies,

Indians on their way to Canada.
Take the redhead—yours for just a word,
a promise that the wind will warm
and all the saints come back for laughs.

("Three Poems on the Same Theme" 48)

Indians appear immediately in Welch's poem. We are told in the first line that "These Indians once imitated life," a statement rife with complexity. The identity of "These Indians" is not offered. After reading Hugo's poem we might envision his Indians "depressed on Thunderbird." Welch handles these Indians gently, without explicit judgment: "Whatever made them warm / they called wine, song or sleep, / a lucky number on the tribal roll." But what does it signify that they "once imitated life"? The phrase suggests a kind of inauthenticity—mere imitation, a facsimile of living. Is Welch implying that such imitation belongs to their past? That they now live actual life rather than imitate it? If so, it's a strange and ambiguous sort of authenticity, a "warmth" made possible by wine, song, sleep, or luck. And is the observation aimed at particular individuals, specific Indians seen in or around the Dixon Bar? How can the poet claim to know their past? Or is it a more general claim, these specific Indians standing in metonymic relationship to the tribes native to Western Montana, the Salish, Kootenai, and Pend d'Oreille, the Flathead Nation? At what point in the past would these tribes have "imitated life"? A more conventional historical perspective would suggest the tribes lived more authentically in the past, prior to contact with white Americans and the ensuing cultural onslaught (not to mention the creation of the Flathead Reservation, and the town of Dixon).

Another possibility is that Welch intends "life" here to mean, implicitly, something like "white life," or "life as defined by the dominant white culture." Thus the claim might point to Indians, individually or collectively, who tried, for a time, to live and work within an alien cultural context. Having failed at the project of "imitating" such a life, these Indians are now defined by the pursuit of "warmth" through various stratagems. On this reading, there is no claim of current authenticity, only an accounting of a kind of "life" imitated unsuccessfully.

Like Hugo, Welch registers the fading of Dixon's architecture: "Now the stores have gone the gray / of this November sky." (The "November Sky" here represents some poetic license, as the ice fishing trip most likely occurred sometime during the winter months. Welch needed a gray sky, and a "January sky," say, would have broken the iambic beat.) And also like Hugo, Welch images cars in his poem: "Cars / whistle past / chrome wind, knowing / something lethal in the dust." These cars appear somewhat more realistic than Hugo's, and the metaphor of the rushing cars as a "chrome wind" is evocative of actual highway traffic, but then again Welch's cars are also anthropomorphized machines capable of "knowing / something lethal in the dust." We can naturalize the image by seeing the cars themselves as a lethal force kicking up highway dust in their passing. A stranger and more ominous reading is the more literal one: there is something lethal in the dust itself, blown by the chrome wind, exposing the residents of Dixon to an environmental hazard.

"A man could build a reputation here." Welch's choice of verb is crucial. Reputations can be made, but some are built, painstakingly, over time. There is something about Dixon, this place where one might go after abandoning the struggle to imitate life, its dust the dust of endings, of death, that affords the crafting of notoriety. "Take that redhead at the bar," the poet says. To "Take the redhead" would be to regard her clearly. Suddenly we find ourselves in the Dixon Bar. But the imperative "Take that redhead" also carries with it the implication of sexual conquest, if not rape. Here, Welch deploys his own outlaw rhetoric, even more sensational than Hugo's "gangsters": "she knows we're thugs, killers / on a fishing trip with luck." Welch's eruption into melodrama undercuts itself; "on a fishing trip with luck" is too over-the-top to be taken seriously, by the redhead whose perceptions he is imagining, and certainly by the reader, especially a reader who knows the poem's genesis is a real fishing trip. The speaker and his colleagues may be "thugs" and "killers," but only to the trout one assumes they pulled through the ice earlier that day.

"No luck," the poet concludes, referring both to the ostensible result of their "fishing trip with luck" and, syntactically at least, to his conviction that "A man could build a reputation here." "No room for those / sensitive enough to know they're beat." Unlike the Indians seeking warmth at the beginning of the poem, and perhaps the bartender, the speaker and his poetic fishing buddies are seemingly sensitive enough to know when they've been beaten. And this knowing marks their estrangement from the world of the Dixon Bar, marks their literal displacement. As in Hugo's poem, for Welch Dixon's promise of home proves eminently elusive.

Welch then turns to the river across the highway and railroad tracks. Like those "sensitive enough to know they're beat," the Flathead finds no home in Dixon: "Even the Flathead turns away, / a river thick with bodies,

/ Indians on their way to Canada." The Flathead River carries the sensi-tive knowledge of suffering and death as it carries the bodies of Indians toward Canada, a macabre and ironic echo, I believe, of Chief Joseph's unsuccessful attempt to evacuate the Nez Perce through Montana to the safety of Canada in 1877.

"Take the redhead," he concludes, "yours for just a word, / a promise that the wind will warm / and all the saints come back for laughs." Again, Welch's syntax contributes to the poem's rich ambiguity. The redhead, an object of desire, may be had "for just a word," if your word serves as a "promise" that the wind will (always?) keep one warm, a "promise" that suffering and death can be transformed by divine warrant, in the knowing laughter of the saints. In the absence of such meteorological and meta-physical certainty—that is, in the realm of our ordinary humanity—such promises necessarily ring hollow, an imitation of truth lying outside our ken. Or maybe the redhead herself represents such promises, and in the fantasy of taking her with our word(s) we fool ourselves into believing in the possibility of their fulfillment. Not sensitive enough to know when we are beaten, by our own desire and limitation, or by an at times brutal world, we crawl inside our warm dreams, forgetting while we can the cold seeping in at the edges.

Hugo places himself and the reader directly in the Dixon Bar. Welch's approach is more oblique, glancing as it does at the Indians, the fatigued buildings of Dixon, and the ominous highway that serves as the bar's doorstep. Reed's poem begins at a further remove:

THE ONLY BAR IN DIXON

Dixon gleams through a six-power
scope on a deer rifle, bar lights wink
in the cross hairs, footprints of drunk braves
weave in bone-dust snow,
a wine-stained version of fox-and-geese:
this shack-pocked village a lumbar vertebra in the spine
of the Rockies grates on its cartilage neighbor, death.

Trucks creak in frost,
white-faced cattle stare

at the blizzard cloud massing near the valley's rim.
Hay freezes from inside-out—
a failure of combustion in the gut.
For sale in the bar: a shotgun, an electric guitar,
wine by the glass, some medals from a war, ten minutes' warmth.

The deck of night shuffles
its sad, animated face
over fields of thistles and sage, over trout
lined up like exclamation points
under ice. The moon nestles in dank hair,
in the black hair of Flatheads sweating
in a pickup truck, whooping against the windows.

The dance on earth's crust throbs,
beaver hear it on the dams,
otters in their muddy slides. The ankle bells chatter,
bone bracelets clack,
a gourd beats its seeds to death,
and the chief shines with bear fat under a skull;
ghost dancers swaying from the hips—cartridges in a belt.

("Three Poems on the Same Theme" 48)

"Dixon gleams through a six-power / scope on a deer rifle, bar lights
wink / in the cross hairs." In Montana, the deer rifle is a practical tool,
not menacing in itself. But as Reed trains it on the lights of Dixon, the
rifle begins to suggest murderous possibility as it emphasizes the physical
and emotional distance between the speaker and his subject. The now-
inevitable Indians first appear in their absence: "footprints of drunk braves
/ weave in bone-dust snow, / a wine-stained version of fox-and-geese."
Reed's "drunk braves" can be seen as a more playful, oxymoronic version of
Hugo's Thunderbird-drinkers. And the "bone-dust snow" artfully captures
the quality of snow during extreme cold. (Ice fishing is a frigid business,
of course, so it's no wonder that all three poets were attentive to warmth
and its absence in their poems.)

At this point Reed risks an obviously poetic conceit, a melodramatic
metaphor that attempts to capture the unique character of Dixon: "this

shack-pocked village a lumbar vertebra in the spine / of the Rockies grates on its cartilage neighbor, death." (Dixon lies roughly a hundred miles west of the Continental Divide; a geographical purist is unlikely to place Dixon on the spine of the Rockies.) As in the poems by Hugo and Welch, death haunts Dixon; here it is a "cartilage neighbor."

In place of the menacing cars of Hugo and Welch, Reed offers vehicles more at home in an agricultural landscape: "Trucks creak in frost, / white-faced cattle stare / at the blizzard cloud massing near the valley's rim." The emphasis again is on the cold, the trucks creaking in the frost. "Hay freezes from inside-out," he writes, "a failure of combustion in the gut."

When he finally turns to the bar, Reed captures more specific details than either Hugo or Welch (and, like Welch, the bar's role as a haven from the cold): "For sale in the bar: a shotgun, an electric guitar, / wine by the glass, some medals from a war, ten minutes' warmth."

But Reed's treatment of the bar itself is quite brief; indeed, as the balance of the poem demonstrates, he seems much more interested in Dixon's mythopoetic potential. In setting up the end of the poem, Reed again chooses self-consciously poetic language, moving steadily away from the realism the poem initially embraced:

The deck of night shuffles
its sad, animated face
over fields of thistles and sage, over trout
lined up like exclamation points
under ice.

As metaphor, "The deck of night" shuffling "its sad, animated face" doesn't really work (after all, a deck of cards has many faces), especially next to the lucid image of the "trout / lined up like exclamation points / under ice." Reed needs to remind the reader that it is night, a fact probably misplaced earlier (the cows must have pretty good night vision to see "the blizzard cloud massing near the valley's rim"). But then again, we are told, there is a night light: "The moon nestles in the dank hair, / in the black hair of Flatheads sweating / in a pickup truck, whooping against the windows." Reed's Indians fare better than either Hugo's or Welch's. They seem happily, and noisily, ensconced in the cab of a pickup, together (unlike Hugo's solitary Thunderbird drinkers) and very much alive (unlike Welch's floaters).

Blessed by the moon nestling in their "dank hair," these Indians share a warmth that derives more from song, and wine, perhaps, than any sense of desperation or hopelessness; they are "sweating," a carefully chosen verb that suggests the pickup has been transformed into a kind of sweat lodge, a place of communion, vision, and renewal. (As such, wine would have no place in the ceremony.)

Indeed, in the final lines of the poem Reed leaves the bar, and Dixon, far behind, engaged now in the mythic space of the Ghost Dance:

The dance on earth's crust throbs,
beaver hear it on the dams,
others in their muddy slides. The ankle bells chatter,
bone bracelets clack
a gourd beats its seeds to death,
and the chief shines with bear fat under a skull;
ghost dancers swaying from the hips—cartridges in a belt.

It is here that Reed's poem becomes overtly, if somewhat incoherently, political in ways that distinguish it from the other Dixon Bar poems. (As I've noted, except for two somewhat incidental lines, Reed's poem doesn't really concern itself with the Dixon Bar.) The Ghost Dance was a last-ditch attempt by Indians throughout the West to redress the tragic consequences of the incursion of white Americans into Indian Country. Reed's sweating and whooping Indians conjure Ghost Dancers powerful enough to make the earth's crust throb (and beavers take notice). Presiding over the dance is a shining chief "with bear fat under a skull," the embodiment of autonomous Indian authority. He watches "ghost dancers swaying from the hips—cartridges in a belt." This last line brings us back to the beginning of the poem, the deer rifle trained on the lights of Dixon. The Ghost Dancers are "cartridges" in the sense that they represent a threat to American cultural and military hegemony.

Reed's poem elicits the question: whose "deer rifle" is this, scoping the Dixon Bar? Is the white graduate student from Michigan "playing Injun," holding that rifle himself, entertaining a violent fantasy of heroic Indian resistance? Or in a gesture of imagined solidarity is he lending potency and agency to those spiritualized Indians in the pickup?

These are difficult questions to answer. We might wonder, too, how readers of *The New Yorker* in October of 1970 would have interpreted Reed's gesture here, two years before the take-over of the BIA building in Washington by Indian activists, and three years before the occupation of Wounded Knee (and Marlon Brando's refusal to accept his Academy Award for *The Godfather* [1972]) drew attention to Native American rights in the public consciousness.

AN ENDURING PARAMOUR

Perhaps predictably, the tension between poetic realism and the creative imagination served to focus the reception of "The Only Bar in Dixon" in Dixon itself.[3] In a very brief letter to the editor of the *Missoulian* in late April of 1973, JoAnne Schmauch, the redheaded owner of the Dixon Bar, took Hugo's representation of Dixon and its bar to task:

> Mr. Hugo's unflattering poetry about the Dixon area has prompted the mayor and me to attempt to write, "An Ode to Five Bourbon Hugo." We sincerely hope he turns blue over OUR contemporary style.
>
> Had he researched his subject properly he would know there are only two kinds of people in this world, those who live in Dixon and those who wish they did.
>
> Surely he has heard the immortal words of an early-day Dixonite who wrote, "Dixon, the delightful land of plums and plenty, only 26 miles from Paradise and 42 miles to Hellgate. (4)[4]

It is somewhat curious that Schmauch singled out Hugo as the target of her good-natured objection. After all, it was Welch who suggestively references the "redhead at the bar" in his poem. In his 2002 *Missoulian* article, Vince Devlin interviewed Schmauch, who struck a fairly generous tone regarding Hugo and his poetry. "Some locals took exception," she acknowledged, adding that she "wasn't all that impressed either." Noting that Hugo patronized the Dixon Bar "quite a bit," Schmauch confessed

....

3   The summary that follows is drawn largely from Vince Devlin's *Missoulian* article and especially McCue's lively and detailed treatment in *The Car That Brought You Here Still Runs* (90–99).

4   McCue describes Schmauch's rhetoric in this letter as "Witty, sarcastic, and inflamed by the verses" (90).

that she actually enjoyed Hugo. "He was very intelligent, I think a kindly man, too. I think he meant (the poem) in a good way, but contemporary poetry doesn't register with every reader."

Hugo replied to Schmauch in a much longer letter to the editor published on May 7, 1973. In his letter Hugo takes refuge in the poetic imagination, faulting Schmauch for assuming that his poetry, or any poetry, trades in reality: "JoAnne Schmauch finds my poems unflattering to Dixon but my poems are not about Dixon," he writes. Hugo then proceeds to lecture Schmauch. "For Schamuch's edification, poems are works of imagination and are not intended to be factual accounts. If I wanted to write about Dixon, I would write an article" ("Not About Dixon" 4).

Hugo's position here may be consistent with his poetics, his sense that real places can serve to "trigger" the creative imagination, but it is also a self-serving evasion, a principle that invites "misreadings" like Schmauch's. One might reasonably ask: if "The Only Bar in Dixon" is purely a work of the imagination, and not a "factual account," why does Hugo insist on its realistic elements, including the town name and its human and geographical details? For that matter, are we to believe that Hugo's many, many poems that address specific places in Montana (and elsewhere) are completely unmoored from reality, signifying only in his personal poetic vision?

Hugo goes on to challenge Schmauch's implication that he is belittling Dixon in his poetry. "I love Dixon," he writes, "as I love all places that trigger my imagination and lead me to truth about the human condition that I can reveal." Dixon is special, Hugo argues, but not for the reasons Schmauch believes. "Schmauch's claim that all people who don't live in Dixon wish they did is nonsense and unless she is bananas she knows it. I love Dixon because a lot of people would not want to live there and many would not even notice it in any detail as they drove through." Interestingly, Hugo's defense of his love for Dixon is grounded in an appreciation for its real characteristics (as he sees them). Unlike Schmauch, Hugo sees and loves Dixon on its own terms, for what it actually is. And Dixon's reality is the grist for Hugo's poetic mill. "If I'm unflattering," he writes, "it's because I reserve flattery for places and people I'm indifferent about." Turning the tables, Hugo argues that it is Schmauch herself who is guilty of "mak[ing] moral judgments of loneliness and despair"; "I am, like any artist, only presenting," he writes ("Not About Dixon" 4).

So, on the one hand Hugo claims to be "presenting" only objective, unvarnished facts about Dixon, details he uniquely perceives, unlike the town's blinkered residents and those who drive through without really seeing. On the other hand, Hugo insists that his poetry is reflective only of his imaginative treatment and the "truth of the human condition." Hugo concludes by attacking "Schmauch's chamber of commerce platitudes" that "only cheapen what Dixon really is." "We often fool ourselves about the value of an acquaintance," counsels Hugo, "never about the value of an enduring paramour" ("Not About Dixon" 4).

McCue generously describes Hugo's response to Schmauch as "a clever retort, clipped and pedantic at the same time" (90). I find it to be both conceptually disjointed and, frankly, more than a little nasty. He is clearly not trying to communicate with Schmauch, and while McCue might be correct when she argues that "some phrasing in his *Missoulian* letter is geared toward an academic crowd" (90–91), I'm guessing that most of Hugo's colleagues in and out of the academy were likely unimpressed by the incoherence of his argument and appalled by his rhetorical excesses. McCue notes that Hugo characterized his exchange with Schmauch in self-servingly heroic terms. In a note to Jim and Lois Welch, Hugo wrote, "'Jim, Lo—Just to say that when the forces of righteousness strike, they strike hard'" (qtd. in McCue 91). Rather than righteousness, I would argue that in this instance Hugo struck only a rather low and public blow in defense of muddled and ultimately incompatible poetic principles.

IN ITS NAME ITS PURPOSE

I would like to add one final poem to this discussion of the Dixon Bar and its poems, "Epłčt eťʔu Sčilip" by Heather Cahoon, a member of the Confederated Salish and Kootenai tribes:

EPŁČT EŤʔU SČILIP

Dixon wasn't always known for its only bar.
It was a place the Pend d'Oreille
would go for plums. In its name
its purpose, *plums at junction of two rivers.*

Where the Jocko pours itself
into the Flathead, the trees,

heavy with deep purple fruit,
grew in excess. Their limbs
hung low to the ground,
under the weight of their world.

Over-ripe plums like so many things
dropped to a life of decay. The second
they fell they began to die. The end
of one life, the beginning of another.
It was a place
where plums were known to grow. (Cahoon 15; italics in original)

A range of implicit and explicit poetic strategies allow Cahoon to peel back layers of cultural and natural history in this deceptively simple poem. Standing here, where the Jocko and Flathead rivers come together—what is this place? Is it Dixon, named after former governor Joseph Dixon? Or, we might ask, is it Jocko City, its name before Dixon? Before either of these, the poem reminds us, it was, and still is, Epłčt eťu Sčilip.

It's a nifty bit of cultural reclamation, made all the niftier when we consider Cahoon's poem in the context of the Dixon Bards.

Given the iconic status of Hugo and Welch in Montana's literary circles, Cahoon's little poem is wonderfully subversive. To remind the reader in the first line that "Dixon wasn't always known for its only bar" is to insist on a deeper and more complex cultural context than that afforded by "The Only Bar in Dixon" in any of its boozy iterations. Not only was Dixon a place before Hugo, Welch, and Reed put it on the literary map, it wasn't even called Dixon. Between the title and the first line, Cahoon effectively reinforces the fact that "Dixon," as portrayed in the Dixon Bar poems, is an imaginary, fictional construct on several levels of personal and cultural history.

But is Cahoon's "Epłčt eťu Sčilip" substantively less imaginary than the Bards' Dixon? To the extent that any name is at least somewhat arbitrary, Epłčt eťu Sčilip is as unmotivated as Dixon (or Jocko City). And like the Bards, Cahoon is certainly (re)imagining this place to suit her own cultural and poetical purposes.

Even so, the poem tells us that this name is *purposeful* in ways neither Dixon nor Jocko City can claim:

It was a place the Pend d'Oreille
would go for plums. In its name
its purpose, *plums at junction of two rivers.*

The name Epłčł eťʔu Sčilip is literally grounded in a very particular eco-
logical and cultural context. As a name with a purpose, Epłčł eťʔu Sčilip
does work in the world. If you are interested in plums (and who among
us will confess not to be interested in plums?), THIS is the place to find
them, summer waxing to its fullness, where two rivers become one. We
can imagine the Pend d'Oreille imagining the sweet, juicy flesh in the
mouth, turning consciously toward Epłčł eťʔu Sčilip.

As Hugo is right to note in his letter to the editor, there are in fact many
ways to see, to know a place, some warped by familiarity, some little more
than passing fancy. With "Epłčł eťʔu Sčilip," Cahoon evokes a powerful
knowledge of place and time capable of feeding both body and soul:

Over-ripe plums like so many things
dropped to a life of decay. The second
they fell they began to die. The end
of one life, the beginning of another.
It was a place
where plums were known to grow.

In her poem, Cahoon is conscious of cycles both natural and poetic—that
what applies to plums applies equally to poets. What we desire commands
our attention, and what we love invites gratitude expressed sometimes in
words (as in poetry, or letters to the editor, or, perhaps, essays), some-
times in deeds (purple flesh dripping juice on our chin). It is a mature
vision that sees death as prerequisite and consummation. Poems begin
and end. Poets live, and write, and die, some fortunate enough to do so
under the Big Sky, their words falling like ripe plums into the fertile soil
of our collective imaginations, making Montana a place where poetry is
known to grow, and thrive.

I would like to thank Lois Welch and Dwight Yates for their invaluable
insights and generous assistance.

WORKS CITED

Cahoon, Heather. "Epłčt eỉʔu Sčilip." *Poems Across the Big Sky: An Anthology of Montana Poets*. Ed. Lowell Jaeger. Kalispell: Many Voices Press, 2007. 15. Print.

Devlin, Vince. "One Bar, two weeks, three poets, one title." *Missoulian* [Missoula, MT] 10 March 2002. Web. 15 January 2012.

Hugo, Richard. "Not About Dixon." *Missoulian* [Missoula, MT] 7 May 1973: 4. Print.

——. "Writing off the Subject." *The Triggering Town: Lectures and Essays on Poetry and Writing*. New York: W. W. Norton & Company, Inc., 1979. 3–10. Print.

Hugo, Richard F., J. D. Reed and James Welch. "Three Poems on the Same Theme." *The New Yorker* 10 October 1970: 48. Print.

Lee, Don. "About James Welch: A Profile." *Ploughshares* 20.1 (Spring 1994): 193–99. Print.

McCue, Frances. *The Car That Brought You Here Still Runs: Revisiting the Northwest Towns of Richard Hugo*. Seattle: University of Washington Press, 2010. Print.

Schmauch, JoAnne. "Land of Plums." *Missoulian* [Missoula, MT] 26 April 1973: 4. Print.

Yates, Dwight. "The Only Bar in Dixon." Message to Annick Smith. 5 Nov. 2004. E-mail.

CHAPTER 16

The Entire Poet: Patricia Goedicke's Surreal Homage to Richard Hugo

CASEY CHARLES (*Missoula, Montana*)

"And what did Dick think of THE ENTIRE CATCH?" Patricia Goedicke wrote to Ripley and Dick Hugo on May 22, 1982. "I'm still stunned at myself for daring to send it. But I had to, so I did" ("Letter to Richard Hugo"). Goedicke had recently written the poem at her home in San Miguel de Allende, Mexico, where she had returned after teaching at the University of Montana that academic year. Remarkably, given—as we shall see—the content of this work, Hugo was flattered by it. "The poem of course makes me look more heroic than I feel," he wrote back in July, "but by all means publish it—where the most will see it, ham that I am" ("Letter to Patricia Goedicke"). The ailing Hugo, who had dominated the Creative Writing program in Missoula since the 1960s, died four months later. "None of us out here have really come to grips with his going yet," Goedicke wrote to poet and editor Stephen Berg the month of Hugo's death. "[I]t was so unexpected, and so swift. It leaves much too large a hole in the landscape. He was such a dear man. And one of the greatest, too" ("Letter to Stephen Berg").

Though written shortly before his death, "The Entire Catch" captures a sense of Hugo's Montana landscape in ways that are both representational and at the same time inimitable to Goedicke's image-laden and surreal poetics. Influenced by poets like Octavio Paz and García-Lorca, Goedicke brought an element of internationalism to the Montana program, more particularly an indebtedness to the free play of thought in verse, typified by the juxtaposition of often unexpected, unrealistic, or incongruous imagery (e.g. "clear streams of association" discussed below).[1] While never as radical as the Lorca of "Poeta en Nueva York" where "furious coins" are devouring "abandoned children," Goedicke's "Entire Catch" employs its own form of surreal imagery as a means of moving beyond the confines of the regionalism often believed more indicative of Montana writers' invest-ment in the particularities of landscape and culture in the so-called "last best place."[2] Of course, Goedicke also studied with the naturalist Robert Frost, and Richard Hugo was more than capable of moving beyond the straightforward methods of realism (e.g. "[t]he blood still begs direction home" (*Making Certain* 369)), but "The Entire Catch," I will argue, uses sur-realistic technique to twist the metaphors of the iconic Montana fishing trip into a trenchant portrait of one of the Northwest's most influential writers.

Published first in *Poetry East*, Goedicke's Hugo poem later became part of her seventh collection, *The Wind of Our Going* (1985). She had returned to the University of Montana from Mexico in the fall of 1982, where she would soon join the faculty permanently until her death in 2006. Born in Boston in 1931, Goedicke studied with Robert Frost at Middlebury College and later spent over ten years living in San Miguel with her second husband,

....

1   We would be hard-pressed to create a direct link between the automatic writing or "self-induced hallucinations" that align the methodology of Andre Breton's 1924 "Manifesto of Surrealism" with Goedicke's poetry, but post-World War II surrealism brought strains of this movement that were associated more generally with a poetics of incongruous and irrational juxtapositions produced to create a new, penetrating version of reality (See Surrealism, *poets.org*).

2   Regionalism, naturalism, and realism are generic literary designations with long and complicated definitions and histories (See Pizer). In this essay, I use these terms more generally to refer to writing that retains an investment in an accurate depiction of the world, or as the Poetry Foundation describes Stephen Crane's work, representation that employs "keen observation as well as personal experience to achieve a narrative vividness and sense of immediacy" (Biography of Stephen Crane). Frost, Robert Lowell, and more recently Donald Hall come to mind. In this essay, I juxtapose the regionalism of Montana writing to Goedicke's more surreal worldview. For Lorca's New York poem, see "The Poet in New York."

writer and editor Leonard Robinson, returning in the 1980s to the States. She would publish eight of her thirteen volumes of poetry while living in Montana, including, posthumously, *Baseball Field at Night* (2009). After publishing *The Wind of Our Going* (1985), her volume, *The Tongues We Speak* (1989), became one of the *New York Times Book Review*'s best books of the year in 1990, and a decade later the American Library Association named *As Earth Begins to End* (2000) one of the best books of 2000. In reviewing Goedicke's *The Wind of Our Going* (1985) for *Small Press Review*, Hans Ostrom wrote, "More than any contemporary woman poet, perhaps, she exhibits a Whitmanesque exuberance" in her "vital and engaging work" (qtd. in "Biography of Patricia Goedicke"). *Western American Literature* called the volume "distinguished by its use of lavish images and multiple comparisons," and Hayden Carruth in *Harper's* affirmed "her good poems have a hard, truthful ring, like parables of survival" (qtd. in "Biography of Patricia Goedicke").

Goedicke later wrote her archived "Note on 'The Entire Catch'" as an introduction to a reading of the poem, a short memoir in which she conveys, in her wryly metaphoric tone, the sense of awe she felt upon arriving in Missoula. "The first time I laid eyes on the large, powerfully soft bulk of Dick Hugo, the strange rolling gait that made him look like a mound of clean laundry billowing down the hall," she noted, "I turned in the opposite direction and fled. A sort of primordial Fear of the Great, I suppose. Fortunately, though, at that point he didn't know me from a semi-colon (Note on "Catch"). But when the semicolon finally met the mound of clean laundry, Goedicke found her colleague disarming: "Dick was one of the least intimidating, most easy-going and sympathetic of men . . . he was always as pleasant and accommodating as could be." What grabbed the visiting professor, however, and what gives us a sense of the complexities of this poem's conceit, was Hugo's combination of kindness and unflinching realism. "For Dick Hugo—driven, hunkered down, darkly self-mired though he may have been in private—was a man of enormous compassion for others," Goedicke noted. "I believe he saw loss, solitude, suffering as at the very center of the human situation, for he himself as well as for others."

Goedicke's observation of Hugo's unique admixture of self-mockery, brilliance, and vulnerability may have spawned the sense of poetic license that gave rise to a poem that begins:

Flopped on the bed, in the sodden overshoe flap
Of a large heart pounding, grown too big for its chest cavity,
Below scabbed hillsides he scowls but still wallows
In gold pools of beer, in the shallows of downtown bars
Hunched over shadowy counters he casts his long lines
Warily, warily, embraces the failed slug
Each of us knows himself to be, in jagged riffs of pain
That is pure cutthroat, moody, scathing, extravagant
But never sentimental . . . (*Wind* 107)

In Goedicke's homage to her formidable predecessor—the drunk genius who put Philipsburg on the poetic map—her style brings to the raw eyes of Hugo's world her own unflinching edge, one that in its finest moments nods to a Lorca-esque surrealism while elucidating the Montana landscape she had begun to assimilate during her first teaching assignment in Missoula. Written in four dense stanzas of nine lines each, "The Entire Catch" is a surprising formal deviation from the more typical couplets of "Gloria Davila" that precedes "Catch" in the collection ("Many times I have seen innocence asleep / Beside me in the calm bedroom") or the Williams-ian short lines of the subsequent poem ("the interior music, waking / collects itself into small fluent eddies / piled up against the fence of morning").[3] "The Entire Catch" is a different kind of lyrical encomium in a collection named after a wind that "passes above us" should we ever die (*Wind* 117).

"Flopped," "hunched," and wallowing in "gold pools of beer," the scathing poet of this first stanza is casting "long lines" warily, confirming himself to be perhaps a kind of bait ("failed slug"), but also becoming the extravagant cutthroat that the angler poet sought to catch within the riffs in rivers of pain beneath "scabbed" or clearcut mountains that mark the legacy of the Montana forest products industry.[4] In Goedicke's version of Richard

....

3 "No Judgment," a poem that begins with a description of New England houses that "stand up like tombstones," is the other work in *The Wind* that adopts this long stanzaic form, unusual in this collection.

4 Drafts of the poem in the Archive show how "gold pools of beer" began as "green pools of alcohol" and in later revisions turned into this striking image of lager ("Revisions").

Hugo, we cannot tell the fisher from the fish, entangled as they are in the moody "shadows of downtown bars" in Dixon and Milltown—the haunts where Hugo found inspiration for his depiction of a different kind of Western environs.

The major conceit of the poem—poet as angler and angled—finds confirmation in Goedicke's "Letter to Hugo from Wells College," a later poem that expatiates on a Hugo diary entry, in which he is quartered in a dormitory called the Prophet's Chambers, writing about imaginary erotic encounters with Wells College co-eds ("Letter to Hugo from Wells College"). This epistolary lyric, après Hugo's own letter poems, tells Dick that he "would have been a pillowy dream in bed" no doubt, except "when the mean booze was on you." In the end, Goedicke writes, the girls never came but it really didn't matter because "the lake / is what really drew you, the girls never came / but the magical trout did." Though alluding to a New England lake in this case, Goedicke, by invoking trout fishing, reconfirms her association of Hugo with a *River Runs Through It* (1977) state of mind, where the magic of fishing almost trumps the magic of sex. "The Entire Catch" builds on that magic, with some of the same fanciful inventiveness that put Brautigan on the map with his *Trout Fishing in America* (1967).[5]

If Goedicke's dubious panegyric adopts some of Hugo's own scathing qualities in its representation of the poet as cutthroat, flop, slug, and drunk, "The Entire Catch" regains a more laudable tone in its second stanza:

> For this is no laziness but a slow, serious settling
> Into the true, the voluminous shape of a man mountain
> At home wherever he is, at typewriter or baseball diamond
> Slumped on the sidelines, in the inlets the sly ears wag
> Like fins, the gills breathe naturally, feeding
> On whatever passes by, rich sediment slipping downstream
> From derelict ranches, railroad stations, small towns,

....

5 Richard Brautigan, who owned property in Montana (near Pine Creek south of Livingston), also wrote *The Tokyo-Montana Express* (1980), a series of vignettes mostly about Tokyo, just as the counterculture classic *Trout Fishing in America* is hardly a book about angling. But Brautigan also taught at Montana State University briefly, before returning to his notorious seclusion. He committed suicide in Bolinas, California in 1984.

The outposts of all our lives crumbled into heavy silt
But picking up speed now, a distant waterfall whispers
Louder and louder, white lace speckles the brown (*Wind* 107)

Goedicke extends her conceit by turning the poet's ears into fins, his lung into a gill, his artistic observation into a "feeding / On whatever passes by, rich sediment slipping downstream." But if Hugo's trenchant depictions of rural life in the West remind Goedicke of a trout feeding near a river's inlet, her poem at the beginning of this stanza reminds us that the seemingly sodden barfly is actually settling into the shape of "man mountain," who with his typewriter is recording the travails and dereliction that characterize the "ranches, railroad stations," and "small towns" that constitute a Western landscape buried beneath myths of homes on the range under cloudless skies, a landscape that Goedicke calls the "outposts of all our lives crumbled into heavy silt." She had read enough of her predecessor's work to know how Hugo pulls no punches in describing his beloved Montana: "With so few Negroes and Jews," he writes in his famous "Map of Montana in Italy," "we've been reduced / to hating each other, dumping our crud / in our rivers, mistreating the Indians" (*Making Certain* 165). The silt Goedicke invokes harbors a struggling trout population trying to survive in arsenic-laced rivers that hold the remains of crumbled buildings in the Dixons and Milltowns Hugo immortalized in his verse, a silt carried ultimately to the waterfall of our own inevitable demise.

In the third stanza, we begin to realize that Goedicke's lyric is as much about Hugo's poetics as about the poet himself, inextricably linked as those two may be:

And suddenly he turns it, with a quick flick of the wrist
That is pure rainbow, in these rushing Montana
Clear streams of association the heart heals itself,
Tough as a pro football or a boiled egg
Quivering in its own tan jelly, a vague
Huge hunger to escape rumbles up from the boots
But the words come straight from the belt,
Buckling under to no colorless net
Of smooth nylon connections, fashionably pale polish (*Wind* 107)

The formal "turn" at this juncture of "The Entire Catch" refers to both a shift or resolution of argument, as in a sonnet, or in the case of the fly fisherman, the turn that comes with wrist action in casting. The "[c]lear streams of association" or consciousness that give Goedicke license to equate the action of the caster to the "rainbow" trout itself (which is similar to the beautiful *arco de iris* that adorns both the big sky and rupture of water in the stream) allows the poem to open up to an aesthetics of the imagination, a creative healing for the "heart" that is embedded in the clear streams which keep the myth of the Last Best Place alive, even amidst the disintegrating ranches of the previous stanza. Unfortunately, the poem's associative license produces a set of metaphoric flights ("pro football" and quivery hard-boiled eggs), which evince Goedicke's penchant for over-exuberant simile. Some of the same baroque imagining appears in "The Lap of the Body," another title in this section of *The Wind of Our Going* (1985) called "Entering the Garden." "The mind an eggplant in high heels!" (*Wind* 114), the poem begins, starting with an image, which, while fanciful and surreal, also may seem strained and outlandish to some.

For sure, boiled eggs and pro football may well be the stuff of Hugo-esque bars like The Ox in Missoula (not to speak of Rocky Mountain Oysters), but Goedicke's poem for some readers may gain a stronger foothold as it anticipates a fish rising to a fly, comparing that breach to Hugo's poetic venture, insofar as it represents "a huge hunger to escape"—what the "Note on the Entire Catch" describes as Hugo's deep understanding of the way the poet is "helpless over the misfortunes of other people, sometimes over his own." These are the words that "come straight from the belt," those Hugo lines that refuse to buckle under an easy net of "nylon connections" like regionalism and realism. No one, Goedicke tells us, can "catch" the brute force of lines like the opening of Hugo's "To Die in Milltown":

> The Blackfoot stops, funereal
> and green, and eagles headed north
> for sanctuary wait for our applause
> to fly them home. At 6 A.M.
> the fast train east divides the town,
> one half, grocery store and mill,
> the other, gin and bitter loss. (*Making Certain* 173)

In the final stanza of "The Catch," Goedicke captures some of the Anglo-Saxon diction that gives Hugo's work its power, but the thematic focus of her poem continues to be an analogy between angling and Hugo's creative cast. Remarkably, the finale of this homage also seeks to collapse poetic creation into the landscape it depicts—turning Hugo's literary heritage into a river that runs through Montana, bringing together fish, fisherman, and rivers as a vehicle for the tenor of the triad poet, poetry, and Montana:

> They leap straight up into the air, the spank
> And wily slap of their tails sweeps up casual insects, seeds
> Until there is no surface left, each facet
> Churns into downdrafts, the blunt upturned logs
> Of feelings he will not avoid rupture themselves and stand up
> So skillfully in the rapids each twig of detail
> Weaves itself to the other until the entire catch
> Is raw, lyrical, unabashed, bleeding on bright gravel
> And pulsing on the river bank, multiplying
> From shadow into sunlight the subtle sheaves thrash. (*Wind* 107–08)

The "[t]hey" that opens this stanza has as its antecedent "words [that] come straight from the belt" in the previous one, but these words are leaping in the air, slapping, spanking, and sweeping like hungry rainbows. In the next lines, these poetic "words" will transform, through Goedicke's free association, into "downdrafts" of rapids, weaving "twig[s] of detail," and finally "raw, lyrical, unabashed, bleeding on . . . gravel," each stream of metaphors exploring both the world of rivers and the process of composition—the "subtle sheaves" of poetry that multiply and thrash through the poet's career.

In "The Entire Catch," Goedicke weaves her own net, her unique poetics of a Montana where Hugo caught fish and landed a sense of people and place, loading his poems with the raw bleeding of a hooked cutthroat "pulsing on the river bank." Yet Goedicke's own freewheeling imagery takes the reader to a place where metaphors merge and coalesce in ways that Hugo's poems rarely attempted. As a result, from the leaping fish, she turns to the "blunt upturned logs / Of feelings he will not avoid," which "rupture" and "stand up / So skillfully in the rapids." For Goedicke, these snags in the river represent the emotion that often rises up in the middle of Hugo's razor-sharp portraits. They are the "the ancient kiss" that still burns out your eyes in "Degrees of Gray in Philipsburg," the vague "hope" that rises at the end of a line about a reservoir filling:

In her Note on the "Catch," Patricia was amazed how easily Dick Hugo could come to tears, though never sentimentally. "He seemed *all* heart to me," she writes, "generous, kind, full of feeling that was also clearly and intricately precise, the powerful urgent pulse of his being warmly, dazzlingly brilliant, but totally and forever vulnerable." In her poetic homage, these emotional logjams, skillfully placed and timed in Hugo's lyrics, rupture amid the twigs of details as hope emerges between multiplying bison and snowfall in "Lady in Kicking Horse Reservoir." The result, Goedicke's poem suggests, is the "raw," "pulsing" lyrics of Hugo's best work, which bleeds on the "bright gravel" like a landed trout.[6] In the protean image-shifting of the poem's final stanza, Goedicke "catches" the entire sense of Hugo and his work: the river under strain from development and industry, the angler struggling to reel in his fish, the "lyrical, unabashed" rainbow of verse thrashing on the shore.

The final line of Goedicke's poem presents a curious case study in the struggles of revision. Though the poem minimalizes punctuation throughout its thirty-six lines, giving the reader only an occasional comma to interrupt the flow of the verse, the syntax of the final two lines mimics the rupture of a tangled bank in the river. After we witness the catch on the bank, a new clause begins with the multiplying "sheaves" that "thrash" from "shadow into sunlight." This convoluted word order imitates the complex image switching that the poem has boldly undertaken throughout its exposition. In Hugo's letter to Patricia in July of 1982, his only criticism of the poem related to this final line: "The only negative thing I can say," Hugo wrote, "is that the last line is very hard to say—too many "s" sounds I think. It's odd to see it because you are a sort of master when it comes to lyrical diction, I think. But don't you think those last three words are a mouthful together?" ("Letter to Patricia Goedicke"). Goedicke's alliterative

....

6 For a look at Hugo's gravel, see Annick Smith's *Richard Hugo: Kicking the Loose Gravel Home: Richard Hugo* (1976) a popular documentary at the time of Goedicke's arrival in Missoula.

abundance, on display in this final line, underwent many attempts at revision, as the archival manuscripts demonstrate. The sheaves became "quiet" in one draft, "glittering" was added to the line in another.[7] Ultimately, the poet retains her adherence to an aesthetic that relies on a lavish exuberance for its effect, picturing sheaves that create a pattern of shadow and sun in the wind. In the end, the sheaves of Hugo's work have become the bundle of her own prolific poem making.

Goedicke's "The Entire Catch," though trenchant and unflinching in its portrait, ultimately emerges as a praise poem, aligning itself with a lyric tradition that dates back at least as far as the Surrey's "Wyatt, Rested Here," and moves forward from Keats's famous sonnet on Chapman's Homer to Auden's "In Memory of W. B. Yeats." In his now-canonical study of Shakespeare's sonnets, Joel Fineman wrote, "the poetics of the poetry of praise is important for a literary history of poetic subjectivity, for it can be shown that the assumptions of epideixis determine in particular ways not only the techniques and conceits of the praising poet but also his literary personality, i.e. the way the poet presents poetic self" (6).[8] Fineman reminds us that the poetics of praise is a kind of demonstrative speech (deixis) that foregrounds (epi) or emphasizes its own technique as much as it describes its object, thus revealing as much about the writer's poetic method as about the subject of the lyric. His observation seems particularly true in Goedicke's portrait of Hugo in "The Entire Catch." Arguably, all poetic language is at some level derivative, but the best derivation—which curiously has its root in the French *dériver* (from the river)—establishes its own unique tributary and attribution. Goedicke's poem presents a vivid portrait of Hugo and his Montana landscape, but it paints that portrait

....

7 The drafts of the poems are typed. One of the many handwritten revisions reads: "From shadow into sunlight the sheaves heave and thrash" ("Revisions").

8 In *Shakespeare's Perjured Eye* (1986), Joel Fineman's complicated argument draws on the Greek rhetorical theory of epideixis, which makes the case that praise speech, like eulogy, does more than "point to" or "show forth" the person praised (deictics are pointing words like "you" and "I," "here" and "there"); it also shows forth the demonstrative capacity of the praiser. "[P]raise is a demonstrative speech that works by showing its own showing" (6). My argument is that Goedicke's Hugo poem allows her to show off her own formidable poetic skills while at the same time admiring his.

through the wonderful extravagance of Goedicke's skill with diction as well as her bold willingness to experiment with a surrealism rare in an era nursed on the Frost-ian naturalism. "The Entire Catch" in the end introduces us to the "techniques and conceits" of a poet whose legacy and literary personality were formed by both regional and international influences, by realism and surrealism, by a Montana landscape seen through the kaleidoscope eyes of a poet who pulsed with her incomparable stream of poetic consciousness. "The Entire Catch" gives us Patricia Goedicke in her entirety.

WORKS CITED

"Biography of Patricia Goedicke." *poetryfoundation.org*. Poetry Foundation, n.d. Web. 29 May 2013.

"Biography of Stephen Crane." *poetryfoundation.org*. Poetry Foundation, n.d. Web. 29 May 2013.

Brautigan, Richard. *The Tokyo-Montana Express*. New York: Delacorte Press, 1980. Print.

"A Brief Guide to Surrealism." *Poets.org*. The Academy of American Poets, n.d. Web. 29 May 2013.

Fineman, Joel. *Shakespeare's Perjured Eye: The Invention of Poetic Subjectivity in The Sonnets*. Berkeley: University of California Press, 1986. Print.

García Lorca, Frederico. *Poet in New York: A Bilingual Edition*. Trans. Greg Simon and Steven F. White. New York: The Noonday Press, 1988. Print.

Goedicke, Patricia. "Letter to Hugo from Wells College" and Notes. 1 June 1985. Patricia Goedicke and Leonard Wallace Robinson Collection. MSS 739 Series 1, Box 17. Archives and Special Collections, Maureen and Mike Mansfield Library, The University of Montana.

———. "Letter to Richard Hugo." 22 May 1982. Patricia Goedicke and Leonard Wallace Robinson Collection. MSS 739 Series III, Box 86. Archives and Special Collections, Maureen and Mike Mansfield Library, The University of Montana.

———. "Letter to Stephen Berg." October 1982. Patricia Goedicke and Leonard Wallace Robinson Collection. MSS 739 GR Paper Series 1, Box 9. Archives and Special Collections, Maureen and Mike Mansfield Library, The University of Montana.

———. "Note on 'The Entire Catch.'" Patricia Goedicke and Leonard Wallace Robinson Collection. MSS 739 GR Paper Series 1, Box 9. Archives and Special Collections, Maureen and Mike Mansfield Library, The University of Montana.

———. "Revisions." Patricia Goedicke and Leonard Wallace Robinson Collection. MSS 739 GR Paper Series 1, Box 9. Archives and Special Collections, Maureen and Mike Mansfield Library, The University of Montana.

———. *The Wind of Our Going*. Port Townsend: Copper Canyon Press, 1985. Print.

Hugo, Richard. "Letter to Patricia Goedicke." July 1982. Patricia Goedicke and Leonard Wallace Robinson Collection. MSS 739 Series III, Box 86. Archives and Special Collections, Maureen and Mike Mansfield Library, The University of Montana.

———. *Making Certain It Goes On: The Collected Poems of Richard Hugo.* New York: W. W. Norton & Company, 1991. Print.

Pizer, Donald. *The Cambridge Companion to American Realism and Naturalism.* Cambridge: Cambridge University Press, 2012. Print.

Richard Hugo: Kicking the Loose Gravel Home. Dir. Annick Smith. Annick Smith and Beth Chadwick Films, 2006. Film.

CHAPTER 17

Riding the Right Wind Home:
Reading Ripley Schemm Hugo

KIM ANDERSON *(Missoula, Montana)*

Ripley Schemm Hugo (1929–2012) grew up in one eminent literary land-scape and lived a good part of her adult life in a second one. A respected poet and teacher who wrote and published for over forty years, she was perhaps better known as the daughter of prolific novelist Mildred Walker, as the wife of poet Richard Hugo, and as fierce friend to the West's best known writers. In her youth these included Joseph Kinsey Howard and A. B. Guthrie, Jr., friends of her famous mother and prominent physician father. After travels as a young adult and a first marriage took her away from Montana, she returned years later and became central to a literary community that included Richard Hugo, James and Lois Welch, William Kittredge and Annick Smith, Paul Zarzyski, and many others.

I can imagine how daunting it would be to take on the label poet, given these surroundings. And while her work appeared in many journals and anthologies, and although she published two collections of poetry and a memoir of her mother, she was reluctant to fully embrace the role of writer. In fact, much of her energy in later years was directed to efforts to shepherd her mother's novels into new editions, oversee her husband's and mother's archives, and preserve the legacy of her son, a poet and environmental biologist who died in his early twenties.

Her battle with self-regard most likely had its start with her demanding and occasionally critical mother. Ripley Hugo's "memoir of a writer," *Writing for Her Life* (2003), describes Mildred Walker admiringly as a disciplined and driven woman and artist, but not often as a warm maternal figure:

> When people exclaim to me about the privilege of growing up with my mother, the writer, I think of how my brothers and I grew up more keenly aware of a mother who insisted in her role . . . of a doctor's wife in a Montana town; a mother whose merriment or pleasure in shared moments seemed reserved for an occasion; a mother who insisted on decorum, performance of correctness in front of those outside the family. . . . A mother who was not easy to live up to." (*Writing* xiii)

By all accounts Ripley Hugo had a very warm and comfortable relationship with her father, a respected doctor in Great Falls, MT. She writes: "While I understood that I was 'a difficult child' in my mother's eyes, I had no such feeling about that with my father" (*Writing* xvii). She devotes several pages in the introduction to *Writing for Her Life* (2003) detailing how emotionally opposed her parents were, and favorably describing her father's compassion, respect for others no matter their station in life, and natural ease with people. Her identification with her father is underscored by the fact that her first collection of poetry takes its title from the poem, "Mapping My Father."

Ripley Schemm Hugo wrote many beautiful poems, most of them deeply tied to and inspired by the landscape of the West, the great high plains and eastern front of the Rockies where she grew up; many of them dedicated to or about dear friends and family. But a handful of poems that are either reprinted or appear for the first time in her last collection, *On the Right Wind* (2008) forego her usual style and focus, and instead feature an internal battle over voice and a desire for and anxiety about breaking free. The title of the collection itself seems to reference soaring away, and the poems that fascinate me describe an imagined leave-taking—leaving home, leaving the country, going for a walk in a strange land, the scenario of escape plays itself out in many different guises. These same poems also reference, over and over, lack of, or dissatisfaction with, voice. Of course, concerns about voice and imaginings of escape are frequent artistic themes, and every writer grapples with the bonds of the past. What's unusual, to me, in Ripley Schemm Hugo's poems is that her attempts at imaginary escape are almost always unsuccessful, not because she fails but because she ultimately turns her back on the wider world and returns home. Perhaps it's a theme that calls to me because I, too, left Montana at an early age, returning with young children years later, as she did. And, like her, my preoccupation with voice seemed linked to an early desire to flee.

These two concerns—fantasies of leave-taking and a preoccupation with voice—occur almost immediately in her last collection. "Rules" is a five-section poem that follows the trajectory of a woman's life, the first two sections describing scenes from childhood, the middle two sections set at the brink of adulthood, and the final section detailing what happens when the woman becomes an adult, a young mother. The entire poem builds to the act of leaving and returns frequently to images of voice.

In the first section, the narrator, a young girl, ponders the future.

1. SCHOOL BUS

I wait in the frozen rut
by the gate, huddled
in a red scarf wound tight
around my chin. My breath
wets the wool, wind stiffens the wool.
I figure by the shadow I stand in
how sun could reach over the rimrock
before the bus, in time
to warm my nose. I wait
for the thing to happen, the thing
I'm reaching for. I have a lot
to figure with. Whether the cow
will calve before I'm back home,
whether the hollow-cheeked kids
From Hound Creek had breakfast,
and if I can toss
my fresh-made curls
when I pass the seat
where Jim Johnson sits. (*On the Right Wind* 17)

The young girl waits not just for the school bus on a cold winter morning but for her life to begin. She is in a "frozen rut" and muffled. The dual focus of voice and being on the brink of action, of leaving, is immediate. Not only is the poet frozen and muffled, she is also standing in shadow. This seems clearly to be a metaphoric nod to both her parents and second husband, all of whom cast quite long shadows (although, not, perhaps, as long as the rimrock). Further, rather than moving into sunshine, the young girl stands and calculates how long it will take the sun to reach her and warm the tip of her nose—a passive stance that seems partly to be a game she plays but also a sign that she is frozen and without agency.

The crux of the poem arrives like the sun over the rimrock. For the second time she signals her lack of action, this time contrasting waiting with reaching: "I wait / for the thing to happen, the thing / I'm reaching for. I have a lot / to figure with." Waiting for the sun to reach her becomes a yearning for her future and already she knows that she'll get there through her mind. That curious country phrase, "I have a lot to figure with," is also the perfect description of the inner life of the introspective child.

The details of this figuring come out in the final moments of the section. While her immediate concerns are believably those of a young child— whether cows will calve, whether other kids are fed properly, whether her curls will attract the attention of a young boy—they are also the stuff of a very adult world—birth, hunger, and sex.

The second section of the poem relates another incident from childhood, again in winter. A central image involves being frozen, again concerned with speech and what it means to the poet. This time, however, the writer is more active, if, in the end, essentially mute.

2. SPEECH

To have speech perfect
rising in pitch
leading the way to my mind,
I take the pipe, the iron pipe
that shuts the corral gate
after we've milked. I take
the iron pipe in my mouth.
Thirty below and I am eight.
My brother is so afraid for me
he grabs the pipe, yanks it
out of my mouth,

the lining with it.
Then to have pain and no words
hurts less. My bloody mouth
is a kind of speech
the whole school understands. (*On the Right Wind* 18)

The section is almost hallucinatory, the language explodes in a long list of plosive p's (perfect, pitch, pipe, pipe, pipe, pain). The repetition and the rhythmic drive of the short lines add to the poem's intensity. The initial clause invites the reader into the poet's thoughts, midway. The next two lines show an eight-year-old wishing feverishly for a perfect meld of voice and thought. In her conception, "perfect" speech rises (like smoke) to her mind, rather than the more usual idea of thoughts travelling down to be spoken. Rather than ideas being vocalized, the perfect voice emerges as the written word, rather than ordinary speech.

Stranger yet, in order to achieve this union the child takes the freezing iron gate pipe and puts it in her mouth. The actualization of this common childhood horror story here takes on an almost ritualized aspect and the repetitive nature of the description of the act implies a hypnotic purposefulness. Unspoken, but somehow evoked for me, is the pure ringing of cold iron in winter—the sound the corral gate makes as it's swung shut, a vibrating peal closer to truth and perfect speech than her young voice.

Most striking, of course, is the pure visceral nature of the episode. Her brother's fear, the blood, the lining of her mouth removed, and then the startling line: "My bloody mouth is a kind of speech." By mutilating herself she achieves another kind of speech (of blood, of violence): "Then to have pain and no words / hurts less." There is a connection between muting her voice and realizing perfect speech. The pain of ripping skin from her mouth is less than the pain of not being able to express her thoughts. And there is a safety in being mute. What the school sees is simply a bloody mouth, certainly a far more ordinary and understandable sight than the strangeness this young girl feels inside.

Sections 3 and 4 of the poem are coming-of-age vignettes. Both deal with growing maturity and awareness of sexuality and the outside world. In Section 3, titled "Scales," the young woman is buying cracked corn for her 4-H calf, dealing with the old man who works at the seed store. She's nervous that he'll overcharge her, but she takes into account "I'm a tall girl in tight jeans, / small breasts bearing July sun, / eyes level with the old man's" (*On the Right Wind* 19). She knows her 4-H days are nearing an end, and almost mournfully repeats the club's mantra—"head heart hands health." As the poem concludes she watches him hook two fingers over the side of the scale to increase the weight, while she, surreptitiously, pushes up her side with a thumb. It's an adult arrangement, and the rule seems to be that everyone cheats, that you use what you can, that is what leaving 4-H behind means. The scales have fallen from her eyes.

This transition into adulthood becomes more somber and fearful in the Section 4, titled "Fire on the North Fork." The speaker is serving a meal to eighteen fire fighters on break from battling a wildfire. "Gliding" back and forth from the kitchen she feels that she is "thin help." Eventually, the reality of this particular adult world becomes clear to her:

> carry how they've been recruited
> hopeless from 2nd Street South,
> their burnt-out lives just right
> to save a canyon, a forest,
> game they'll never hunt. (*On the Right Wind* 20)

The picture of these men hunched over the long tables is not valiant or romantic. Long before this fire, their lives were "burnt-out." They are here because they have nothing better. If this is adulthood she wants no part of it. The slim young girl with braids takes in and is, "glad / my belt lies flat on my hips, / glad my mouth knows the rules" (*On the Right Wind* 20). This is the first time "the rules" are actually referred to in the poem, and they seem to include silent serving and good behavior. The rejection of the life these men embody is also a rejection of adult sexuality. She's glad she's not pregnant—her belly flat—glad she has apparently not broken any rules.

Together the first four sections of the poem seem to tremble on the rim (rimrocks) of action, of flight, of some great event. In the culminating Section, we finally get to see the great leave-taking that the first four sections have been building to. The poem begins in an exultant mode:

5. LEAVING

> One spring I leave for town,
> I leave for love,

for learning, for all
the lives I want.

Those opening four lines contain the lure of longing and yet they remain curiously abstract. Her leaving, realized after four sections of childhood and adolescence, seems unreal. While this section begins in a sense of openness and possibility, the experience seems to be almost entirely in her imagination.

Town brings a bigger town,
after that cities too big
to beg. I live all the lives
I pass on the stairs,
in the street, in the park.
I hardly know which of the women
is pushing this child in a swing. (*On the Right Wind* 21)

The town, the bigger town, the cities, are anonymous and proud ("too big to beg"). The task of living "all the lives / I pass on the street" carries a sense of claustrophobia and disorientation. These opening lines have an amazing resonance for me, recalling immediately my own move to New York City from Montana as a young woman. Both the longing to leave and, then, the sense of unreality brought on by being anonymous in a strange place exactly describe my experience.

The poet's response to this disorientation, however, is startling. Halfway through the "Leaving" she jerks herself out of her uncomfortable here and now and pays an imaginary visit to her "own life," which is still going on back at home.

My own life gets along at home
by itself. Stubs its toe
on a willow root,
coils old rope in the shed,
cuts the engine when a quail's
limp feathers fly up with the hay,
races against my heart
to the house to save the nest
of hatchlings. I leave
the morning to mold in the field. (*On the Right Wind* 21)

The poem's language instantly becomes concrete and vivid—the life she has left behind is the only one she actually knows. She describes in intense detail a daydream of morning work, coiling old rope, haying, dramatically saving a nest of quail hatchlings. In her "own life," the one she is not living, she is a central player, she is active and necessary. She doesn't have to wonder which woman she is as she pushes her child on a swing—she can see herself clearly.

The dramatic rescue described in the last half of the section refers to the narrator herself—she is the hatchling who needs to be saved, and the incident gives a nod to the act of leaving the nest. Heart racing, the narrator swoops in and saves herself from an anonymous life in the city. She leaves the morning to mold in the field.

The long poem, then, is a progression along three early stages of the poet's life, all leading toward independence and voice. In the first two sections she longs for voice, longs for "the thing to happen," the thing she's reaching for. The next two sections detail the growing awareness of adolescence, as if the poet is peeking into the adult world. In the first of these she's confident that she can operate in this world of chicanery. In the second she recoils from a grimmer reality. In the end, the writer retreats from the brink, and finds her sense of self and reality in a melodramatic fantasy of saving herself from adulthood. The quail is cut down, but the fledglings are saved.

"Rules" first appeared in Hugo's much earlier collection, *Mapping My Father* (1981), as did another poem about the allure/danger of leaving home, "View from the Kitchen." This time the cautionary tale of leaving home happens to someone else. The poem begins with an overheard anecdote, "[t]he way I heard it," and the narrator who is listening to the tale is a young girl or woman, "my feet hooked over a rung." In the shared kitchen gossip an unidentified "she" is tired of ranching, so abandons her husband and child, to escape with a travelling preacher. But,

> She came back years later
> to the same field, land
> her married daughter ranched,
> to park her pink trailer house
> with a view of the mountains.
> And maybe she sleeps without shame
> in a herd of blue lupine,
> humming hymns of the road.

A plains wind can turn us,
turn us all around. (*Mapping* 24)

While the poem starts with the disapproving tone of scandal, it takes a turn (like the wind) that tells us something about how the poet regards the impulse to escape. The abandoning woman— even more shocking, a mother—eventually returns home and is accepted back by her daughter. There is an almost wistful appreciation of this woman, as the narrator imagines her not feeling shame, parking her pink (lurid) trailer house with a view of the mountains and continuing to hum hymns of the road. The description is painterly, reminiscent of Monet with the pink house, the purple lupine, the mountains.

The final lines certainly seem ones of forgiveness, and contain a sense one comes across often in the hard lands of the West. "A plains wind can turn us / turn us all around." People in northern and eastern Montana, in particular, understand that the harshness of the land, the weather, bad fortune can overwhelm even the most stalwart. What starts as reprehensible turns to a homecoming and an acceptance of running, leaving, abandoning. The poem suggests all may be forgiven if one only returns.

As they appear in *On the Right Wind* (2008), these two poems are surrounded by many lovely paeans to the landscape and the familiar people that Ripley Hugo loved first and foremost. But the fantasy of leaving, of escape, of imagining a different life and the longing for/ambivalence about claiming a voice persists like a slow steady pulse throughout the collection. In a poem touchingly titled "Bravado," and dedicated to her mother, she writes of her mixed feelings about travel. The poem begins "Planning to go to new country / I tie the details of travel / tight in a knot my throat won't undo" (*On the Right Wind* 47). Again the poet refers to a distrust of her voice ("my throat won't undo.") linked to travel. And as in the final section of "Rules," while this poem begins with the excitement/anxiety induced by a trip, immediately after these lines the poet describes in great detail a memory of childhood in Montana.

In another poem titled "Say You Go for a Walk," an homage to Richard Hugo that takes on his conversational tone, the poet starts out in a jaunty vein as the title indicates. Before the poem's end, however, this thought experiment in being a casual, experienced traveler devolves into the same fear of anonymity and isolation that the narrator experienced in the last section of "Rules."

As the poem begins, the writer once again sets a scenario of departure:

SAY YOU GO FOR A WALK

in country not your own
one indifferent afternoon
but you leave yourself open
to the off-chance of a stray
sheep or an unpicked apple,
the off-chance this afternoon
might be startling. You use
the guile of counting on nothing. (*On the Right Wind* 51)

The narrator is determinedly unconcerned in this instance of imaginary leave-taking, the afternoon is "indifferent," off-chance is repeated twice, she uses the guile of counting on nothing. It's as if this stance will protect her from the anxiety being in a country not her own usually induces. Lovely things may happen this time around, a stray sheep or an unpicked apple.

The narration becomes increasingly anxious. In the second stanza, only three lines long, the sassy voice tightens to sound slightly desperate.

Say it's chancy, raunchy—what you
got t' lose? Such a walk requires
nonchalance in country not your own. (*On the Right Wind* 51)

The repeated "ch" sound, seven times in three lines, is like smart alecky gum smacking, a defensive attempt at that nonchalance the narrator is willing herself to have. Then, in the final stanza the facade comes crashing down:

You return to your rented
house, your table on loan.
Your stack of books waits,
says it's your place. You wish
yourself fun at some turn between
threshold and water faucet
in this country not your own. (*On the Right Wind* 51)

The promising adventure turns into a lonely, disassociated experience. What starts out as a daydream testing another life circles back inward to a sense of disconnectedness and isolation. Now, rather than an unexpected delight, an unpicked apple or stray sheep on a country lane, the poet is reduced to hoping for fun between the doorway and the sink in her depressing room, sounding more like someone trapped in a witness protection program than a jaunty wanderer in a country not her own.

Obviously, Ripley Schemm Hugo isn't literally struggling with a fear of travel in these poems. Other poems in *On the Right Wind* (2008) detail time in Europe, both before and after her marriage to Richard Hugo. And while she did spend most of her last forty years in Missoula and at her beloved family cabin on the eastern front of the Rockies, she had lived far from Montana for years before that. So what does this preoccupation with leaving really mean? The abstract nature of the fantasy suggests that the underlying desire isn't, actually, to travel someplace else. It's the thrill and excitement of being on the brink, about to take off, that seems to be the point of these fantasies. There are no detailed dreams of leaving home *for* any place. We never learn where the woman who runs off with a preacher has run off to.

These fretful visions of escape are stoked by her concerns about the legitimacy of her voice. Again, this is an anxiety that isn't supported by the body of her work—her Montana and Isle of Sky poems have a full, consistent, confident voice, an assured point of view. Perhaps that's why I find these other poems so compelling. I love the bravery the poet shows by allowing us to see her attempts to break free of influence and self-doubt.

There is a poem in *On the Right Wind* (2008) that, for me, brilliantly combines her desire to take flight with an assuredness of voice. The poet allows herself to successfully break free, and, not surprisingly, it is a place-based poem set in her beloved West. It is another imagining of travel, leave-taking. But this time, rather than stopping, the poet allows herself—in the shape of first moonlight, then water—to roam free without concern. It is as if, by freeing herself of the burden of her human construct, she can, finally, escape, free in spirit, strong in voice.

MOON MUST HAVE RIDDEN THIS RIVER

Let me down slow under the call
of whistling swan. I give him
my earbone in praise.

Here dark settles
over dark water. Long lines

of water easing the base
of these high bare hills.
Let me down easy down their slope. (*On the Right Wind* 61)

The poem begins with an exaggerated slowness. As if hypnotizing herself, the poet gives instructions: "Let me down slow" and "Let me down easy." These first two stanzas are like sinking into a not-too-hot bath, the lulling repetitions become a murmur. We're unsure what's going on, but it's clear that the poet is settling herself into a scene the way "dark settles / over dark water." And it is as if the narrative voice were looking down from a distance, testing the water, easing herself into the scene, not as a human, but as part of the landscape.

The mood shifts in the third stanza. Rather than a contemplative pastoral, the poem's rhythms quicken and consonants harden:

Once, before dams, this river
owned ridges, turned sharp, cut
bends, took curves, left cliffs—
quick with light, quicker with dark.

Moon must have ridden this river
high, low—ricocheted sly
off Swallows Nest, leaving Asotin.
Down river, passing Clarkston,
moon must have skidded to stop
at these high bare hills.
It had to, to light the Clearwater
into the Snake, already turning west.

Take me along, each curve, each stretch,
along each roll of these high bare hills. (*On the Right Wind* 61)

The poet begins the stanza with a dispassionate authorial voice, the voice of the teacher. But as the words are shortened and sharpened, the voice is no longer describing the river but is taking the river like a carnival ride. The words tumble over each other, the voice seems exhilarated, thrilled with speed and danger.

In the fourth stanza, the writer takes another tiny step back to consider the scene—"Moon must have ridden this river"—but by line two, again, the voice is one with the action, this time the moon's passage as it rides the river. The voice is the moon's, tagging place names in its wild ride with the river, Swallow's Nest, Asotin, Clarkston. Until, suddenly, the moon skids to a stop to light, again, those "high bare hills" and other rivers, the Clearwater, the Snake, turning, ever turning, west on the border of Idaho and Washington.

Finally, the poet steps back to reclaim her consciousness in the final stanza—"Take me along"—but in fact she's been on the ride, she is the ride, curling through those "high bare hills."

Unlike the other poems of travel, of escape, this one is almost purely exultant. By disembodying herself, by becoming the river and the moon, the poet has been able to finally escape the constraints of expectations, responsibilities, mindfulness.

. . .

I met Ripley Hugo in 1975, when I was eighteen. I was taking a class from her husband, Richard Hugo, and dating one of his graduate students. The Hugos were renowned for opening their homes to students, and I must have shown up there with my boyfriend—it seems like a Sunday afternoon. There was some kind of simple meal, most of the guys were in the den watching football or something. I went into the kitchen to see if I could help.

Ripley, ever gracious, tried to engage a tongue-tied near-child in conversation. I was struck, as much as anything, by her remarkable voice— somewhere between a whisper and a sexy growl. When she asked about my plans for the future I must have stammered something about considering moving to New York City with my boyfriend. She stopped slicing tomatoes, wiped her hands on a kitchen towel, and turned toward me full-on. "Oh, but you must go," she whispered, staring into my eyes.

Ripley saw me leave my hometown several months later. And then, with a smile, after fifteen years, she saw me return.

WORKS CITED

Hugo, Ripley. *On the Right Wind*. Friday Harbor: Cedar House Books, 2008. Print.
———. *Writing for Her Life: The Novelist Mildred Walker*. Lincoln: University of Nebraska Press, 2003. Print.
Schemm, Ripley. *Mapping My Father*. Story: Dooryard Press, 1981. Print.

PART 6   POETRY ACTIVISM

Photo by Brian Herbel

CHAPTER 18

The In-Betweenness of Home:
The Poetry of Judy Blunt and Paul Zarzyski

NANCY S. COOK *(Missoula, Montana)*

It is hard to overstate the effects of Dana Gioia's now-infamous essay, "Can Poetry Matter?" First published in *The Atlantic Monthly* in 1991, widely circulated, then republished many times, it laments the creation of a "large professional class for the production and reception of new poetry, comprising legions of teachers, graduate students, editors, publishers, and administrators" (219). One problem stemming from this trend is that "as American poetry's specialist audience has steadily expanded, its general readership has declined" (220). Gioia goes on to criticize poets for becoming too egocentric and insular, as he extols the virtues of recitation. Of his "six modest proposals" to help poetry "again become a part of American public culture," one asks that "*teachers . . . spend less time on analysis and more on performance*" (236–37; italics in original). Many poets and critics have taken up Gioia's essay in an effort to make a case for the validity and vivacity of cowboy poetry, a genre that engages non-specialists, sells books, and honors oral traditions.[1] Both Judy Blunt and Paul Zarzyski are, in part,

....

1   Proponents and defenders of cowboy poetry have used Gioia's essay extensively. I cite the reprinted text in McDowell's *Cowboy Poetry Matters* (2000), for as the title suggests, Gioa's essay is central to the conception of the collection.

a product of the professionalization Gioia derides, for both earned MFA degrees from the creative writing program at the University of Montana. While arguably the program at Montana, like many others, increasingly produces poets and poetry that circulate in a rarified atmosphere of other universities, journals with very small circulation, and a world disdainful of mass appeal, Blunt and Zarzyski represent a different tradition. Blunt remains in academe, but not as a poet, and Zarzyski hasn't taught at a university in decades. Their tradition, nominally housed in academe to be sure, is one that values a writer's emotional investment in place, in physical work, in working-class culture, and in the hard choices people in places like rural Montana often have to make. While both Blunt and Zarzyski have published their poetry in traditional creative writing journals, and sometimes in prestigious ones, they have also been published in *Western Horseman* and by the cowboy-centric Dry Crik Press.

This essay focuses on the "in-betweenness" of Blunt and Zarzyski's work as it relates both to the distance between academic poetry and cowboy poetry, and to the representation of what each identifies as a home place. Judy Blunt is a product of Montana ranching culture, while Zarzyski embraced it as an adult; both feature ranch and rodeo life in their poetry. While both trained in academic poetry, neither has sought a career as an academic poet. Moreover, while neither fits the standard "cowboy poetry" mold, both writers address an audience that includes regulars at Elko, Nevada's annual national Cowboy Poetry Gathering, where both have appeared on the program. Both poets engage two traditions without fully inhabiting either one.

Both Blunt and Zarzyski draw on images and experiences from the working rural West, but neither offers the standard relation toward a mythic West and neither works in the conservative formal and ideological modes associated with cowboy poetry. Both present a challenge to readers of cowboy poetry and academic poetry alike as they negotiate a space in between these two poetic practices. Both connect to a mythic West, but both work to complicate, as well as provide flesh to, the myths about the rural working West. Both poets bridge ideologically oppositional communities in the contemporary West. In so doing, they translate values and experiences from one group to the other, linking insider and outsider, wannabe and detractor. With their commitment to both the material life of rural working people and the ethics associated with that life, they express authenticity in ways that encourage cowboy poetry audiences to stay with them as they produce poetry that uses the techniques of academic poetry. In this way, they move cowboy poetry audiences into an aesthetic experience with contemporary forms of academic poetry. At the same time, both consciously push against persistent stereotypes of both rural-centric Western poetry and a preconceived audience for that poetry. In other words, while their subject matter and ethical alliances suggest cowboy poetry, their technique suggests academic poetry, altering cowboy poetry practice while at the same time honoring rural audiences as intelligent and receptive to alternative aesthetics. They manage to surprise readers at both ends of the spectrum. As if in answer to the question posed by the song in the musical *Camelot*, "What Do the Simple Folk Do?," Judy Blunt and Paul Zarzkyski show that the simple folk may *do* what urban people imagine they do, but they think about what they do in complex, artful, and beautiful ways.

Beginning with the first National Cowboy Poetry Gathering in 1985, cowboy poetry regained national attention, and that renewed interest has prompted the publication of several collections as well as some critical work. Characterizing cowboy poetry's interest in "a disappearing way of life under assault from industrialized society and "its parallel celebration of organic wholeness, camaraderie, and individualism" (2), David Stanley offers an overview of the tradition in his *Cowboy Poets & Cowboy Poetry* (2000). Along with a focus on ranch and livestock work, a commemoration of traditions, enunciation of authenticity and "the system of values prevalent among cowboys (usually referred to as 'the code of the West')" (11) constitute key aspects of cowboy poetry. In her characterization of women poets within the tradition, Elaine Thatcher claims:

> Ultimately, the test of whether a poem is "cowboy" or not is whether the poem is accepted as such by cowboys and ranching people. Its content and language will make it expressive of the values of the group. To listen attentively to cowboy poetry is to discover a strong sense of community and the love of a way of life. (239)

Blunt's poetry sits uneasily with such definitions, while Zarzyski's work endorses these aspects of cowboy poetry in much, but not all, of his poetry.

Stanley goes on to say that there is an "awareness of poetry as speaking for an entire regional occupational group" (13), which sets up an ethical obligation for poets who choose to write for or about ranching and rural people in the West. Both Robert McDowell and Barney Nelson recognize that an essential aspect of cowboy poetry is that it takes up "proximity to animals" (McDowell xvii). It is in these last two claims that Blunt and Zarzyski both engage their readers and ally themselves with the project of cowboy poetry. In the ranch life poems of her collection, *Not Quite Stone* (1992), Blunt begins the process of critique, particularly of gender roles, that continues powerfully in her memoir, *Breaking Clean* (2002).

In part, I propose an argument for closer attention to poets who write from within the culture, an approach that counters simplistic readings of Richard Hugo's advice in *The Triggering Town* (1979). In the essay, "Writing off the Subject," Hugo says, of "the places that trigger my poems": "[k]nowing can be a limiting thing" (6). He goes on to clarify: "[t]he poet's relation to the triggering subject should never be as strong as (must be weaker than) his relation to his words" (6). While both Blunt and Zarzyski are competent and often very strong poets, and while both exhibit care with their words and offer poems rich with the love of language carefully deployed, neither regularly lets go of the insider position, an attachment to the facticity—that is, things grounded in concrete facts— of event, place, and lifeway. It is in this aspect that they resemble cowboy poets rather than academic poets.

To push the idea of in-betweenness, I have paired poems by Blunt with two by Zarzyski, hoping to show that while they have taken up similar situations associated with cowboy, rodeo, and rural life, they come to these topics with different sensibilities and methods. Judy Blunt gave up the ranching life in order to get an education, create opportunities for her children, and to write. Several of the poems in *Not Quite Stone* (1992) take a retrospective view of her childhood on an eastern Montana ranch, while others concern her life as a working-class single parent in Missoula. Here I look at two of her poems about ranch life.

Women are always already in an ironic relationship with the cowboy West. "Sisters," the opening poem in Blunt's only book of poetry, plays with time as it works with and against Western myths. The setting is a round corral, made of log poles, at a cow camp a long way from any town. Except for the mention of a pickup truck in the second line, the scene is one that has figured in Western legend for well over a hundred years. Except the speaker is a girl. The poem considers what happens when girls enter this iconic space: the corral where men catch "roughstock" (horses bred for the rodeo circuit as buckers), the old-fashioned way. No Pat Parelli-style natural horsemanship here. It is an iconic Western scene, a tough masculine space, serving rodeo with "bands of broomtail mares and yearling colts / bred to buck." Throughout the poem Blunt shows the way these sisters fit and don't fit in this world, and in some ways, the threat they represent. While the adults in the opening stanza, "Jack," the "Crooked Cross riders," and the "men," don't merit any details, readers get a clear sense of the speaker's emotional state from the opening lines:

One whine shy of a forced march
to the pick-up, I hung a long face
between the third and fourth rails
of Jack's Larb Hills cow camp corral,
picking at scabs of dry Lodgepole bark[.]

The speaker recollects herself as a child, and a pouty one at that. As the first stanza develops, readers move from wondering if the speaker doesn't want to be there, to supposing it's envy that drives the sulk, with the speaker outside the corral, watching what goes on within, waiting. And then we get a very clear portrait of the speaker's sister:

A fidget alongside the men,
my older sister waited, grown-up in stiff
boots, straw hat brim clean and barely
crimped, her knuckles braided white
around a pint-sized hackamore.

Will the sister be taking one of the "yearling colts / bred to buck" with the "pint-sized hackamore"? The poem offers an array of differences, species, gender, and age. The speaker recalls herself as a young girl, while recognizing that the sister is poised between child and adult, just as she stands between the speaker and the men. She's a "fidget alongside the men," but "grown-up in stiff / boots." Both the line endings and breaks emphasize the sister's difference from the men. She is "grown-up" but her boots are stiff, her hat is new, and she stands "stiff" in this new role. Moreover, this first stanza works to link the girls and the horses, with the sister's white knuckles braided "around a pint-sized hackamore" duplicating a braided nose of the hackamore itself. And, like the girls, the horses vary in age—some fillies and some mares.

The second stanza presents Jack at its center, a competent, old-school horseman,

> pivoting slow
> and sure, center of a pinwheel blur
> of bays and roans, reds and wall-eyed
> blacks, his lariat coiled in one leather glove.

Snaking his lariat loop "past / future Cannonballs and Widow Makers," he "snagged / both front feet of a palomino filly, / popped the slack and dropped her flat, breathless." Jack, powerful and calm and very much in control, shares the second stanza with the "palomino filly" in action that sounds like violent seduction, his leather glove, lariat, and "snaked" loop suggestive of BDSM (Bondage Discipline Sadism Masochism). For Jack, the horse's submission is integral to the sorting process.

The filly, we learn in the third stanza, is "too light to buck" "and quartered like a cow horse. My sister / didn't hear a word, beside herself in love" with the filly. Blunt emphasizes the filly's age and vulnerability—"snowy / stockings tied in a bunch, the baby fringe / of mane and tail to match." The sister draws the speaker from the fence, inviting her into the corral, now emptied of "future Cannonballs and Widow Makers" and they go to the filly, still "dazed / and hog-tied" in the dirt. The sister's "hands shook / like the colt's own hide" as it

> hunkered
> down close enough to touch, our faces
> and the clouds behind us mirrored
> in the dark, wild eye of her colt.

In "Sisters," the girls don't express the mastery and dominance of the able horseman, Jack; rather, they seek intimacy and identification with the filly. No longer separated by age or the fence, the girls' intimacy with each other is manifest in their reflection, "our faces" "mirrored" in the filly's eye, as well as by the use of the pronoun "our." That gender plays an enormous difference in responses to ranch life is a central theme in *Graining the Mare: The Poetry of Ranch Women* (1994) by Teresa Jordan. As a tomboy herself, Jordan recalls:

> I realize that I knew early that women inhabited secret territories. I often had the sense of living in two worlds—a sense that is shared by many ranch women I know. . . . When I was with boys, we rode horses. When I had girls to play with, we actually became horses. (3)

Indeed, in this moment of intimacy with the filly, the worlds of sister and speaker, filly, and sky come together, creating an entirely new scene, excluding from sensation and view the frenetic world of men. The sister, in spite of having to play the cowboy role to be in the company of these men, reveals both their difference from them and her subversion of that world in the final stanza's final lines:

> Cream Puff, she said, glancing back
> for fear the men would hear and laugh,
> I'm going to name her Cream Puff. (Blunt 1–2)

Blunt not only leaves her readers with a parting act of defiance—one that renders Jack's control and dominance almost silly—but she also shifts temporality. Here, at the end of the poem, in the assertion, "I'm going to name her Cream Puff," we move out of the round pen and past tense and set off into a future that hijacks a "roughstock" filly and refashions her into a beloved and sweet companion, a confection. Blunt's poem, then, speaks to "cowboys and ranching people," incorporating the precise language of their work, but it also subverts traditions as much as it honors them. It has the richness and subtextual life of many academic poems, while it maintains an allegiance to the actual work of livestock handling.

Compare Blunt's treatment of the inner sanctum of the cowboy, the round corral with wild "roughstock," to the rodeo world offered by Paul Zarzyski in "Retiring Ol' Gray," from his collection, *Roughstock Sonnets* (1989):

> "Tailor-made," we'd say
> each time the chutegate cracked

and she'd buck honest—
a jump-'n'-kick rocking-chair
bronc, not a "dirty" in her, (Zarzyski, *Roughstock Sonnets* 11)

There's a "we" here, human co-conspirators, the bronc riders. And there's an ethic at work, here, too, with some broncs "honest" and some "dirty." The speaker continues:

That campaigner
taught us heart, those moments
she'd hang high
enough for us to dream
fancy filigree with ruby
inlays on the sun—the silver
buckle to win Cheyenne, like heaven,
"Daddy of 'em All." (Zarzyski, *Roughstock Sonnets* 11)

In this world of men and competition, the bronc is female, the bronc busters are males, as is "the Daddy of 'em All," the major rodeo at Cheyenne. Zarzyski deftly employs gender distinction here, as he also links "Ol' Gray" to the world of emotion (taught us heart) and in the next stanza, to sex:

I'll always crave and miss
her acrobatic kick
to kiss the earth,
the way she'd break in two,
come up again for air
and float: back to back,
we'd take wing, my high
spurring stroke lifting
and lifting her, from horizon
to horizon—"The Bronco Pegasus"
soaring to love
every inch of sky—rainbowing
and high rolling for the clouds
going stark-raving
wild in a crowd. (Zarzyski, *Roughstock Sonnets* 11)

It's an eroticized ride, and the bronc rider's ability to turn the competition in "The Daddy of 'em All" into an athletic and synchronized set of spurring strokes, reveals both the domination and the difference at the heart of rodeo performance. The bronc rider must demonstrate that, far from being truly one with the bronc or mirrors of each other, he must find her rhythm while spurring her into a good performance that will win him the silver buckle. It is dominance as performance, with points scored for animation in both rider and bronc. It's also voyeuristic, public. Compare the ride on "Ol' Gray" with the gendered treatment of the palomino filly in Blunt's poem. In "Sisters," where the men work to master, the girls seek to meld: "our faces / and the clouds behind us mirrored / in the dark, wild eye of her colt" (2). While the crowd at the rodeo might go as "stark-raving / wild" as "Ol' Gray," cheering the performances of bronc and bronc rider, in "Sisters," the girls eschew the audience of men, who "would hear and laugh" at the un bronc-like name, "Cream Puff." Instead, they look for intimacy with the filly and between themselves, with their faces, separated by age and a fence in the earlier parts of the poem, coming together as they are reflected in the eye of the filly. The difference in the representation of a horse bred to buck in these two poems suggests the distinctions between these two poets' relation to their material and to their readers. Both poems evoke a Western livestock-centered sensibility, but Zarzyski's poem sits more comfortably within the ideologies of rodeo culture. Both offer complexity for the reader of academic poetry, but neither moves away from the "triggering" event. Both remain committed to the facticity of the event.

Both writers' work requires either knowledge of rodeo, ranching and livestock, or the willingness to do a little research in order to make the poems intelligible. Students who are not from the rural West often have trouble with the work of both these poets, for it's a world unfamiliar to them. In class, I sometimes pair an "old hand" with a "tenderfoot" and then watch the tenderfoot blanch when he discovers what, exactly, is eaten at the potluck in Zarzyski's poem, "Escorting Grammy to the Potluck Rocky Mountain Oyster Feed at Bowman's Corner." Similarly, they have trouble parsing the language and imaging the scene in "Sisters." I believe that, in part, the subject matter, the use of colloquial speech and the Montana setting convinces many students that these are not the poems of academic or canonical poets, and therefore not subject to the same research that might be applied to explicating a poem by Eliot or Ashbery. It's that in-betweenness at work, with the poem's subject declaring accessibility, but the language resisting ready transparency.

Blunt's ranching culture poems speak of her experiences growing up on a ranch, of what happens to girl children, of the indoctrination into Montana rural folkways, of measuring up against such rules. Zarzyki's poems of Montana rural culture are the work of a man who has chosen the life, who lives in rural Montana, but whose livelihood is not solely derived from that world. These differences play out in many poems, but perhaps most glaringly in their poems about animals. In "Barn Cats," a 46-line poem, Blunt spends the first 25 lines describing, in sensual detail and with childhood's sensibility, new litters of kittens and the way the speaker imagines both the kittens' ability to return to the womb and her own desire to feel the maternal warmth of the "smooth cradles snug full / of kittens jig-sawed together." The poem turns, and the speaker, now grown, finds:

> Even now
> it's hard to think beyond the birth
> to a day in late spring
> or fall when my parents thinned carrots
> and kittens with the same sure sense of timing.

The rancher logic is at work here. "Dad" knows when there are too many cats, and that if left on their own, worse fates befall them. In this world, it is too expensive and too much trouble to neuter cats, but it is also a rancher's responsibility to cull any overpopulation, regardless of species. The speaker goes on to affirm the soundness of Dad's logic, presenting two alternatives: "winter kill" or:

> the way the boys two farms away hang
> gunny sacks of half-grown cats over a clothes line,
> and shoot .22s until the sack is still,
> and even after.

But the logic takes its toll on emotions, sensitivity, and, to some degree, on humanity, for the speaker has also learned of death

as a time that came, a distance
measured in units of mercy, the arm's length
that separates a man's heart from his hand
when cries and claws sliver through burlap (Blunt 18–19),

and that drowning kittens, while more merciful than the alternatives set forth, costs both the rancher, in the separation of heart from hand, as well as his family. On the ranch mercy must be measured, doled out in units, and killing animals happens seasonally and repeatedly. In this world, Blunt suggests, there is no room for the warmth of any cradle or nest, no place for emotion, and for the girls and women in this world, no room for a kind of mothering that resembles coddling in any way. The kittens are destined for regular culling, the barn cats for a life of endless reproduction and loss.

Paul Zarzyski has many poems about life and death, human and animal, with several appearing in the collection *Wolf Tracks on the Welcome Mat* (2004). The brief bio on the dust jacket describes his home as "west of Great Falls" (Zarzyski, *Wolf Tracks* 137) and the poems suggest a small ranch or acreage. In "Playing Favorites," the speaker describes watching and photographing a hatch of great horned owls nested just outside the window of his home. Like Blunt's kittens, Zarzyski's owl chicks offer the speaker the pleasure of close observation of new life and, like Blunt's speaker, the speaker in "Playing Favorites" recognizes the gap between appearances and destiny, as he recalls:

> we loved
> the eight-moon lure of their eyes,
> rejoiced in this brief innocence—peace
> bloomed so near our lives. (Zarzyski, *Wolf Tracks* 18)

The turn, as the title and use of past tense anticipates, comes in the next stanza, as the speaker hears "the shrill panic-squeal of a rabbit" as the owl chicks fledge and start to hunt. No longer the "we" who watched the chicks, it is the speaker alone who takes action to protect the rabbits, "shooting like a lunatic from the hip" with his shotgun. The shots are only warning shots, "toward God" and not aimed to kill the owls; rather, they are fired "to stop the nocturnal loss of cottontails / we loved counting each morning from the kitchen" (Zarzyski, *Wolf Tracks* 18). Unlike in Blunt's "Barn Cats," lethal pragmatism does not reign here. But the speaker is no naïve suburbanite either. Zarzyski carefully exposes the ways in which poetic imagery, subject position, and even the poem itself conspire to involve the speaker and the observer partner in the workings of nature. The poem opens with the "great horned owl quartet," at once suggesting the way humans pattern, link, and compose their observations of other species. The second line offers a comparison of the hatchlings to "voluptuous mums," and Easter lilies in lines seven and eight, as if they are garden flowers, grown for the humans' pleasure. The stanza continues with the development of mutual spectatorship, the hatchlings "gawked at us all spring," while the humans click "snapshot after snapshot," and the hen owl makes a "clacking" sound in response to the camera shutter's click (Zarzyski, *Wolf Tracks* 18).

The second stanza pushes spectatorship further, with the owlets watching the humans' TV through "our picture-tube window," and the humans see both the owlets through the window and their own reflected faces there, looking. The "late-show violence on the Zenith" in line three prefigures the violence that begins outside in the next stanza, as does the qualifying "brief" that precedes the word "innocence," as the humans "rejoiced" in the connection and that "peace / bloomed so near our lives" (Zarzyski, *Wolf Tracks* 18).

By the third stanza, quoted above, the speaker intercedes, plays favorites, and defends the rabbits with his shotgun. The shotgun blast kills nothing, but unsettles the speaker, leaves him "shivering." In the fourth stanza, a house window reappears, their "favorite," where "each morning" they count the cottontails:

> their ears turning pink-
> veined as Christmas poinsettia
> with first sun, my favorite time for plant
> and animal, when I write, in favor
> of prey, this one page outliving the night. (Zarzyski, *Wolf Tracks* 18)

The cottontails, too, have been rendered as decorative plants, and the humans' habitual morning activities as well as the view from this favorite window give the advantage to the rabbits. It is not, however, an actual advantage, the product of successful human intervention into the world of predator and prey outside the house. Rather, the advantage, the speaker informs us, is rhetorical, and the bunnies triumph on the page rather than in the yard. Zarzyski describes a natural world that is the product of his own reflection, and, since his business is poetry, he need not engage in the jaded pragmatism and measured mercy of the rancher in "Barn Cats." While Blunt, as poet, can articulate that pragmatism and can suggest its costs, she will not, even rhetorically, alter the outcome. The facticity of the "triggering" event stands. Zarzyski, while his sentiment moves him away from central concerns of cowboy poetry, does offer a view within one tradition of cowboy poetry wherein the speaker carefully observes predator and prey. In his use of cultivated flowers, among other images, he shows his training in and commitment to more academic traditions of poetry.

Zarzyski is fond of quoting his mentor, Richard Hugo. In *The Triggering Town* (1979), Hugo writes:

> A poem can be said to have two subjects, the initiating or triggering subject, which starts the poem or "causes" the poem to be written, and the real or generated subject, which the poem comes to say or mean, and which is generated or discovered in the poem during the writing. (4)

Both poets hang on to the "triggering" subject or event more than we might expect in "academic" poetry, but both, as we have seen, have the accomplished poet's attentiveness to words and the music of the poem. I want to re-assert here that each resides in that in-betweenness, a space of poetic practice between the facticity of cowboy poetry and the primacy of the words, as articulated by Hugo and quoted earlier. Both Blunt and Zarzyski understand that words represent things, and neither plays with words to a degree that might unmoor them from standard meanings or ready intelligibility. It is this grounded quality found in cowboy poetry that poet and publisher, John C. Dofflemyer, describes this way:

> Lingering perhaps in redundancy, the contemporary vision of many cowboy writers may be less cluttered than their urban or academic counterparts. As such, their expression is more lucid and uses old terms and language with common work-related meanings, lending a more visual and intellectual accessibility to the page. . . . The most original and innovative force within the genre is Paul Zarzyski, an ex-rodeo cowboy

and a student of Richard Hugo, who effectively explores the margins between academic and cowboy poetry. Exposure to his work inspires more experimentation and illustrates that cowboy poetry is no longer isolated, although it was never a totally free or pure expression that popped mystically out of the heads of cowboys on cattle drives. (359–60)

A little later in *The Triggering Town*, Hugo makes another distinction that might help us see the relationship between cowboy poetry and academic poetry:

> Please don't take this too seriously, but for the purposes of discussion we can consider two kinds of poets, public and private. . . . The distinction lies in the relation of the poet to language. With the public poet the intellectual and emotional contents of the words are the same for the reader as for the writer. With the private poet . . . the words, at least certain key words, mean something to the poet they don't mean to the reader. (14)[2]

Zarzyski has been pulled toward the position of public poet by his audience and his choice to make a career as a performer, largely in cowboy poetry circles and in cowboy music. But he has also pulled his audience in the direction of the academic or private poet, introducing audiences at cowboy poetry gatherings to free verse, at times (as in "Playing Favorites") different ethics, and broader themes. Zarzyski, then, has not been lassoing his readers as much as he has been "graining the mare" all along, coaxing readers to follow him away from strictly rhymed verse and traditional cowboy topics to a broader notion of what poetry can do, a poetry that takes the rural West and small town Montana as "triggering towns."

While Blunt may more closely resemble the private poet, she, too, has edged a cowboy poetry readership and audience closer to an appreciation of academic poetry through her accurate *and* revisionist treatments of hardscrabble ranching life. We might recall Teresa Jordan's comments, quoted earlier, about the way many ranch women "inhabited secret territories,"

....

2 As Lisa Simon suggests, even the title of Hugo's book, *The Triggering Town* (1979), offers one of those "in-between" terms. It's a term that belongs to the West, bringing "triggers" into poetic terminology (Communication with author).

with a sense of "living in two worlds" (3). We have seen those "secret territories" in both of Blunt's poems, in the longing to merge with animals as well as an understanding of the impossibility of doing so. We might now expand the idea of "living in two worlds," a skill acquired early for a ranch girl, to a sense of the way her work straddles different aesthetics and different audiences.

Both Blunt and Zarzyski have cultivated an "in-betweenness," stylistically and in their publication choices. Readers can find poems by these poets in *Poetry* and any number of academically centered small journals, as well as in venues for the rancher/cowboy poetry audience such as *Western Horseman*. In so doing, they have made the creative-writing program poetry disparaged by Dana Gioia appealing to those now elusive "general readers," and in the process each has created a more complex version of what is all too often seen as life in the mythic American West.

WORKS CITED

Blunt, Judy. *Not Quite Stone*. Missoula: University of Montana, 1992. Print.

Dofflemyer, John C. "Cowboy Poetics at the Millennium." *Cowboy Poets & Cowboy Poetry*. Eds. David Stanley and Elaine Thatcher. Urbana: University of Illinois Press, 2000. 351–62. Print.

Gioia, Dana. "Can Poetry Matter?" *Cowboy Poetry Matters: From Abilene to the Mainstream*. Ed. Robert McDowell. Ashland: Story Line Press, 2000. 219–38. Print.

Hugo, Richard. *The Triggering Town: Lectures and Essays on Poetry and Writing*. New York: W.W. Norton & Company, Inc., 1979. Print.

Jordan, Teresa, ed. *Graining the Mare: The Poetry of Ranch Women*. Salt Lake City: Gibbs Smith, 1994. Print.

McDowell, Robert, ed. *Cowboy Poetry Matters: From Abilene to the Mainstream*. Ashland: Story Line Press, 2000. Print.

Simon, Lisa. "Notes to You" Message to the author 4 May 2013. Email.

Stanley, David, and Elaine Thatcher, eds. *Cowboy Poets & Cowboy Poetry*. Urbana: University of Illinois Press, 2000. Print.

Zarzyski, Paul. *51: 30 Poems, 20 Lyrics, 1 Self-Interview*. Bozeman: Bangtail Press, 2011. Print.

———. *Roughstock Sonnets*. Kansas City: The Lowell Press, 1989. Print.

———. *Wolf Tracks on the Welcome Mat*. Cedarville: Oreana Books/Carmel Publishing, 2004. Print.

CHAPTER 19

Poetry for Life's Sake: On the Road
with Montana's Poets Laureate

KEN EGAN, JR. *(Missoula, Montana)*

My neighbor introduced me to her grandson: she's the poet laureate; it's like the state bird.
—*Sandra Alcosser*, Montana's First Poet Laureate

Montanans are storytellers, fond of sharing creation myths, tall tales, and intimate fables. They embrace and celebrate gifted prose writers such as A. B. Guthrie Jr., D'Arcy McNickle, Mildred Walker, Dorothy Johnson, Ivan Doig, James Welch, Deirdre McNamer, Mary Clearman Blew, David Quammen, Rick Bass, and Debra Magpie Earling. They communicate that love through lively book festivals, book clubs throughout the state, and impromptu conversations in places urban and rural about writers who have made a difference to their lives, to their way of thinking about themselves.

More complicated would seem to be Montanans' relationship with poetry and poets. This apparent ambivalence is of a piece with American attitudes in general. Twenty years ago Dana Gioia famously asked, "Can Poetry Matter?" It was both a plea for attention and an assertion of relevance. Certainly the state has featured major, influential poets, the most prominent being Richard Hugo. And Montanans relish the words of the "cowboy poets," including Wally McCrae and Paul Zarzyski. Yet when asked to name the state's most important writers, they default to the prose artists. Perhaps it's the sheer scale of Montana, encouraging attraction to extended narrative rather than finite lyric. Or perhaps Montanans, used to driving the long roads of their state, are drawn to the narrative pulse of prose. It's also possible citizens are reluctant to acknowledge publicly their scandalous delight in poetry's spots of time, moments saturated with beauty and emotional intensity.

Yet an experiment in public poetry conducted since 2005 suggests the state's citizens are far more engaged with lyric than might be supposed. Montana's poets laureate travel to reservations, schools, libraries, festivals, and more to promote poetry as a public good, a vital source of self-understanding, shared wisdom, and joy in language. They do so with modest funding and the guile of saints. In the process they have come to realize Montanans not only read but practice poetry, often in private, and poets laureate serve as a conduit for passion and belief hardly glimpsed on the surface of our culture. The laureates prove time and again that poetry is for life's sake. They make it respectable to be ravished by profligate nature and human ties.

To gain a deeper sense of poetry's importance in Montana, I interviewed the four poets laureate to date: Sandra Alcosser (2005–2007); Greg Pape (2007–2009); Henry Real Bird (2009–2011); and Sheryl Noethe (2011–2013). They shared vivid stories of poetry on the road, tales of epiphanies, wonder, and doubt. Their accounts illuminate poetry's value to Montanans' public and private lives.

ORIGINS

Like many a good poem, the poet laureate position emerged mysteriously, surprisingly, uncannily. This role was created by the state legislature in 2005 and is now included in the state's statutes as Montana Code Annotated 2-15-242. The initial promoters of the legislation included then-current and former legislators and Montana citizens passionate about poetry's place in our daily lives. The statutory language is impressively spare in its requirements. It makes clear that the position is honorary, that is, no state funding can be used to support the poets laureate during their two-year terms. Further, the Montana Arts Council is required to submit the names of three nominees for the position to the governor every other year. As for the laureate's reason for being, this crucial information is more implied than asserted in the code's emphasis on the Montana Arts Council's role in administering the position, inasmuch as the Council exists to "encourage throughout the state the study and presentation of the arts and stimulate public interest and participation therein" (Montana Arts Council website).

Montana is not the only state that recognizes a laureate. In fact, forty states do so, though the terms, compensation, and public commitment to the position vary from state to state ("Current State Poets Laureate"). Wyoming's poet laureate serves co-terminous with each governor; North Dakota's laureate, Larry Woiwode, is named for life. The laureate role has deep roots in the Western tradition, reaching back to ancient Greece, re-emerging in the British bardic tradition, and taking on added luster with the naming of national poets laureate such as John Dryden, William Wordsworth, and Alfred Lord Tennyson. The United States has had a poet laureate since 1937. The role usually includes public celebration of nation and leader, a task noticeably absent from Montana's poet laureate legislation, yet one the poets laureate have performed in ways overt and subtle.

Alcosser, as the original laureate, provides the definitive account of how the Montana Arts Council and its partners set about putting feet on the ground, getting a live poet on the road promoting poetry as a public good:

> When the legacy appointment was announced by the governor, Arni Fishbaugh of the Montana Arts Council in Helena, Mark Sherouse and Kim Anderson of Montana Center for the Book and Montana Committee for the Humanities [now Humanities Montana], Corby Skinner of Billings' Writers Voice, and Barbara Theroux of Fact and Fiction Bookstore gathered for a day in Missoula to discuss what we might build with the laureateship. Rick Newby of *Drumlummon Review* joined us by speakerphone. This group remained enthusiastic and supportive through [my] entire two-year term. Tami Haaland, a poet and professor at MSU Billings, drove across the state on more than one occasion to help organize and moderate events—what friends, what blessings. (Personal Message)

The planning group faced a crucial question: Is the laureateship primarily intended to honor the poet's achievement or to promote poetry as public art? The founders decided to split the difference, as the position description on the Montana Arts Council's website reads, "The Montana Poet Laureate recognizes and honors a citizen poet of exceptional talent and accomplishment. The Poet Laureate also encourages appreciation of poetry and literary life in Montana" (Montana Arts Council website). Or as Anderson expresses this second responsibility, the laureate provides "populist outreach that demystifies poetry" (Anderson).

The laureate's official duties are few: participate in a public reading during the Governor's Arts Awards ceremony and travel the state through Humanities Montana's Speakers Bureau program. The poets laureate have applied their remarkable imaginations to defining, amplifying, giving flesh and blood to these duties. Not surprisingly, that work has entailed long hours on the road of this state that remains a small town with long streets. Also not surprisingly, the poets light up in prose and in person when recounting these journey stories.

ON THE ROAD, BY HORSE, BUS, AND CAR

Going on the road is an American tradition, a rite of passage, a cultural icon. Yet typically road stories focus on the migrating self, accounting for lessons learned and insights gleaned by the quester. Montana's poets laureate tell different road stories: their journeys have brought them into contact with remarkable people who represent and disclose unique places throughout the state, connecting the poets to unfamiliar landscapes and communities. Time and again the road has led to home.

Henry Real Bird's journey by horse along the Hi-Line during the summer of 2010 will no doubt serve as the definitive road story for years to come, and not simply because it garnered national attention. As one reporter described Real Bird's travels,

> He is handing out books of poetry to the people he meets along his route, which will take him through Indian country where his grandfather rode a century ago. This is not a press stunt, but rather a demonstration of Henry's life, culture and poetry: a journey of horse and horseman slowly making their way across a vast ancestral landscape. (Western Folklife Center website)

In Real Bird's own words, "I especially enjoyed riding from the gateway of the West where steamboats have been and explorers headed to the mountains. The railroad towns and rivers of Montana where life has been and still is were beautiful places to deliver poetry" (Personal Letter).

Real Bird's ride is of a piece with his published poetry, which often returns to travels that bring his personae into contact with cherished places, magical states, and crucial beings. His poem "Vision" begins, "The promise of love and life in the moon / Beckons our rider to cinch real loose / For an easy day of riding through Yellowstone" (*Horse Tracks* 101). That journey leads to a meeting with "the beautiful Woman-of-the-Mountain," a journey into spring, into possibility, into rebirth at the end of a sad winter. The persona hauntingly describes how "people hide / From themselves in thick underbrush, / In the shadows of their hearts." The persona's abiding desire: "I want nothing to cling to your heart / As you go riding in life" (*Horse Tracks* 101). In this way Real Bird's poem uses a common Montana experience—riding through a stunning landscape—to invoke the possibility of freeing ourselves from inhibition, repression, and doubt. In this way the poet laureate becomes the means to open ourselves to expression and connection. He serves as cheerleader for our souls.

Noethe's travels by Greyhound bus provide a striking counterpoint to Real Bird's journey by horse: "Whoever thought a woman sitting in the back of the bus, which is where the troublemakers choose to sit, scribbling away with an ink pen, listening, watching, conversing, would result in poems that bring out the kindred spirit of all of us. These commonalities are as basic as bread" (Personal Message).

As the paradigm-maker, Alcosser embraced poetry on the road with gusto. She recounts a dizzying array of places and people met in her travels, yet her poetic impulse to anchor in the concrete and the immediate leads to this epiphany in Billings:

The shoes on the stage of MSU Billings' gymnasium remain indelible. Professor Sue Hart...invited me to deliver the commencement address where surely four-time- Pulitzer-prize winning poet Robert Frost was the last poet to deliver this address on May 1952, at graduation ceremonies for his granddaughter Robin Fraser. Thousands of mud-puttied work boots passed by that day, as they might also have passed the great poet whose commencement address carried the advisory *that one must be well versed in country things to understand the deeper things of life.* (Personal Message)

Pape's road stories take on an incantatory quality as he names the many towns that welcomed him: Dillon, Great Falls, Kalispell, Bozeman, Stevensville. He was willing to go anywhere he was invited, and he was apparently invited everywhere. And "everywhere I went people were hungry to listen to poetry and to share" (Personal Interview).

ART FOR LIFE'S SAKE

What has compelled these talented artists to spend time on the road? Was the life of the itinerant poet a burden, an imposition, a rupture in their daily routines? What, after all, is poetry's role in the lives of Montanans, and how do the poets laureate serve that role?

Pape speaks for all the poets laureate when he asserts that in contrast to the notion of poetry as "art for art's sake" it should be "art for life's sake": "Poetry is not an aesthetic practice of the elite. I hope my audiences discovered art comes from lived experience. It is vital inside us and around us" (Personal Interview). He compares his work to the Slow Food Movement, proposing that Montanans participate in the Slow Poetry Movement (SPM): find out who your local poets are, celebrate them, and grow poetry yourselves. He asserts that SPM has clear health benefits: increased powers of observation and imagination; reducing stress and increasing receptivity to insights; preserving and strengthening brain function; and encouraging connection and empathy with others.

Pape's poetry often instructs the reader in these health benefits, though with a strong dose of delight:

An owl calls across the river.

Another answers farther downstream.

Stars glitter through the branches of the pines
and on the back of the river.

He sits still, leaning against a tree.
The river comes a little closer. (Pape, *American Flamingo* 8)

The poem's character shows the virtues of full immersion in a place, sitting still to experience the owls and the stars and the pines and the flowing river. This moment truly becomes a Wordsworthian spot of time, saturated with a sense of the interconnection of things and self. Given Montanans' heavy workload—the state frequently leads the nation per capita in number of citizens holding more than one job at a time—"The River Comes Closer" becomes an elixir of pleasure and an invitation to suspend the normal rules of busyness and anxiety.

Pape reinforces these themes through his remarkable rhythms and sound effects. The reader experiences the river's flow through the movement of syllables, and echoes such as "owl calls" and "stars glitter" reproduce at the auditory level the very condition of interconnection with natural phenomena. The poem's closing lines bring home this moment of satisfying unity of being:

> He listens, slips his hand into the cold river,
> turns it over, palm up, to cup the water
> to hold stars. (Pape, *American Flamingo* 8)

Pape's vision of poetry's health benefits, in part earnest, in part playful, suggests a deeper need to suspend the press of work to recognize the wonder around us. These poets share a Romantic confidence in the imaginative and attentive faculties in all of us. It is as if they would jump back across the gulf created by the technically brilliant but difficult Modernist period of Stevens, Crane, and Eliot to return us to the publicly vital poetry of the nineteenth-century United States. In that sense Alcosser's neighbor comparing the poet laureate to the state bird makes perfect analogic sense: like the meadowlark, the laureate would be a memorable songster, of a piece with the wild world of Montana.

Alcosser demonstrates lyric's bond with place through many of her precisely located, sensory-rich poems:

> June and finally snowpeas
> sweeten the Mission Valley.
> High behind the numinous meadows
> ladybugs swarm, like huge
> lacquered fans from Hong Kong,
> like the serrated skirts
> of blown poppies,
> whole mountains turn red. (*Except* 47)

The poet deploys near metaphysical conceits (swarming ladybugs compared with fans and skirts) to link exotic, extreme nature to our domestic lives. The implication is clear: Montanans live in this wondrous natural world, find home here, and, as the poem goes on to argue, can participate fully in that home life.

> And in the blue penstemon
> grizzly bears swirl
> as they bat snags of color
> against their ragged mouths. (*Except* 47)

The gorgeously red scene takes on new tones and frenetic energy with the entrance of the grizzly, a creature usually treated as dangerous, uncanny. Yet here the persona emphasizes the bear's playfulness, ungainliness, and delight in wild nature's bounty.

And then, in the most electric move of all, the persona links the grizzlies' dance to our own lives:

> Have you never wanted
> to spin like that
> on hairy, leathered feet,
> amid the swelling berries
> as you tasted a language
> of early summer? Shaping
> the lazy operatic vowels,
> cracking the hard-shelled
> consonants like speckled
> insects between your teeth,
> have you never wanted
> to waltz the hills
> like a beast? (*Except* 47)

Suddenly the terrifying grizzly becomes the avatar of full human engagement with Montana's wonder world, the bear's zest for color and food becoming the symbol of the human need for bridging self to world through language. Of course the poem demonstrates the very act of celebrating summer through language in its exquisite performance. In other words, "What Makes the Grizzlies Dance" embodies the very behavior it would encourage, the lustful, playful, sensuous immersion in this wild place called Montana. Similar to Real Bird, Alcosser would encourage readers to let go of emotional and aesthetic inhibitions that block release into the joy of being. She also demonstrates again the truth of Frost's injunction *"that one must be well versed in country things to understand the deeper things of life."*

These public poets reinforce the belief that their work as laureates has flowed organically, meaningfully from their daily lives as poets. Poetry is not apart from life—it is a representation, amplification, and clarification of life (to paraphrase that iconic American poet Frost once again). Or as Real Bird has expressed this faith, "The duty of Poet Laureate was an honor greatly appreciated, for I asked my grandfather where thought was from at an early age. He said thought is from the shadow of flame and that my thoughts were from his shadow of the sacred fire" (Personal Letter). Therefore, poetry should be accessible, both in the nature of the poems offered and the places where they are shared. Noethe captures this conviction when she observes, "I feel the most important work I can do is to make poetry friendly and familiar to everyone I meet, to show them that poetry is available and accessible and is a human right and privilege" (Personal Message). These Montana bards emphasize that they have not focused exclusively on their own work. Instead, they have seen their mission as promoting the work of the full community of poets, both published and unknown. They have featured published poetry by friends throughout Montana, student writers, classic poets such as Wislawa Szymborska and Elizabeth Bishop, and the furtive writings of audience members.

Perhaps because all four poets laureate have been teachers, they have taken special joy in encouraging composition during and after their travels. All four testify to wonder at the outpouring of creativity to which they bore witness. Montanans, it turns out, are deeply lyrical people. Pape counsels those ready to join the Slow Poetry Movement to practice the six R's: Research, Remember, Relax, Release, Revise, and Rejoice (Personal Interview).

These itinerant mentors provide moving instances of citizens producing first-rate verse under the Laureate's inspiration. Here, Virginia Howell testifies to the difference Alcosser made to her own poetic strivings:

Living in Roundup, Montana, back in 1971, poetry came to me mysteriously in the night. So thrilled by it I tried to capture family and friends to listen, but they looked at me with skeptical eyes and escaped. Over one hundred poems I wrote in a few months and no one to hear them! I was like a Meadowlark with no spring in sight! No one to look at them until Sandra Alcosser came to Billings in 2006. . . . she encouraged me and I thank her. (qtd. in Alcosser, Personal Message)

Real Bird adds another note to the teacher's joy: the sheer pleasure of offering published poetry to unsuspecting Montanans:

They're surprised and they just browse through it right there, and they don't know what to think and so I'm gone by the next day so I don't know what they think. I just put my name on there and everything else. I just want them to enjoy the thought, enjoy the thought and go for the ride into the feeling whatever it is. (Western Folklife Center website)

Noethe communicates this pedagogical duty and joy with unusual gusto. Her poetry often recreates scenes of education, providing inside accounts of children freed into themselves by the poet's empathy and encouragement:

The poet asks the children to hold their breath and keep still.
Eyes wide, hands covering mouths, they look around at each other.
Not wanting to break the moment until they gasp and laugh.

Now, he says, write about the silence.
Silence is a rock not moving in a lake.

Says the brown haired 4th grader in a whisper.
I nod, and a few children like that, they begin
Nodding their heads at beautiful thoughts.

In lyric moments such as this the reader returns to a stillness that reveals the metaphors, the analogies by which we live. Noethe is exceptional at representing the physical challenge of such silence for children humming with the zest for living. Yet similar to Pape's character in "The River Comes Closer," that moment of silence yields a profound connection to others:

We smile tenderly at each other.

Nod. In this sudden outbreak of splendor we are happy to be
  together.
Finally, the boy who was working on his drawing says,
Silence is in a bottle and a basket.

In this instant of shared trust, one of the more reluctant students yields his revelatory metaphor.

In her unpublished poem "Reservation School," the poet concludes with that most Romantic notion of all, the innate genius of children, and in this way Noethe reinforces the poet's special obligation to young citizens:

I roll this afternoon around in my mouth.
Something sweeter than a ripe peach or custard.
How close the soul can come to the skin
When the body is still so new.

The implication is clear: If teachers can nurture such self-expression in children, they prepare the ground for full lives of wonder and engagement.

In addition to their duties as teachers, the laureates have also served an official function informally. The poets laureate have seen themselves as representative Montanans, speaking to and for community needs. Alcosser reports that Governor Schweitzer challenged her "to capture in poems the essence of the first Montanans—the seven tribes and the eighth tribe: Butte" (Personal Message). Pape describes with relish participating in the harvesting of the national Christmas tree in the Sapphire Mountains south of Missoula. He was honored to read a poem for the occasion in the company of Blackfeet storyteller Jack Gladstone and 600 fellow citizens (Personal Interview). The laureates have also offered poetry—their own and others—during book festivals in Billings, Great Falls, Helena, and Missoula. Finally, they have served as judges for Poetry Out Loud, an annual competition hosted by the Montana Arts Council that gives voice (literally) to youthful creativity and performance.

GIFTS

And what of compensation? What have these poets gained in return for their travels, their teaching, their inspiration, their wonder?

The question answers itself: more than they could possibly give. The poets laureate believe they have participated in a gift economy, an exchange of presents physical, spiritual, social, and imaginative. Their journeys have brought them into community, into graciousness, into grace. And so Real Bird recounts one of the great gifts during his ride along the Hi-Line: "On the trail along the Milk River an old Gros Ventre woman cooked the best elk tenderloin and Bannack bread I have ever tasted" (Personal Letter). Alcosser manifests this sense of profound gratitude when she writes,

Everyone points out that the poet laureateship is a non-paying job, but that's not exactly true. For love of poetry, one man brought a book to my house to sign and carried a loaf of homemade Italian bread leavened with plum rust yeast; at Hamilton Farmer's Market the woman from Wild Rose Emu Ranch gave me Emu Oil Soap. The participants of a workshop at Bozeman Library, knowing that I was off to work in New York, collected $55 for me to buy a new dress. (Personal Message)

Pape articulates a common pleasure for these poets when he observes that writing is both possible and necessary while serving as poet laureate, noting that he "found" many poems during his preparation and travels (Personal Interview).

Noethe, in the midst of her service as laureate, writes with passionate intensity of these gifts:

Every poet longs for contact, someone to share in the experience of words transforming life into the realm of the inner landscape, bringing contemplation, introspection and beauty into an indifferent world. What surprised me most was the kindness and respect I received wherever I went: Montanans love books and telling stories and commemorating the wild pristine glory of these mountains that shelter us. (Personal Message)

Can poetry matter in Montana? Based on the testimony of the poets laureate, absolutely. Poetry thrives in the state, often in a shy reticence or cautious withholding. These official representatives of the state's poetic tradition bear witness to the depth and breadth of lyric expression. They encourage stillness, attention, playfulness, and compassion in a state of hard-working folks. Their poetry demonstrates the benefits of lyric expression and vision, witnessing the wonder of Montana's natural world and the need for connection to the other beings inhabiting this daunting, beautiful place. Rightly, then, in the beginning is our end, for the first poet laureate, Sandra Alcosser, testifies to the vibrancy, the health, the necessity of Montana poetry:

> I have lived in Montana for thirty-five years and cannot remember a time of greater arts and cultural opportunities. I believe the creation of the laureateship brought focus and energy to the discipline of poetry from the media, from arts organizations, as well as from the citizens of Montana. . . . Along the way I made new friendships with many people like retired fisheries biologist Geoff Moser from Bozeman or 86-year-old Vergie Howell who, after I read and helped her publish one of her manuscripts, presented me with a family bullet from Custer Battlefield. (Personal Message)

WORKS CITED

Alcosser, Sandra. *Except by Nature*. Saint Paul: Graywolf Press, 1998. Print.
——. Personal Message. 15 March 2012.
Anderson, Kim. Personal interview. 14 March 2012.
"Current State Poets Laureate." *The Library of Congress*. The Library of Congress, n.d. Web. 25 March 2012.
Gioia, Dana. "Can Poetry Matter?" *The Atlantic Monthly* 267.5 (May 1991): 94–106. Print.
Montana Arts Council website. State of Montana and the National Endowment for the Arts, n.d. Web. 14 March 2012.
Noethe, Sheryl. Personal Message. 29 February 2012.
——. "Reservation School." Unpublished manuscript. Used by permission of author.
Pape, Greg. *American Flamingo*. Co-publishers: Carbondale: Southern Illinois University Press and *Crab Orchard Review*, 2005. Print.
——. Personal interview. 20 March 2012.
Real Bird, Henry. *Horse Tracks*. Sandpoint: Lost Horse Press, 2010. Print.
——. Personal Letter. 29 February 2012.
Western Folklife Center website. Accessed 25 March 2012.

CHAPTER 20

From Love to Activism:
Bringing Advocacy to Montana's Poetry

LISA D. SIMON *(Alberton, Montana)*

"To have great poets, there must be great audiences too."
—Walt Whitman

I am a poetry advocate. I'm also a lover of poems. Poems open my eyes, make me see entirely new things as well as old things in new ways. They wake me up to new experiences, encourage me to listen closely, make me more conscious of how to activate those invisible antennae we all use but seldom acknowledge to feel our way through our lives. Poems lend a reflective gravity to grand events, and they teach me to linger over the unsung moments of everyday life. In the springtime, when Montana is restless for color, I like to read plucky plum blossom haikus. In the depths of winter, I look for heavy, snow-sodden stanzas, meditative and suited for torpor. I love the pleasures of poetry, but it isn't love that makes me an advocate.

My fondness for the varied expressions I find within individual poems is strengthened by a gratification of the larger, social potency of the genre. As a mere lover of poems, I see no problem with poetry. The essays in this book are a testament to the quality, diversity, and abundance of interesting poetry in Montana. My shelves are full of volumes I have enjoyed and more are waiting to be read. If I lived in isolation, I wouldn't need to be an advocate. But the facts of dwindling readership are undeniable and it is that reality that impels me to put aside my reading and enter the murky frontier of advocacy. If you're reading this as a lover of poetry, then you've probably seen similar articles, too often accompanied with forecasts of poetry's end of days. I confess I find most of them inaccurate in regard to to my own experience and often lacking in practical responses. I especially take exception when they suggest poetry itself is dying. I don't believe there's anything wrong with the quality of poetry being produced in Montana, in America, or in the world. But the condition under which that poetry is being received has changed and we have yet to recalibrate our thinking. To adjust, the definition of advocate needs to be sharpened to signify *activism*. Currently, "poetry advocate" conveys anyone loosely affirming poetry—readers of poems, writers of poems, buyers of books, attendees at readings, as well as anyone not purposefully fleeing a room after discerning a poem is about to be read. In other words, it's pretty broad. The reality is that those writing poetry, publishing books, teaching literature, holding readings, may be advocates or *not*. I've known many well-published poets and teachers of poetry who take no part in advocacy, as counterintuitive as that may seem. In fact, the counterintuitive is more often the norm. This isn't because these poets and teachers don't believe in advocacy. For the most part, it seems, it simply hasn't occurred to them. Their efforts are invested in being good teachers and poets—time-consuming endeavors. Yet this balance will have to change and we'll all have to take up the cause of literary activism if we want to revive the social potency of the genre.

Under this more specific definition, an advocate acts to encourage reading poetry as a lifelong practice. Advocates nourish new readers and act to create a vibrant and dynamic community of appreciators from all sectors of society. To call oneself an advocate means agreeing that it is not sufficient to write poetry or secondary books about poetry (like this one), teach a literature class, or to host readings *without also* concerning ourselves with building audiences beyond that specific task or event. I've come to understand that the audience, the reader, is the most grossly underestimated, if not neglected, player in the realm of the literary arts. And it shows.

A decade ago a survey by the National Endowment for the Arts (NEA) revealed the surprising statistic that only twelve percent of adults had read any poetry in the previous year. According to the same report, "less than half of the adult population now reads literature" (1). A comprehensive follow-up study conducted in 2007 showed the decline worsening despite popular advocacy programs aimed at school-age readers such as "Poetry Out Loud" and "The Big Read." The study showed drops in readership regardless of gender, race, and education level. This is about the same timeframe that I began adjusting my own definition of advocacy. At the release of the next NEA survey two years later I was braced for more bad news; instead I was greeted with the amazing statistic that the reading of literature was on the rise for the first time in twenty-five years! This was not only fantastic news for literature but also a validation for the steady work of advocacy. Yet my hopes were dashed as the fine print showed that the increase did not include poetry, which actually continued to decline, especially among women readers. These statistics highlight the urgent need for poetry-specific advocacy. To make a difference, those of us who support poetry by buying books and regularly attending readings must adjust our lens to this wide angle and address the diminished social value of poetry. The formation of great audiences has become something we can no longer take for granted. We need current lovers of poems to extend themselves into activists in order to grow more lovers of poems.

WHAT DRIVES ADVOCACY?

The social promotion of poetry, if you ask around, is generally assumed to fall upon schools, arts and humanities councils, poets, book publishers, and university English and Creative Writing departments. These are the hubs wherein the love and social role of poetry is assumed to rest. The responsibility seems to lie here largely because, in Montana, we have no specific organization, center, house, press, or bookstore that dedicates itself to advocacy as some other states are fortunate enough to have. Yet if we look at our organizations closely we see that explicit advocacy is not within their primary goals or mission statements. Their articulated goals take up learning objectives, cultural or art awareness in the community, revenue streams, or, at a practical level, with the coordination of cultural events—scheduling, publicity, podiums and whatnot. Often the only thought of advocacy—that is, actively fostering readers or paying attention to audience *experience*—is in the accounting and arrangement of chairs.

Although I can't be too critical of these institutions because, truth is, the need for literary activism is somewhat new. Twenty years ago audiences didn't need explicit tending because collectively audiences were already somewhat familiar with and fluent in the genre. That is no longer true.

As the numbers of readers diminish, the less we can take for granted an informed and engaged listenership. And poetry events, that is, readings, are at the top of what ought to be re-thought. Frankly, this recalibration is not just needed in Montana; readings need to be reassessed and re-configured across the United States. I should begin by saying I'm guilty of organizing less-than-successful events and can confirm how socially awkward and depressing they can feel even when the poetry is quite good. Yet the time-honored formula for readings seems so sacred that few dare to tamper with it. It generally runs like this: the event scheduled is for forty-five minutes to an hour, with a reader or two, some cheese and wine. The event has three parts: introduction, reading, and a question-and-answer period. The introduction centers on the poet's life, awards and accomplishments, with little mention of the relevancy or salient features of the work about to be read. Advertising has been largely limited to visually unappealing fliers posted in the expected locations, published in newspaper calendars, and minimally circulated online. The fliers often contain only a photo, bio, and particulars of time and place; very rarely do they contain information about why the work is interesting or relevant. So far, the only part of this perfunctory practice that suggests advocacy is the wine and cheese.

Yet, to be fair, sometimes these events turn out well, if the poet is also a good performer or storyteller who talks directly to the audience about his/her work. Readings also morph to advocacy if someone (poet, organizer, or audience member) generates a conversation in the question-and-answer session. Advocacy emerges in these situations only as the poetry is given the opportunity to invite the audience in, to create something besides a one-way communication. These opportunities are missed when the advertising and introductions emphasize only the poet's resume rather than the poetry. Some people may claim to enjoy the one-way, lecture-like model of conventional readings, but the hard line it draws between the poetry and the audience usually doesn't serve the goals of advocacy. And, if growing a larger readership is the goal, we can give poetry a better chance to find its audience.

Engaged readings and public lectures on poetry require turning the attention towards those chairs and thinking about the experience of sitting in them. Drawing readers in means finding ways to make them feel as included and invested as the poet who is reading (or speaker in the case of poetry-based talks). When I'm giving a talk on poetry, I think about giving the audience a uniquely good time, one that they'll continue to think and talk about, one that contains relevance to their current lives. That means while they're in the chairs I must connect and engage with them. I must start conversations that will linger and in some cases will grow into larger connections and conversations about poetry elsewhere. Importantly, the spotlight cannot solely be on me (as a lecturer) or on the featured poet. We begin being advocates when we make the single event about *all* of us, not one or two of us. These acts of advocacy are often surprisingly simple, inexpensive measures; they tend to be small gestures of thoughtfulness and community inclusiveness.

The transition from being a lover-of-poems to a poetry-activist benefits from a fluency in the allures of poetry. That is, it is useful to consider intellectually—not just at a gut level—what specific things *new* readers often find remarkable in poems. This helps anticipate what to do to make the reception of poetry—life in the chairs—more inclusive and dynamic. To this end, I've produced the following audacious (and sometimes obvious) list of pleasurable experiences poems give readers drawn from my experiences as a lover of poems as well as a teacher of poetry. There's not much textbook guidance available about how to do this, but there is an abundance of compelling evidence that advocates succeed and new lovers of poetry are created every day. Keeping those two factors in mind allows me to transition from the more theoretical aspects of poetry appreciation to the practical, strategic steps that we'll get to next. But first, poetry gives. . . .

- A piercing insight into the unspoken workings of our interior selves and/or the world. This isn't about delightful wording (that's coming up), but the sharp, often surprising revelation of a hidden or shadowy truth made suddenly apparent.
- Perfect turns of phrase for common thoughts. Or as Alexander Pope put it, "what oft' was thought, but ne'er so well expressed." Poetry elevates mundane thought, adding a sense of significance and cultural value.

- A slowing down of time to fully appreciate a moment otherwise lost. This quality is what the nineteenth-century poet Dante Gabriel Rossetti called "the moment's monument." An otherwise mundane experience—the windshield wipers sticking, a trip to the airport, an overheard conversation—is imbued with significance and becomes elevated by the poetic eye and language. There's a poem in the volume of *New Poets of the American West* (2010) called "Gate C22" by Ellen Bass that enacts this quality marvelously by word-painting a scene in an airport where a middle-aged couple greet one another in what unfolds to be a profound embrace of awe and wonder to bystanders. For thirty-five lines the poem describes both the mundanity of their outward appearance and the palpable, nearly spiritual, transcendence of the kiss. What we recognize is the human potential for great passion in all of us, even within our beleaguered, aging selves. A kiss that in real time might have lasted five, maybe ten, seconds stretches into multiple minutes and into a work of art. That's a moment's monument. These poems are deeply pleasurable, I think, because they replicate a recognizable mental activity. We all have defining moments in our memories that we fondly replay in the mind's eye. So without ever having studied poetry or knowing Rossetti, this technique of poetry feels mentally familiar.

Poetry also offers:

- A collapsing of historic time and distance that can seem magical and breathtaking. It can make us feel close, even intimate, with writers who lived centuries before us. For instance, many readers, without any experience with poetry, discover the ancient poets, Sappho and Catullus, speak with a surprising immediacy and contemporary ease. Their words, in contemporary translations, are as accessible as popular songs to most teenagers. These poems act as messages in a bottle conveying, inexplicably, that we're not alone, we're not too weird, that neither our identities nor paths are fixed, and that human feeling is broad, diverse, and, for a large part, waiting to be written. This aspect helps clarify poetry's special power to reach young people who are forming identities, resisting pressures, and finding their own means of expression. They're hungry for the message that poetry brings from outside their peer groups.

Continuing with our list, poetry provides:

- A way to empathize with conflicts of another time where factual content pales. For instance, the visceral poetry about the battlefield horrors penned by the young (and doomed) British poet, Wilfred Owen, have ushered millions of readers into the harshest experiences of World War I. Owen's courageous, truth-telling poems have helped many soldiers and civilians deal with dark aspects of war downplayed by mainstream culture. Through Montana's Speakers Bureau, I've presented many talks on Owen's work around the state—in museums, historical centers, libraries as well as campgrounds. I've seen first-hand how his work brings together liberals and conservatives, young and old, those in favor of our recent wars and those against, highly decorated veterans and conscientious objectors. Somehow a thirty-line poem about a different country, a different war using different technology in a different era enables larger and very personal conversations between and about Montanans. The power of the poem allows us to talk powerfully about the connections between us—our parents' wars, our children's futures, our region's contributions, sacrifices, and even missteps. I've been surprised to find how conversations with Montanans about the tragedy of war from the viewpoint of the soldier almost always drifts to other tragedies and open wounds shared by people of this region, namely the white European treatment of Native Americans. In other words, we end up talking about the things that are particular about living in this region, about our own experiences of being human here in a place where notions of "belonging" and "ownership" are contested at the deepest levels.

The last item on our list of poetry's allures is, perhaps, my favorite attribute. Poetry exploits our intuitive and largely unarticulated associations between sound and feeling. This is a pleasure rooted in the rhythms of human biology—breath, heartbeats, footsteps, chewing, swallowing. From our earliest days we've learned these are not merely static sounds but signifiers of life itself. In harmonious verses, like Edgar Allen Poe's "Annabel Lee," this pleasure soothes. In the repetition and staccato of another of his famous poems, "The Raven," he builds heart-pounding suspense. Rhythmic pleasure also comes from short vibrant lines, as we've seen in the works in this volume by Grace Stone Coates and Marjorie Frost-Fraser. Poems sometimes present a recreation of psychological processes as poets follow familiar patterns of interiority—the slow aches of human longing, the short, erratic surges of passion. These pleasurable rhythms might also suddenly break to signal the confusion of heartbreak and anger, like the discordant sounds of rebellious music. These sonic signifiers convey meaning in subtle ways, but they are familiar to the human experience and even new readers recognize them.

I add this as the last item of our list because too often we forget that poetry, more than any other written form, works with the physicality of sound, both the tangible beat of it as well as the emotions we've come to associate with different sonic cues. It is tacit knowledge of the human experience that poetry brings into language, and thus, into awareness. This capacity, above all the others on the list, is why I love poetry. But collectively they are all why I feel compelled to be an advocate. I want these insights into human feeling, emotional literacy, and empathic attention to humanity to be valued more in our culture.

PRACTICAL TIPS ON THE INTANGIBLE

As I've said, poetry is best introduced through experiences personal to the receiver. Yet, we must be prepared to realize that those conveyed messages are not always obvious. New readers tend to gravitate towards what they can instantly discern. They often treat the poem as a reading comprehension test and rush to what it means. Be gentle. Don't roll your eyes. That's how they've been trained by our test-giving and answer-rewarding education system and it is difficult to unlearn. As teachers of art know, our education system puts at disadvantage fields that cross into the intangible, where the moral of the story, the right answer, the "deliverable," doesn't pop out with all the subtlety of a jack-in-the-box. Deep, sensory reading is a learned skill, not an intrinsic trait. The personal engagement that I keep emphasizing and returning to in this essay is necessary when fostering new readers because it gives them something to find where they've been taught to look. Redirection to finer points can happen later, but first it must be personally rewarding.

Poetry, like all the arts, can move us outside a zone of mainstream "messaging" into the realm of evocation and association, into the subtleties of human experience. These subtleties can be viewed as unknown fields, waiting to be discovered by artists and thinkers. I greatly admire the descriptions in this vein offered by modernist poet H. D. She describes the poet as that of a "research worker in another dimension" (*Tribute to Freud* x) and "a sort of scientific lyricist" (*Nights* 24). She believed that what the creative mind sees may be slightly ahead of what conventional science can validate, but that poets can be "a Galileo, a Newton, [who] may make discoveries that the human mind has not yet, so far, been in a position to make" (*Within the Walls* 14). The rewards of poetry may be more difficult to measure quantitatively, but they are nonetheless important. As an advocate, whenever I can, I call to mind this human potential and encourage resistance to the idea that overt messaging is the primary connection between humans. Through small, strategic reminders, I try to assert artful thinking into mainstream living. This is both the work of poetry and the work of advocacy.

I have come to understand that, as advocates, we have no choice but to be a self-propelled, grass-roots movement. Until we are able to achieve major funding for a Poetry House and direct poetry programming in Montana, there's no organization to turn this work over to. To be done at all, advocacy must take place in small, strategic steps carried out by dedicated lovers of poetry. To aid this community activism, I've compiled a list of practical to-dos, which is, by no means, exhaustive. But if selectively undertaken, they might lead to other ways to integrate activism into our routines of living, to demonstrate how art is present and relevant to life. I've separated these into categories of "Easy peasy advocacy" and "Full-on activism." The most important thing to remember is to create *connections*—that is, rewards—where there is currently silence, lecture, or one-dimensional communication.

EASY PEASY ADVOCACY

- When you come across a poem you find relevant, share it with people around you who would understand its relevancy. Strategic, thoughtful gestures are more effective than blanket distribution.
- Surprise a friend with a poem that is especially relevant to his/her life.
- Frame a favorite poem and hang it in your house, especially where guests will see it—entryways, bathrooms, guest bedrooms.

- Frame a favorite poem and give it to someone for whom it would be meaningful.
- Include poems in occasional cards (again, aim at relevancy to life events).
- Post a short poem as your social networking (Facebook, Twitter, etc.) status now and again.
- Pin poems around your workplace—in the break room, bathroom, and your office.
- Give a volume of love poems with a wedding gift or, as the case may be, a volume of nursery rhymes for a new baby or children's birthdays.
- Subscribe to a local literary magazine; there are some terrific ones in Montana, including *Cutbank*, *The Whitefish Review*, *Aerie International*, *Camas*, and *The Oval*.
- Send an email to Montana Public Radio and/or Yellowstone Public Radio in support of literary programming, especially during their pledge drives.
- Subscribe to *The Writer's Almanac* and receive a poem in your e-mail inbox each day. These are thoughtfully selected—short, seasonal, and occasional. I often find poems here to circulate.
- Purchase a book by a Montana poet each year. More if you can afford to.

FULL-ON ACTIVISM!

The ideas in this section involve ways to *start conversations* about poetry, which is a terrific way to get people accustomed to listening or reading to enter more directly into the reflective process.

- Invite the Montana poet laureate to read in your community. The poet laureateship is the only official advocacy in Montana. Support it! Each laureate brings unique advocacy (See Ken Egan's article for more on this).
- Attend a local reading, but look at the author's work first and formulate questions you might ask to initiate a discussion during the Q & A. You can preview the book in stores, online reviews, and the "Look Inside" feature on Amazon.com.
- At readings, inquire what other poets the featured writer is currently reading. After the reading, ask the same question of someone near you in the audience
- Include Montana poetry in your book club . . . or start a book club.
- Turn a dinner party into a poetry salon, asking everyone to bring a favorite poem on a particular topic like love, springtime, war, or nature.

- If planning a reading, ask the poet to begin with a favorite poem of a writer who influenced her/him.
- Write reviews of local poetry for blogs, newspapers, and magazines.
- Respond to other reviews in comment sections or bring them up to friends. Whenever you come across a good conversation about poetry, circulate it.
- Invite a speaker from the Humanities Montana Speakers bureau to give a poetry talk on in your community.
- Help pass the word and support the poetry readings and talks in your area.
- If asked to give a speech or a reading, begin or end it with a poem by someone else, demonstrating support for the community and normalizing reading poetry.
- Donate to literary champions—Humanities Montana, public radio stations, the Missoula Writing Collaborative (which brings professional writers, often poets, into schools) and other groups in your area.
- Support the literary radio programs, especially local ones like Reflections West and The Write Question. Send notes to the producers, the radio programs, and to the funders expressing appreciation for whatever it is you admire about the program. As the producer for Reflections West, I've found myself buoyed by such messages at times when I wondered if we could continue the program. They work because they show advocates that they aren't alone. In essence, those listeners who take the moment to send me an e-mail, validate that we're reaching an audience. I always appreciate that.

The list could continue with other ways to connect, start conversations, foster engagement, and show social relevancy. Once you get started, you will think of your own ways. Share them.

WHAT'S AT STAKE IN ADVOCACY?

I began this essay with a quote by the great American bard Walt Whitman: "[t]o have great poets, there must be great audiences too" (319). Whitman points to "audience" as a direct corollary to great poetry, implying not just a personal value or enjoyment, but a cultural value. This value has diminished in the population of everyday Americans in the last century.

In 1912, while launching her literary journal, *Poetry*, Harriett Monroe chose this same Whitman quote as the credo for her risky endeavor to embrace the innovative work of new poets, among them T. S. Eliot, Ezra Pound, H. D., and D. H. Lawrence. But Monroe knew it wasn't enough to just publish these works; she had to create an audience for this new type of poetry, which radically eschewed rhyme and metered stanzas. Monroe's foresight to tend to audience as well as the poets paid off; *Poetry* magazine recently celebrated its 100th anniversary, outlasting dozens of other coterie, celebrity-based, and even wealthier literary journals of the time. It has grown into one of the largest operations in support of poetry and become a national leader in advocacy. I find it telling that Monroe was, until recently, largely written out of this history. These great poets have often been presented in textbooks as if they popped out of history as fully formed sophisticates and were met, in kind, by equally sophisticated readers. History shows that Monroe not only gave them space and income to experiment, she cultivated a reading audience to be open to and accepting of their experimentation. She encouraged the journal's readers to take risks, to follow these poets into unknown and untried territories. What Whitman, Monroe, and successive editors of *Poetry* have realized is the necessity to work both sides of the line, supporting both the art of poetry and the cultivation of readers.

The grand objective of advocacy is the more significant goal of bringing poetry back into cultural vitality. We do this generally for a healthier literary community, but there's something much greater at stake that ought to be of concern to lovers of poetry. That is, advocacy preserves poetry's capacity to be radical. At its best, its very highest state, art has social impact. As a poetry lover, I'm most concerned with the loss of this impact. It is what drives me to move beyond my personal experiences with poetry (I could happily enjoy poems by myself) and enter into this trial-and-error social work of advocacy. Someone today could write the equivalent of T. S. Eliot's modernist masterpiece "The Waste Land," but it would lack the cultural register that it had in 1922. With diminished social relevance, poetry loses its capacity to critique culture in a meaningful way. Advocacy fosters an environment in which more complex poetry can thrive. It begins in the realm of accessibility and the personal, which some deem unsophisticated in the way representational painting is often snidely regarded by aficionados of the abstract. Yet ultimately advocacy garners widespread support, and in doing so it preserves poetry's capacity to be radical in the wildest, most idealistic sense. Without this cultural traction, poetry is not bad—certainly not dead or dying—but it is less effective as a social force.

If we don't cultivate the experiences of reflection and pleasure, if we don't encourage the accessibility of poems in the larger population, the overall cultural value of poetry will continue to be diminished. If we want poetry to be read, we must build communities of readers. We must do that work in addition to the work we owe our own art and professions. This is our challenge as members of the community who value poetry and want to preserve its potency.

It is said that, in every era, artists and thinkers must rise to the calling of their time. In our time and in this state, literary activism is calling. There is no one else to ask; there is no one else to blame. It's our work, our line in an ongoing cultural struggle, which, if we profess to care about poetry, we must pick up, take hold, and begin to pull. We must do this each in our own way, each with our own network of people, each in our own communities and without waiting for a leader or an organization to guide us. Just begin today with a poem you love.

WORKS CITED

Bass, Ellen. "Gate C22." *New Poets of the American West*. Ed. Lowell Jaeger. Kalispell: Many Voices Press, 2010. 61. Print.

H. D. (Hilda Doolittle). *Nights*. New York: New Directions Publishing, 1986. Print.

——. *Tribute to Freud*. Boston: David R. Godine, 1974. Print.

——. *Within the Walls*. Iowa City: Windhover Press, 1993. Print.

National Endowment for the Arts Website. National Endowment for the Arts, n.d. Web. 29 Aug. 2013. <http://www.nea.gov/research/>.

——. *Reading at Risk: A Survey of Literacy Reading in America*. Research Division Report #46. Washington: NEA, 2004. Web. 29 Aug. 2013. <http://www.nea.gov/research/>.

——. *Reading on the Rise: A New Chapter in American Literacy*. Washington: NEA, 2009. Web. 29 Aug. 2013. <http://www.nea.gov/research/>.

——. *To Read or Not to Read: A Question of National Consequence*. Research Division Report #47. Washington: NEA, 2007. 29 Aug. 2013. <http://www.nea.gov/research/>.

Whitman, Walt. "Notes Left Over." *Complete Prose Works*. Boston: Small, Maynard & Company, 1907. 317–19. Print.

CONTRIBUTORS

DAVID ABRAMS is the author of *Fobbit* (2012), a comedy about the Iraq War, which was named a *New York Times* Notable Book of 2012 and a Montana Honor Book. His short stories have also appeared in *Fire and Forget: Short Stories from the Long War* (2013) and *Home of the Brave: Somewhere in the Sand* (2013), anthologies of short fiction about the wars in Iraq and Afghanistan. His short stories have also appeared in *Esquire, Narrative, Salon, Salamander, Connecticut Review, The Greensboro Review, Consequence Magazine,* and many other publications. He earned a BA in English from The University of Oregon and an MFA in Creative Writing from The University of Alaska-Fairbanks.

KIM ANDERSON is the Associate Director for Programs at Humanities Montana and the Director of the Humanities Montana Festival of the Book. She returned to her hometown of Missoula in 1989 after living and working in New York City for fifteen years—as the Editor for an international business newspaper, *The Journal of Commerce,* an Associate Editor for a national magazine, *Quest,* an Associate Editor at Arbor House Publishing, and as Subsidiary Rights Agent for the literary agency, Lescher & Lescher, Ltd.

CASEY CHARLES is Professor of English at the University of Montana-Missoula where he teaches Shakespeare as well as lesbian and gay studies. He is the author of *Critical Queer Studies: Law, Film, and Fiction in Contemporary America* (2012) and a novel, *The Times of Christopher Mann* (2013). He has also published two poetry chapbooks: *Controlled Burn* (2007) and *Blood Work* (2012).

NANCY S. COOK is an Associate Professor of English at the University of Montana, Missoula where she teaches courses in Western American Studies, Literature and Environment, and American culture. She has published articles on U.S. ranching cultures, water policy, Montana writers, social class, and place. Her work has appeared in books and journals in the U.S., the U.K., and Spain. She is Past President of the Western Literature Association. When not teaching, she manages a ranch near Clyde Park, Montana.

KEN EGAN, JR. is Executive Director of Humanities Montana, the organization that sponsors the poets laureates' travel through its Speakers Bureau. He previously taught literature and writing at Rocky Mountain College in Billings, Montana, for seventeen years. He has published *Hope and Dread in Montana Literature* (2003) and many articles focused on Western American literature. His book *Montana 1864*, a panorama of characters and events during the year of Montana's founding, will be published September, 2014 by Riverbend Publishing.

KATHLEEN FLENNIKEN is the 2012–2014 Washington State Poet Laureate. She is the author of two poetry collections: *Plume* (2012), a meditation on the Hanford Nuclear Site and a finalist for the William Carlos Williams Award from the Poetry Society of America, and *Famous* (2006), winner of the Prairie Schooner Book Prize and named a Notable Book by the American Library Association. Her honors include a fellowship from the National Endowment for the Arts and a Pushcart Prize. She teaches poetry through Writers in the Schools and other arts agencies, and is an editor and president of Floating Bridge Press.

DAVID GILCREST teaches American literature, poetics, and critical theory at The University of Montana-Missoula. He is a graduate of Dartmouth College and holds advanced degrees from The University of Utah, The University of Montana-Missoula, and The University of Oregon. He is the author of several chapters and essays focusing on poetry, ethics, and the environment. His book, *Greening the Lyre: Environmental Poetics and Ethics* (2002) was named an "Outstanding Academic Title" by the American Library Association.

TAMI HAALAND is the author of two books of poetry: *Breath in Every Room* (2001) and *When We Wake in the Night* (2012). She is a Professor of

Creative Writing at Montana State University-Billings. Among her awards are the Nicholas Roerich First Book Award and the Artist's Innovation Award from the Montana Arts Council. She received an MA in English from The University of Montana-Missoula and an MFA in Creative Writing and Literature from Bennington College. She is the current Montana Poet Laureate, 2013–2015.

BRADY HARRISON is a Professor of English at The University of Montana-Missoula, where he teaches courses in American, Canadian, and World Literatures. He is the author of *Agent of Empire: William Walker and the Imperial Self in American Literature* (2004), editor of *All Our Stories Are Here: Critical Perspectives on Montana Literature* (2009), and co-editor of *Punk Rock Warlord: The Life and Work of Joe Strummer* (2014). His stories, essays, and articles have appeared in journals and books in the U.S., Canada, Mexico, Puerto Rico, France, Germany, and Australia.

SUE HART is a Professor Emerita of English at Montana State University-Billings, and has been a steadfast reader and promoter of Montana literature. She is the author of *Thomas and Elizabeth Savage* (1995) and numerous articles on such writers as Dorothy Johnson, A. B. Guthrie, Jr., and other Montana literary luminaries. She has also published fiction in a variety of literary journals, including the PEN Syndicated Fiction Award-winning short story, "Star Pattern."

LOWELL JAEGER is the founding editor of Many Voices Press. He has edited two anthologies: *Poems Across the Big Sky: An Anthology of Montana Poets*, and *New Poets of the American West* (2010), an anthology of poets from eleven Western states. His third collection of poems, *Suddenly Out of a Long Sleep* (2009), was a finalist for the Paterson Award. His fourth collection, *WE* (2010), was published by Main Street Rag Press. He is the recipient of fellowships from the National Endowment for the Arts and the Montana Arts Council and winner of the Grolier Poetry Peace Prize. He was also awarded the Montana Governor's Humanities Award for his work in promoting thoughtful civic discourse.

DANELL JONES's poetry, fiction, essays, and reviews have appeared in the *Denver Quarterly, British Writers, Beyond Baroque, Sow's Ear Poetry Review*, and *Gingko Tree Review*. She has a Ph.D. in English from Columbia

University-New York, where she received a Whiting Fellowship and a Bennett Cerf Award for her work on Virginia Woolf. The University of Colorado awarded her the Jovanovich prize for poetry and the U.S. Poet Laureate Louise Glück selected her work as a finalist for the Breadloaf Writers' Conference Poetry Prize. She is the author of *The Virginia Woolf Writers' Workshop: Seven Lessons to Inspire Great Writing* (2007).

DAVID L. MOORE is Professor of English at The University of Montana-Missoula. His fields of research and teaching at graduate and undergraduate levels include: cross-cultural American Studies, Native American literatures, Western American literatures, Peace Studies, Baha'i Studies, literature and the environment, and ecocritical and dialogical critical theory. He has taught previously at The University of South Dakota, Salish Kootenai College, The University of Washington, and Cornell University. He was the recipient of a Post-Doctoral Fellowship at the Society for the Humanities at Cornell University and a Faculty Research Fellowship in Western Studies at the O'Connor Center for the Rocky Mountain West, among other awards. His publications include an edited volume of *American Indian Quarterly*, as well as numerous articles and essays in journals and collected essays. His study, *"That Dream Shall Have a Name:" Native Americans Rewriting America*, was published University of Nebraska Press in 2013.

KARL OLSON is the author of "West of Desire: Queer Ambivalence in Montana Literature" in *All Our Stories Are Here: Critical Perspectives on Montana Literature* (2009). He currently studies English Literature at The University of Montana-Missoula, and is a recipient of the Helen J. Olson Scholarship Award. He works for the Missoula Public Library Foundation.

CAROLINE PATTERSON has published literary fiction in numerous journals, including *Alaska Quarterly Review*, *Epoch*, and *Southwest Review*. She edited the anthology *Montana Women Writers: A Geography of the Heart* (2006), which won the Willa Award. She teaches creative writing at The University of Montana-Missoula and for the Missoula Writing Collaborative. She was a Stegner Fellow in Fiction and has won fellowships from the Montana Arts Council, the San Francisco Foundation, the Ucross Foundation and the Virginia Center for the Creative Arts in Lynchburg, Virginia. She recently completed a novel, *The Stone Sister*.

KATHRYN W. SHANLEY is a Professor of Native American Studies at the University of Montana-Missoula, and also works as the Special Assistant to the Provost for Native American and Indigenous Education. Her most recent publications include, "'An Event of Distance': James Welch's Place in Space and Time," in Native American Renaissance: Literary Imagination and Achievement (2013) and "Intersubjectivity with 'Nature' in Plains Indian Vision-seeking," in Re-imagining Nature (2013). Shanley coedits (with Ned Blackhawk) the Yale University Press Henry Roe Cloud, American Indians and Modernity series, and she served as president of the Native American and Indigenous Studies Association in 2012. She is an enrolled Nakoda from the Ft. Peck Reservation.

JOCELYN SILER is an emeritus professor from the Department of English at the University of Montana-Missoula. She is the author of *The Essential Rhetoric* (1999), *The Responsive Writer* (1996), and co-editor of *The Quill Reader* (1999). She was a student of Madeline DeFrees in the MFA program at UM in the 1970's.

LISA D. SIMON is a humanities scholar, a poetry activist, and a recent recipient of the "Humanities Heroes" award in Montana. She created and produces "Reflections West," a five-minute radio program that celebrates the literature and culture of the American West. Simon holds a PhD in English, specializing in literary modernism, from The University of Washington. She publishes and gives public talks on the topics of Imagism, the poet H. D., as well as the histories of war and love poetry.

TIMOTHY STEELE is the author of several collections of poems, most recently *Toward the Winter Solstice* (2006). He has also published two books of scholarship and literary criticism, *Missing Measures: Modern Poetry and the Revolt against Meter* (1990) and *All the Fun's in How You Say a Thing: An Explanation of Meter and Versification* (1999). He also edited *The Poems of J. V. Cunningham* (1997). His honors include a Stegner Fellowship in Creative Writing from Stanford University, a Guggenheim Fellowship, a Peter I. B. Lavan Younger Poets Award from the Academy of American Poets, the Los Angeles PEN Center's Literary Award for Poetry, and the Robert Fitzgerald Award for the Study of Prosody. He is a Professor Emeritus of English at California State University, Los Angeles.

CAREY R. VOELLER earned an MA in English from The University of Montana and a PhD in English from The University of Kansas. He is currently an Assistant Professor of English at Wofford College, where he teaches Early American and Nineteenth-Century American Literature. He has published articles in *The Hemingway Review*, *Legacy*, and *Western American Literature*.

O. ALAN WELTZIEN is a Professor of English at The University of Montana-Western, in Dillon, Montana, where he teaches courses in American, Western American, and World Literatures, as well as non-fiction and poetry workshops. He has published dozens of articles and has authored, edited, or co-edited seven books, most recently *The Snowpeaks* (2013), his second book of poems. He has also received two Fulbright Fellowships and one University of Montana International Faculty Exchange Award.